W9-CMK-157

Eleanor Roosevelt and the Media

Eleanor Roosevelt and the Media

A Public Quest for Self-Fulfillment

Maurine H. Beasley

UNIVERSITY OF ILLINOIS PRESS
Urbana and Chicago

This book is printed on acid-free paper.

Quotations from oral history interviews in the Columbia Oral History
Collection are used by permission of the Trustees of Columbia University.

Library of Congress Cataloging-in-Publication Data

Beasley, Maurine Hoffman.
    Eleanor Roosevelt and the media.
    Includes index.
    1. Roosevelt, Eleanor, 1884–1962—Career in journalism.
2. Mass media—United States—History—20th century.
3. Press—United States—History—20th century.   I. Title.
E807.1.R48B42   1987   973.917′092′4   86-19281
ISBN 0-252-01376-x (alk. paper)

To my mother, Maurine Hieronymus Hoffman, who thought Eleanor Roosevelt was the "better half" of the Franklin & Eleanor team,

and to my husband, Henry R. Beasley, who I know is the "better half" of our team.

Contents

Illustrations follow pages 50, 152

Preface

I began research for this book in 1977 after discovering that few records of Eleanor Roosevelt's press conferences are preserved among the rest of her papers at the Franklin D. Roosevelt Library at Hyde Park, New York. Consequently I attempted to assemble material by contacting women journalists who had attended the press conferences. I am greatly indebted to many individuals who generously provided information based on their firsthand recollections. Among them are Dorothy Ducas Herzog, Ann Cottrell Free, Ruth Cowan Nash, Malvina Stephenson, Beth Campbell Short, Hope Ridings Miller, Frances M. Lide, and Rosamond Cole. Three others have died since I interviewed them: Mary Hornaday, who offered invaluable insights, Katharine M. Brooks, and Esther Van Wagoner Tufty. Three other women, Mildred Gilman Wohlforth, Dorothy Roe Lewis, and Kathleen McLaughlin, provided material in telephone interviews and by correspondence. Anne Wassell Arnall, who photographed Mrs. Roosevelt in the White House, also graciously agreed to an interview.

In addition, I want to thank relatives of several of the deceased women journalists for sharing their memories and family papers. They include Cornelia J. Motheral, the daughter of Ruby A. Black; Ruth Armstrong, the daughter of Bess Furman Armstrong; and Martha Strayer Sherier Paxton, the niece of Martha Strayer.

I also want to express appreciation for material furnished by Eleanor Roosevelt Seagraves, Mrs. Roosevelt's granddaughter; Dorothy Dow Buttruff, former White House secretary; Sally L. Smith, a friend of Mrs. Roosevelt; Eleanor Zartman, the niece of Malvina Thompson; Jean E. Collins, who permitted me to see transcripts of her oral history interviews with pioneer women journalists; and John F.

McHugh, who compiled a book of Mrs. Roosevelt's obituaries for me. Very special thanks go to William D. Mohr, who transcribed the shorthand notes on Mrs. Roosevelt's press conferences made by Martha Strayer.

As I worked on the press conference phase of Mrs. Roosevelt's activities, it became apparent that it needed to be studied within the broad context of Mrs. Roosevelt's own journalistic career and her emergence as a media personality. Numerous academic colleagues have aided me in endeavoring to understand Eleanor Roosevelt's role in the mass communications process. They include Frank Freidel, Betty H. Winfield, Susan Ware, Marion Marzolf, Richard Lowitt, Mildred Abramowitz, Donna Allen, Jay Blumler, Jay Snorgrass, and Frank J. Krompak.

In particular, I want to thank Carole S. Appel of the University of Illinois Press for her interest in this project. Thanks also go to my editors, Susan L. Patterson and Carol Saller. Extraordinary encouragement and assistance were provided by Ruth K. McClure. Other help was given by Hilda R. Watrous, Ann Davis, and Emily L. Wright.

Much library research has gone into this book. I am grateful for student assistance provided by the University of Maryland College of Journalism headed by Dean Reese Cleghorn and its research center directed by Michael Gurevitch. I am especially indebted to Suzy Chan among the students who helped me.

I also want to acknowledge, with gratitude, the assistance of William R. Emerson, director of the Franklin D. Roosevelt Library, and his staff, especially Frances Seeber, Joseph Marshall, Emily Williams, Robert Parks, and Mark Renovitch; the research librarians at the Library of Congress Manuscript Division, where the Bess Furman papers are located; the staff of the Western History Research Center of the University of Wyoming, where the Martha Strayer papers are housed; the staff of the oral history and special collections divisions of the Columbia University library; Dale C. Mayer, archivist at the Herbert Hoover Presidential Library directed by Robert Wood; and Barbara Vandegrift, librarian-archivist at the National Press Club. A grant from the Eleanor Roosevelt Institute aided me in starting this project. Picture research was done, in part, by Picture Research of Washington, D.C.

I also want to thank Barbara Birney, Barbara Oldroyd, and Patty Colon of Pagemasters, who courteously and capably prepared the manuscript, and Marion Gideon, who carefully photocopied large numbers of yellowed newspaper clippings from the Ruby Black papers. I am also grateful to Barbara Crandall, who typed the first draft.

Finally, I am indebted to my husband, Henry R. Beasley, for his never-failing understanding, encouragement and financial help, and to my daughter, Susan Sook Beasley, for her cooperation.

Introduction

One of the most brilliant weddings of the season took place yesterday afternoon at Calvary Church, at Twenty-first-street and Fourth-avenue. Miss Anna R. Hall, daughter of Valentine Hall, Jr., was married to Mr. Elliott Roosevelt. . . .

The bride carried a bouquet of white roses and lilies of the valley. The corsage bouquet was of orange blossoms. The ornaments were diamonds.

— *New York Times*, December 2, 1883

The one woman of our time whose name was known on every continent and whose face was familiar to countless millions was Eleanor Roosevelt. Her death at the age of 78 will be mourned in many lands where she was revered as a symbol of loving kindness toward persons of every race and creed. . . .

Her speeches, her writings, her unabashed politicking and her appearances in such roles as a United States representative to the General Assembly [of the United Nations] were careers in themselves.

For a dozen years and more she led public opinion polls as the world's most admired woman. Her newspaper column in The Herald often topped all other newspaper features in reader popularity.

— *Miami Herald*, November 9, 1962

In the tight little world of New York society in the 1880s, the elegant young Elliott Roosevelt and his beautiful bride shone like stars among a select group, including the Astors and the Vanderbilts, who were on hand for the Roosevelt wedding. Ten months later, Anna Hall Roosevelt produced her first child, Anna Eleanor, who arrived on October 11, 1884. Sadly she was "a more wrinkled and less attractive baby than the average," or so she described herself years later.[1]

Like her mother, she seemed destined for the constrained life of an upper-class lady, expected to avoid the public spotlight except for dazzling visibility in society. Conventions of the era held that a lady's name appeared in print only three times: when she was born, when she was married, and when she died. No one expected the unprepossessing infant to become the single most publicized woman of her day—an American heroine—who gained her fame via the media of mass communication.

When Eleanor Roosevelt died on November 7, 1962, the news media throughout the world bid farewell to one of its own—one of the greatest personalities and newsmakers of the twentieth century. Her obituaries dramatized the heart-tugging aspects of her life. Merriman Smith of United Press International called her the "shy and self-imagined 'ugly duckling' . . . who found true beauty through service to humanity." The *New York Journal-American* editorialized that she was a "remarkable woman [who] gained in her lifetime a recognition that not many are granted." In its news columns it stressed the poignancy of her widowhood: "Eleanor Roosevelt, regarded by many as the First Lady of the World, was reunited in death today with her husband, President Franklin D. Roosevelt, seventeen and a half years after his passing." Under a headline, "Mrs. Roosevelt, First Lady 12 Years, Often Voted 'World's Most Admired Woman,'" the *New York Times* called her a "noble personality." It declared that "by the end of her life, she was something even rarer than a distinctive First Lady. She was a great lady." The *Washington Star* declared that she was known to "three generations as a woman who never wearied of well-doing."[2]

Yet what was missing from these tributes was a sense of how—and why—Eleanor Roosevelt used the media to make her life stand out before the world. Numerous books have been written about Eleanor Roosevelt, concentrating on various aspects of her multi-faceted life—her marriage, her relationships with her family and friends, her political and humanitarian interests, her personal growth and development, her activities as first lady, her career at the United Nations, her inspiration to others. What has been overlooked is the obvious: that Eleanor Roosevelt emerged as the most influential woman of her day largely because she was able to utilize the media both to advance the causes in which she was interested and to realize her own potential.

Like her husband, she was an individual who dominated her times, yet her perception of the contemporary always was influenced by a sense of history rooted in her personal experiences as a daughter, wife, and mother in a period of shifting social roles for women. Through the media she made herself a role model for others by combining traditional aspects of a woman's role with the requirements of changing times.

Eleanor Roosevelt was not alone among women of her era in her understanding of the importance of the mass media. Although she did not participate in the woman suffrage movement, she came to know women who had been publicists for it through her work in the League of Women Voters and the Democratic party in New York State. Initially Louis McHenry Howe, the newspaperman who was Franklin Roosevelt's political mentor and Eleanor Roosevelt's trusted friend, helped her gain a feel for the journalistic process. Later she received guidance from women with experience in newspaper work and public relations. Against this background Eleanor Roosevelt developed herself, using her warm personality, gracious manner, enthusiasm for new ideas, and genuine interest in others to create her own unique media career. Undaunted by the technology of modern communications, she became its master.

As the niece of one president, Theodore Roosevelt, and as the wife of another, Franklin D. Roosevelt, Eleanor Roosevelt lived in a world of political power that depended increasingly upon the media. Theodore Roosevelt made the presidency a "bully pulpit," relying on newspapers to mobilize public opinion behind Progressive reforms. Franklin D. Roosevelt transformed it into a vehicle of personal communication, speaking directly to the public in radio "fireside" chats. And Eleanor Roosevelt used all forms of the media to make her voice heard throughout a nation unaccustomed to listening to a woman speak from a White House platform.

As first lady, Eleanor Roosevelt, of course, had no official role. In any contest for the holder of the most ambiguous position in American political life, the winner might well be the first lady, who lacks any constitutional authority but wields an intangible amount of public influence. Through the unpredictable operations of fate—the accidents of marriage and the electoral process—presidents' spouses have found themselves in the public eye, whether or not they wished to be there. Without set duties, they nevertheless are expected to improvise suitable roles, knowing they will be scrutinized closely as symbols of administration style or tone. Journalists stand foremost among the scrutinizers. Both influencing and reflecting public opinion, they watch the performances of the presidential spouses, measuring their success or failure by the media's own standards.

Rejecting the pattern set by her predecessors, Eleanor Roosevelt became the first president's wife openly to use her position as first lady to seek access to the media and to turn this access to her own advantage. She became the first president's wife to hold press conferences, to write a syndicated newspaper column, to sell articles to popular magazines, to earn money as a lecturer, and to be a radio commentator. In the process she created intense controversy, not so much over the ideas she expressed as over the example she set. From the days of the first administration, when Martha Washington was accused of behaving too much like a queen, to the most recent one, during which Nancy Reagan initially was berated for more interest in clothes than in causes, first ladies have been the objects of political attacks. But Eleanor Roosevelt remains the only first lady to create controversy by carrying on a money-making media career within the White House.[3]

In recent years questions have been raised about Eleanor Roosevelt's private life, including possible sexual involvements with men and, perhaps, women. The Roosevelt children have stated that their parents did not live together as husband and wife after Eleanor Roosevelt's discovery in 1918 of Franklin Roosevelt's affair with her social secretary, Lucy Page Mercer. Of legitimate interest only to the degree that it may shed light on her development as a public figure, this speculation about her intimate relationships deters study of Mrs. Roosevelt as a major influence in American society. For twelve of the most eventful years of the twentieth century—from 1933 until 1945, while the nation moved from the worst part of the depression through World War II—she held center stage as first lady, easily the single most visible woman in the United States. Undue concentration on her private life obscures and trivializes the more basic issue of what she communicated publicly and how she did it. What is of lasting importance is not what did or did not go on behind closed doors, but what Eleanor Roosevelt did in public.[4]

Public careers have their image-making aspects, and Eleanor Roosevelt's was no exception. As first lady, functioning in a position of symbolic importance, and later at the United Nations, where she occupied a position of actual authority, she presented through the media her own idea of an appropriate role for a woman. True, there may have been a dichotomy between what she advocated—urging women to put family life first although conceding their right to work for personal as well as economic reasons—and her own marriage, which was in effect a business partnership. Nevertheless this did not detract from her importance as a model for millions of women. There always is a difference between images and realities, but as the media assume increased influence in society, the images they offer tend to become the reality for those exposed to them. A difficult question to resolve, however, is to what degree Eleanor Roosevelt used the media and to what degree they used her in the symbiotic process of image making.

Eleanor Roosevelt was born into a world of only one viable news medium—print. When she died, the electronic media had begun to squeeze out the once all-powerful newspaper as the primary transmitters of information. Both as a participant in the media and as a subject for them, she became involved with all their varied forms— newspapers, magazines, photography, film, radio, and television.

The relationship between Eleanor Roosevelt and the media started long before she became exposed to the publicity surrounding the White House. For some presidents' spouses, life in that goldfish bowl represented an abrupt departure from a previous existence. This was not true in the case of Eleanor Roosevelt. Through her family ties, she knew in advance what living in the White House would be like and how the media spotlight would envelop her there.

This is the story of how Eleanor Roosevelt functioned in that spotlight, transforming herself from a potential victim into a renowned world figure. It was during her White House years that she mastered the techniques of mass communication. In her post at the United Nations after she left the White House, she simply put those techniques to excellent use. Therefore, this book is focused primarily on her White House career, providing the first detailed examination of the way she learned to use the media to fulfill her personal needs while carrying out her role as first lady.

1

First Exposure
1905–24

One of the most notable weddings of the year was that celebrated yesterday, when Miss Eleanor Roosevelt, daughter of the only brother of President Roosevelt, and Franklin Delano Roosevelt, a cousin of the President and son of the late James Roosevelt, were married by Rev. Endicott Peabody of Groton, Conn., at the residence of the bride's cousins, Mr. and Mrs. Henry Parish, Jr., 8 East Seventy-sixth Street. . . .

President Roosevelt gave the bride away.

—*New York Times*, March 18, 1905

Washington, July 16—The foodsaving program adopted at the home of Franklin D. Roosevelt, Assistant Secretary of the Navy, has been selected by the conservation section of the Food Administration as a model for other large households. Mrs. Roosevelt on her pledge card said that there were seven in the family, and that ten servants were employed. . . .

"Making the ten servants help me do my saving has not only been possible, but highly profitable," said Mrs. Roosevelt today.

—*New York Times*, July 17, 1917

Of course we know that no formula, no plan, no one idea, no one mechanism of association among nations will immediately procure peace.

—Mrs. Franklin D. Roosevelt
"The American Peace Award,"
Ladies' Home Journal, August, 1923

Eleanor Roosevelt learned the hazards of the publicity process long before she became first lady. Unlike her mother, Eleanor was upstaged at her own wedding. Instead of focusing their attention on the bride, both the socially prominent guests and the crowd outside the Parish residence riveted their eyes on the charismatic President Theodore Roosevelt. While the popular Teddy stole the show, inside and out, the newlyweds were ignored. Press accounts of the president's trip to New York for the wedding emphasized the public acclaim he received. A guest at the wedding reception found Eleanor Roosevelt bore the lack of attention calmly, although it miffed her new husband.[1]

At this point Eleanor Roosevelt was used to being eclipsed by others. Her father, whom she had adored, had died in 1894 shortly before she was ten, following bouts of mental instability and alcoholism, which had prompted her mother to leave him before her own death in 1892. The orphan had been brought up in the gloomy household of her maternal grandmother, who spent winters in New York and summers in her mansion at Tivoli on the Hudson River. On occasional trips to the Theodore Roosevelt home at Oyster Bay, New York, Eleanor had been overshadowed by her more sophisticated cousin Alice.

In her autobiography Eleanor Roosevelt portrayed herself as a shy, plain child, treated indifferently by her mother and loved only by an unreliable father. She wrote of her youthful desire for "attention and admiration" as well as of her fears that nothing about her would attract either. Because of her feelings of inferiority, which she eventually was to describe repeatedly in the mass media, Eleanor Roosevelt pictured her marriage as something of a Cinderella story.[2]

After three years at Allenswood, a girls' boarding school in England headed by Marie Souvestre, a liberal intellectual, Eleanor Roosevelt returned to the United States in 1903, making the conventional debut into New York society. Inspired by Souvestre, she threw herself into settlement-house work and the National Consumers' League, which was committed to securing healthful, safe conditions for workers, especially women. But she was no radical; the woman suffrage campaign failed to interest her, and her activities remained within the acceptable framework of good works by upper-class women.

When the dashing Franklin D. Roosevelt, her fifth cousin once removed, asked her to marry him, over the initial objections of his domineering mother, Sara Delano Roosevelt, she accepted. She was eager, she recalled in her autobiography, "to participate in every experience that might be the lot of women." In later years her children speculated that their father's proposal had been motivated by "pity as well as love."[3]

In the years following her marriage at the age of twenty, Eleanor

Roosevelt immersed herself in motherhood. She gave birth to six children in a decade: Anna (1906); James (1907); Franklin (1909), who died seven months later; Elliott (1910); Franklin Jr. (1914); and John (1916). Either pregnant or recuperating from childbirth for most of this period, she possessed little energy for public activities, but even if she had summoned it, family friction would have ensued.

Roosevelt women, like most of their peers, led sheltered, conventional lives, observing a clear demarcation between their domain and that of men. When Sara Roosevelt, whom Eleanor called "Mama," directed her to stop settlement-house work because she might bring diseases home to her children, the self-effacing young wife obeyed. Her other female relatives eschewed the public arena, except for Theodore Roosevelt's uninhibited daughter, Alice, whose audacious capers, such as smoking cigarettes, made tabloid headlines. While Eleanor eventually followed the example of Theodore Roosevelt and crusaded for social reform, the tart-tongued Alice scorned her cousin's causes and devoted most of her life to Washington society.[4]

Privacy was a passion with Theodore Roosevelt's second wife, Edith Carow Roosevelt, whom he married after his first wife died giving birth to Alice. In her old age she snapped at a reporter, "I haven't talked to the press, not in seventy-one years, and it's too late to begin now."[5]

Similarly Eleanor's aunt Anna Roosevelt, the crippled sister of Theodore and Elliott Roosevelt, held to the Victorian tradition that it was not fitting for a lady to publicize her views even if she was credited with the best mind in the family. An insightful woman who provided affection for both Eleanor and Alice in their growing-up years, "Auntie Bye," or Bamie, as her family called her, would have been president if she had been a man, Alice said in later years. But her character and perceptions remained known only to her intimates.[6]

Eleanor Roosevelt's personal introduction to the newspaper world followed her husband's feat of being elected as a Democrat to the New York State Senate in 1910 from Republican Duchess County, where the family estate at Hyde Park was located. Going with him to the capital at Albany, Eleanor met the gnomelike Louis M. Howe, a newspaper correspondent, who successfully managed Franklin Roosevelt's reelection campaign in 1912 when Roosevelt came down with typhoid fever. Howe's genius lay in political publicity, a point the rigidly moralistic Mrs. Roosevelt did not appreciate at the time. She said she disliked him because he chain-smoked cigarettes.[7]

After the family moved to Washington in 1913, owing to Roosevelt's appointment as assistant secretary of the navy, Mrs. Roosevelt experienced her first bruise from direct contact with the press. It came during World War I when the war provided a patriotic rationale for her to resume social service, although she played no part in the suffrage campaign. To aid the war effort she ran a Red Cross canteen, visited the wounded and tried to improve conditions at St. Elizabeth's hospital, a federal institution for the mentally ill. Spurred by wartime campaigns urging housewives to conserve food, she allowed herself to be interviewed in 1917 by a woman reporter for the *New York Times* with disastrous results.

Headlined "How to Save in Big Homes," the story called attention to the family's "ten servants." It said that Mrs. Roosevelt did "the buying, the cooks see that there is no food wasted, the laundress is sparing in her use of soap; each servant has a watchful eye for evidences of shortcomings in others, and all are encouraged to make suggestions in the use of 'left overs.'" Making a laughingstock of the family, the article added to growing strains in the Roosevelt marriage.[8]

The story appeared after Mrs. Roosevelt, suspicious that her husband was carrying on a romance with her social secretary, Lucy Mercer, had reluctantly left Washington with her children to vacation at the family summer home on Campobello Island in Canada. Franklin Roosevelt immediately sent her a scathing letter: "All I can say is that your latest newspaper campaign is a corker and I am proud to be the husband of the Originator, Discoverer and Inventor of the New Household Economy for Millionaires! Please have a photo taken showing the family, the ten cooperating servants, the scraps saved from the table and the handbook [on food conservation]. I will have it published in the Sunday Times." Sarcastically he declared, "Honestly, you have leaped into public fame, all Washington is talking of the Roosevelt plan."[9]

His wife responded with an abject apology, blaming the unidentified reporter for misquoting her. "I do think it was horrid of that woman to use my name in that way," she wrote from Campobello, "and I feel dreadfully about it because so much is not true and yet some of it I did say. I will never be caught again that's sure and I'd like to crawl away from shame."[10]

Subsequently she refused direct contact with reporters, using Mercer as a go-between. The social secretary continued to work for the Roosevelts until the fall of 1918 when Eleanor Roosevelt, opening her husband's mail while he was ill, stumbled on letters that proved his infidelity. Profoundly hurt, Mrs. Roosevelt agreed to preserve the appearance, but not the reality, of the marriage on condition that the lovers would break off contact.[11]

The next phase of Eleanor Roosevelt's exposure to journalists came in 1920 when she accompanied her husband as the sole woman on his campaign train. As the Democratic candidate for vice president, Franklin Roosevelt made whistle-stop appearances throughout the country with his wife standing at his side, a strategy prompted by the artful Howe. Mindful of votes by women newly empowered to cast ballots by the Nineteenth Amendment, Howe wanted Mrs. Roosevelt, by that time a convert to woman suffrage herself, on display. Determined to mold her into a political asset, he sought her company and tried to make her joke with the hard-drinking, card-playing newspapermen whom Eleanor Roosevelt previously had regarded with awed hostility.[12]

So prodded she began to reevaluate her reactions to the press. She noted in her autobiography: "My grandmother had taught me that a woman's place was not in the public eye, and that had clung to me all through the Washington years. It never occurred to me to do more than answer through my secretary any questions that the reporters asked about social events."[13]

Why did she fail to mention the devastating food-saving story? Perhaps she simply had forgotten the incident, but more likely she deliberately omitted it. What is now known of her marriage makes clear that her autobiography presented a public image at variance with private reality. The fact that she avoided close relationships with journalists until 1932, when Lorena Hickok of the Associated Press was assigned to cover her, casts doubt on her assertion: "Largely because of Louis Howe's early interpretation of the standards and ethics of the newspaper business, I came to look with interest and confidence on the writing fraternity."[14]

Eleanor Roosevelt's personal start in journalism came right after the defeat of the Democratic ticket in 1920. It was a modest endeavor, stemming from her work with the League of Women Voters in New York State. She provided a "comprehensive digest" of proposed changes in the state primary law for readers of the league's *Weekly News* in August 1921. The article appeared the same month her husband was stricken with infantile paralysis, which left him unable to walk for the rest of his life. Although the Eleanor Roosevelt legend holds that she entered politics to keep up her husband's interest after his illness, in actuality Mrs. Roosevelt had moved outside the domestic sphere before the tragedy struck.[15]

Contributing to the league newspaper was one small part of Eleanor Roosevelt's effort to surmount her subservience to her husband and mother-in-law. Sara Roosevelt, appalled at the prospect of well-bred women in the public eye, believed women should subordinate themselves to their husbands. Declaring her independence of "Mama," Eleanor Roosevelt absorbed new ideas of women's roles from her friends in the league and in the women's division of the Democratic party in New York State, which she joined within a year of her husband's illness. For the first time since boarding school, she found herself within a support network of women who lived and worked with other women and committed themselves to social causes.[16]

From their work for suffrage, many of these women were experienced in the use of journalistic and public relations techniques. Among Mrs. Roosevelt's closest friends were Elizabeth Read, a lawyer, and Esther Lape, an educator and publicist. The two shared a Greenwich Village apartment and edited the league's bulletin, *City-State-Nation*. The league stressed the need to provide new women voters with accurate information. By working on league reports, Mrs. Roosevelt gained practice in the journalistic skill of gathering facts systematically and thoroughly.[17]

She also experienced the ego-building satisfaction of seeing her work appear in print. While not the same as a paid job, writing on issues related to political reform represented a start toward self-expression and fulfillment. Like other women before and since, Mrs. Roosevelt found writing, an occupation that could be done within the confines of the home, a demanding and creative activity that enlarged her horizon. In September 1921, the *Weekly News* ran her article on "Common Sense Versus Party Regularity," which admonished league members to vote for the best candidates, regardless of party affiliation. The following summer two more of her articles appeared, one titled "The Fall Election" and the other "Organizing County Women for a Political Party." To facilitate writing them, she employed her newly acquired skill at typing.[18]

The league also furnished Mrs. Roosevelt with more experience in the pitfalls of publicity. Not perceiving the political implications, she introduced a resolution at a Duchess County league meeting defending a Vassar professor assailed in a magazine article by Vice President Calvin Coolidge. The female professor had been criticized as a radical for objecting to the narrowmindedness of congressmen seeking to deport the Soviet representative in Washington. When a local newspaper headlined the story, "Mrs. F. D. Roosevelt Offers Resolution Taking to Task Husband's Victorious Rival," she jotted down in her diary, "Foolish of me ever to do anything of the kind."[19]

League activities, however, were overshadowed by partisan involvement after Howe pushed Mrs. Roosevelt to become active in the Democratic party to keep Franklin Roosevelt's name before the public while he recuperated. She formed an intimate friendship with two women party members who lived together, Marion Dickerman, an educator, and Nancy Cook, the women's division executive secretary. They were among the postsuffragist generation who argued that women were less selfish than men and urged women to enter politics to benefit their families and society as a whole. Consequently the women's agenda became so broad it covered everything from pure milk to peace.[20]

Drawn into this milieu, Eleanor Roosevelt came to see political activity as a way for her to make an individual contribution toward improving the world. Yet because of her husband's condition, her own pursuits, endorsed and guided by Howe, were placed within the socially acceptable framework of acting as a dutiful wife. At this point the stand-in role suited everyone, including Mrs. Roosevelt.[21]

Continuing to write as a form of political activism, Mrs. Roosevelt made her journalistic debut before a national audience in 1923 in connection with the Bok Peace Prize. This competition, organized by Edward W. Bok, former editor of the *Ladies' Home Journal*, offered a $100,000 award to the American citizen who submitted the best plan for United States cooperation in organized world peace. Half was to be paid to the winner on selection of the plan and the other half after either the Senate consented to ratification of the proposal or a substantial percentage of the population approved it in a referendum. Along with two League of Women Voters associates, Lape and Narcissa Vanderlip, Mrs. Roosevelt was picked to run the contest on a day-to-day basis.

As the wife of a former vice presidential candidate, it fell to her to announce details of the contest in the *Ladies' Home Journal* in October 1923. In a full-page article, Eleanor Roosevelt called attention to the novel solicitation of public opinion via mass communications. Stressing that the award was not an attempt to "buy" world peace, she noted, "All that the offer of the award can do is to create a new avenue through which plans can be offered for public consideration."[22]

The public responded with a flood of some 22,000 peace plans, and administration of the contest proved a frustrating experience. The winner, Charles Levermore, retired president of Adelphi College, received $50,000 for recommending cooperation with the League of Nations. But Republican isolationists in the Senate denounced the plan and the resulting referendum. Nine million individual ballots were distributed and arrangements made for others to be published in mass circulation periodicals with a combined readership of thirty-three million. When the referendum ended in the spring of 1924, a disappointing total of only 610,558 ballots had been cast, 87 percent favoring the Levermore plan. By that time the peace award had been attacked as a pro–League of Nations ploy, and public interest dissipated.[23]

With Lape and Vanderlip, she found herself the target of hostile headlines after Lape testified at a Senate hearing that the trio had picked the male members of the contest policy committee. Offended at such feminine effrontery, the Republican *New York Herald* captioned its article: "Three Women Engineered Bok Peace Prize Contest." Even though the outcome was not what was desired, the experience exposed Eleanor Roosevelt to the potential for reaching the public through the mass media.[24]

In view of her future activities, it was a potent appetizer. Three months after her *Journal* debut, an article written by her appeared in another national magazine, the Junior League *Bulletin*. Titled "Why I Am a Democrat," it came out as she increased her partisan political activities. Under Howe's tutelage, she began to speak in public, in spite of a high-pitched, uneven voice, and to edit a political newspaper. Thus the Eleanor Roosevelt saga began. Although piecemeal and seemingly apart from any plan to build a career, her early experiences formed what in retrospect can be seen as a valuable apprenticeship in using the mass media.[25]

2

Finding a Voice
1925–32

You may count your marriage a success as far as your husband is concerned if you feel that you are useful to him in whatever is the most engrossing interest of his life. He may as life goes on have many other helpers besides his wife, particularly if his interests are varied and broad but in the last analysis if he counts on his wife as one of the essential contributors to his success then you have succeeded in establishing a real companionship.
— Mrs. Franklin D. Roosevelt,
"Ten Rules for Success in Marriage,"
Pictorial Review, December 1931

I think that as yet, women are so new in this game of politics and feel themselves so inexperienced, that while there is much in political life as the men have shaped it . . . which they openly criticize, still the serpent in the Garden of Eden did give us a certain kind of wisdom and most of us know that we are not ready to take the great responsibility of the highest places of power.
— Mrs. Franklin D. Roosevelt,
"What Do Ten Million Women Want?"
Home Magazine, March 1932

In the years before Franklin D. Roosevelt's first election as president in 1932, Eleanor Roosevelt established herself as a magazine writer. Her work constituted an unusual kind of personal journalism, based on the value of her name as a symbol of social and political prominence. To gain material, she combed through her personal experiences, writing in the first person. Although her own life was far different from that of the average woman, Eleanor Roosevelt cultivated the knack of identifying with her readers and their problems by alluding to her own.

Overt political considerations motivated some of her journalistic efforts. She saw journalism as a practical tool to strengthen party organization. With Howe's help, she edited a monthly magazine, the *Women's Democratic News*, aimed at women voters in New York State. In three articles for national magazines in 1927 and 1928, she expressed support for Governor Alfred E. Smith, the unsuccessful Democratic presidential candidate in 1928.[1]

As editor of the *Women's Democratic News*, which first appeared in May 1925, Mrs. Roosevelt worked chiefly with Dickerman, Cook, Elinor Morgenthau, whose family estate was located near the Roosevelt home at Hyde Park, and Caroline O'Day, head of the women's division of the New York Democratic party. Under Howe's brusque supervision, the women transformed a mimeographed bulletin into a monthly, 12- to 16-page, slick paper magazine containing articles on and by prominent Democrats, descriptions of legislative proposals, reports of local Democratic clubs, and advertising, solicited by the editor herself. Dependent on Howe's expertise, Mrs. Roosevelt learned from him how to make up a dummy, proofread, and skim newspapers to get news.[2]

At times she was forced to defend Howe's involvement on grounds that his assistance was needed because she was busy with her family. On August 14, 1925, Mrs. Roosevelt sent a note to Dickerman, explaining, "I feel I owe Caroline an apology for injecting such a disturbing element as Louis into the office, particularly as I knew how fussily he worked, how interfering he was, and how full of work for other people and improvements on what everyone else was doing." She added, "It was pure laziness on my part but families and jobs really don't go and I am getting it at last." The note ended with a reference to a memo she had given Howe to make sure the next issue "can be done without trouble." Evidently she was learning to stand up to her mentor as well as to her mother-in-law.[3]

The magazine itself echoed the ideas of the social feminists of the early twentieth century. Unlike radical feminists, social feminists did not view women as a disadvantaged class. Instead they sought greater opportunities for individual women to serve society without altering their traditional family role. The *Women's Democratic News* espoused this philosophy within a political context, asserting that the Democratic party cared for all the people while its Republican opponents were interested only in the rich.[4]

Eleanor Roosevelt's journalistic ventures, however, covered a broader area than the purely political. She definitely was not a jazz-age flapper who broke old-fashioned rules and quaffed bathtub gin. Still Mrs. Roosevelt emerged through the media as a symbol of a "new woman," one able to combine family responsibilities with interests outside the home. From 1928 to 1932, while her husband was governor of New York, Mrs. Roosevelt wrote more than twenty articles for mass periodicals. The majority ran in women's magazines and were loosely tied to a social feminist perspective. Topics included marriage, housekeeping, schooling, the role of older women, preparation for careers, wives of great men, the educational value of the movies, and her own philosophy. Writing on "What I Want Most Out of Life," she gave her answer as "the privilege of being useful."[5]

Most of the articles offered advice and inspiration drawn from her personal knowledge. While she did not reveal the strains in her marriage, a careful reading of her work finds her ideas not totally inconsistent with what is now known about the Roosevelts' relationship. "Who am I to decide what are the tests for a successful wife, for no human being can really judge any other human being?" she began an article on marriage, describing it as a process of adjustment from romance to companionship. The test of companionship, she wrote, lay in a wife's contribution to her husband's success in his most absorbing endeavor. Who could say this did not describe her own marital partnership? Years later she wrote of her husband, "I was one of those who served his purposes." She might have added that he also served her own.[6]

Through writing, as well as public speaking, Eleanor Roosevelt coped with her own tribulations. If her husband had not been Franklin D. Roosevelt, it is doubtful that she would have found an audience. Through his career she built her own, demonstrating an amazing ability to deal constructively with private trials by transforming them into journalistic anecdotes. During the 1920s, as later, she repeatedly interjected autobiographical fragments into her magazine articles— even when they did not fit.

For example, in an article titled "The Ethics of Parents," which she attempted unsuccessfully to sell to *Collier's*, Mrs. Roosevelt alluded to relationships both with her father and her mother-in-law. The magazine, then one of the largest and best-selling, rejected the piece on grounds of poor writing. An editor who attempted to rework it finally told Mrs. Roosevelt, "It was one of those articles which had us defeated." Perhaps it was because of the unwieldy syntax that characterized the barely disguised story of her love for her father: "I knew a child once who adored her father. She was an ugly little thing, keenly conscious of her deficiencies, and her father, the only person who really cared for her, was away much of the time; but he never criticized her or blamed her, instead he wrote her letters and stories, telling her how he dreamed of her growing up and what they would do together in the future, but she must be truthful, loyal, brave, well educated, or the woman he dreamed would not be there when the wonderful day came for them to fare forth together."[7]

After she again painted the child as a pathetic object—"full of fears" and lacking "intellectual stimulus"—Mrs. Roosevelt ended the vignette on a surprisingly upbeat note. She declared that the child had made herself as the years went by "into a fairly good copy of the picture he had painted." So she saw herself, a woman who had survived misfortune to play an active, useful role in the world.[8]

The same article contained a veiled rebuff of her overbearing mother-in-law's efforts to control her and to take charge of her children. Living together did not necessarily mean "inner understanding," she wrote. It was recognition of her unhappy experiences with Sara Roosevelt, who ruled the family both in Hyde Park and in New York City, where she had built twin houses with connecting doors for herself and her son's family. It was written at a time when Eleanor Roosevelt symbolized the break from her mother-in-law by moving out of the Roosevelt mansion and into Val-Kill cottage, which she shared with Cook and Dickerman, on the grounds of the Hyde Park estate.[9]

Although the manuscript was returned, it marked a step toward Eleanor Roosevelt's public presentation of her "ugly duckling" childhood, the story told in the first volume of her autobiography, *This Is My Story*, written a decade later. The Victorian code of separating the public from the private called for her to conceal the tragedies of her family, including her father's wasted life and the dissipation of her maternal uncles. Instead she wove them into the the *Collier's* manuscript, making herself a poor little rich girl who overcame a tortured childhood to emerge as a model woman.

Indeed, she tried repeatedly to treat her own story as fiction. In a 1929 manuscript rejected by *Vogue*, she examined the plight of the middle-aged woman whose children had grown up and left her, by introducing a character named Sally who remembered herself as an "ugly little girl" receiving a "cold glance" from her beautiful mother. Since the incident had little to do with the point of the article, it provided another example of Eleanor Roosevelt's own need to recount the traumatic events of her childhood.[10]

At least one observer found this disquieting. Years later Frances A. Perkins, appointed secretary of labor by Franklin Roosevelt, remembered how Mrs. Roosevelt had confided the sad tale of her childhood one night in the governor's mansion at Albany, New York. For Perkins it appeared to be "the kind of a story that you realized the individual had some need for telling." When Mrs. Roosevelt wrote it in her autobiography, Perkins did not bother to read the book thoroughly because she found it embarrassing. A reticent person who spewed out facts and figures "as if she swallowed a press release," as one reporter put it, Perkins had no sympathy for public airing of private concerns. She lacked the flair and need for catharsis that Eleanor Roosevelt was to exhibit time and time again.[11]

When Mrs. Roosevelt moved beyond her own conflicts in her magazine ventures, she still clung to the personal. In a *Good Housekeeping* interview in 1930, she referred to the social changes confronting women. She recognized that the home was being transformed from a unit for producing food and clothing into one of consuming products purchased from industry. She realized that the occupation of motherhood had been narrowed because of reliance on professional advisors and the expansion of formal education.[12]

Her advice was to follow her own example as a "modern" wife and to develop interests outside the home and family, but she emphasized that the home should come first. After noting that "until all my children were away at school, I stayed at home," she discussed her teaching position at the exclusive Todhunter School for girls in Manhattan. Although she lacked formal teaching credentials, she had been brought into the school by Dickerman, the vice principal, before Roosevelt's election as governor. Having purchased an interest in Todhunter, Mrs. Roosevelt commuted three days a week from Albany to New York to teach history, current events, and literature there.[13]

In line with the general counsel offered in women's magazines, Mrs. Roosevelt called on wives to cultivate their husbands' love by giving of themselves. This too can be construed as a reflection of her experience. To a degree Eleanor Roosevelt had to subordinate herself, "give," as she put it, when her husband was elected governor in spite of his handicap.[14]

James Roosevelt has written that his mother expected his father to lose the 1928 gubernatorial race and that her chief interest in the campaign was to support Smith, who lost the Democratic presidential bid to Herbert Hoover. As national director of women's activities for Smith, Eleanor Roosevelt believed "that if he attained the Presidency she would play an even more important part in public affairs," James Roosevelt commented. She thought this would not happen if her husband won because "she felt father would expect her to slip back into the shadows," he continued. Therefore Eleanor Roosevelt found herself somewhat trapped. She worked to promote her husband's career, but the price she paid for his advancement was the loss of her own independence.[15]

The *Good Housekeeping* article ended with the interviewer asking Governor Roosevelt to name "the one thing which more than any other accounts for the success of Mrs. Roosevelt as a wife and mother." After first replying, "Great Scott," Franklin Roosevelt credited his wife with "that something which every member of the Roosevelt family seems always to have had, a deep and abiding interest in everything and everybody." Asked, "And has she no special abilities of any kind?" the governor answered, "None!" Prodded further by the interviewer, he declared that she had become "a good executive because she is interested in people and in doing things."[16]

The comments presented Franklin Roosevelt himself in the role of public image maker for his wife. Exercising his consummate political skill, he pictured her as a kind of Mrs. Average Woman. Crediting her with no particular abilities, he complimented her only for an aptitude usually considered as feminine—the ability to deal with people, but not ideas. Perhaps the comments were revealing for what he did not say—that he sought and valued her opinions.

According to Perkins, Roosevelt did not consult with his wife, but "liked her as a reporter." Unable to move about freely, "he believed her when she came back and said, 'Now I saw this, and this and this. Somebody said this, and this, and this to me,' " Perkins said. "In fact, on occasion when most men would have asked their wives what they thought, he didn't. Liberal-minded as he was toward women, he tended to think a wife should keep out of those things."[17]

Directed by Howe, the Roosevelts teamed up for public relations purposes to visit state institutions. Since the governor could not walk through prisons, hospitals and schools, the couple parted company on arrival, with Roosevelt speaking to officials while his wife inspected kitchens, dormitories and even closets. After she reported to him on her discoveries, Roosevelt was able to provide the press with accounts of "shocking" conditions encountered on the visits. In one case, this helped offset unfavorable publicity stemming from two prison riots, since Mrs. Roosevelt's report provided information that Roosevelt used to show he was in command of the situation. In checking on cleanliness, food preparation, availability of supplies and treatment of inmates, Mrs. Roosevelt carried out functions traditionally considered appropriate for women.[18]

Complications arose, however, when she tried to move outside the areas of interest believed proper for a wife. According to James Roosevelt, his father encouraged her to resign her own political posts after he was elected governor, because he believed it would look bad for his wife to have too active a role in the administration. Mrs. Roosevelt complied, but this scarcely terminated her political involvement.

Although her name was removed from the masthead of the *Women's Democratic News*, she continued to oversee it. In an unsigned editorial in 1929 she urged women to hold "chicken suppers" or "card parties" to raise funds for the party. Subsequent contributions centered on topics such as tax relief for rural counties, bond issues, criticism of Republican candidates, and pleas to support the state ticket. Her byline appeared on a detailed account of her trip to Europe with Dickerman, Cook, and her two younger sons that ran in eleven installments in 1930 and 1931. Offered to "be helpful to some of our readers" planning European vacations, the travelogue featured the human interest touches that marked Mrs. Roosevelt's writing. For instance, she described her sons as "horrified" when they discovered "bathrooms were not as plentiful as in America."[19]

More important, with Howe as her agent, she wrote for mass circulation magazines as a political representative of American women.

In the article titled "What Do Ten Million Women Want?," which appeared in *Home Magazine* nine months before her husband's election as president in November 1932, she denied that women wanted a woman chief executive. But she suggested that many women "feel that the time has come for a woman to fill a place in the Cabinet," a broad hint that Roosevelt intended to appoint Perkins as secretary of labor. Thus the magazine article served as a trial balloon to test public reaction to the idea.[20]

The *Home* article also outlined areas Mrs. Roosevelt considered of special concern to women: education, Prohibition, then still on the books, uniform marriage and divorce laws, and curtailment of crime partly through the employment of women as police officers, although she said women "would not want a woman at the head of the police department." All of these issues were linked to women's role within the home as guardian of children. They accurately indicated the weak position of women in the social and economic sphere.[21]

As a spokeswoman for her sex, Mrs. Roosevelt articulated ideas of moderation and tokenism. Contrary to the dreams of suffragists, passage of the Nineteenth Amendment had not brought about economic equality between men and women or the coalescence of women as a bloc voting group. By 1924 it was apparent that women, if they ventured to the polls at all, divided on social and economic lines similar to those of their husbands. Political parties needed energetic workers to organize women voters, and Eleanor Roosevelt stood in the forefront of this activity.[22]

During this period most women did not work outside the home unless forced to do so by necessity. In 1930, for example, over 57 percent of the working women were members of nonprivileged groups —blacks or the foreign-born—employed chiefly as household servants or garment industry operatives. Professional women were restricted mainly to "female" occupations—primarily teaching and nursing. Surveys of women in the professions showed clear discrimination based on sex, marital status, and age.[23]

In general, the roles of housewives were glorified in the mass media. This was the message Eleanor Roosevelt conveyed even while she called for women to be more involved in politics. It was social feminist doctrine, yet it held numerous contradictions, as Mrs. Roosevelt's own life illustrated. Traditional marriage almost by definition required a subordination from women that was incompatible with public life, but Mrs. Roosevelt did not address this issue.

Repeatedly Mrs. Roosevelt pictured conventional marriage as the most desirable station in life for women, including her own daughter. Years later Anna Roosevelt remembered how she had been compelled in 1924 to make a debut, the social rite that served to announce that an upper-class young woman was available for marriage. "I grew up in a most inconsistent . . . and a very difficult atmosphere to think through," she said. "Because, on the one hand, here were my parents with their social and political views . . . and, on the other hand, here I was being forced [into society]."[24]

Clearly Mrs. Roosevelt's own pursuit of a career showed that she herself could not be content simply to be known as a wife, no matter how prominent her husband. Continuing to be coached by Howe in writing techniques, she began to make money from her magazine work, "necessary evidence to her that she could go it alone," according to Elliott Roosevelt. Her family did not always applaud her efforts, but she persisted. Ignoring comments from her son James, for example, that he "wouldn't write for such a magazine," she turned out a piece on women and politics for *Redbook*, known at that time chiefly for light fiction.[25]

Her schedule created conflicts between her own role as a governor's wife and her career aspirations. Her Sunday night departures from Albany for New York for three full days of teaching left a void for some occasions requiring a hostess. Living in the governor's mansion, her husband's secretary, Marguerite (Missy) LeHand, filled in for her, becoming Roosevelt's increasingly close confidante.[26]

When Roosevelt became a leading contender for the 1932 Democratic presidential nomination, Mrs. Roosevelt faced with trepidation the prospect of living in the White House. While she took advantage of her position as a wife to influence her husband, to what degree she had so far succeeded was debatable. During his two terms as governor she had pressed him unsuccessfully to sponsor child-labor legislation, argued against his abandonment of Prohibition, and disapproved of his withdrawal of support for the League of Nations and World Court. Once in the White House she would be able to work behind the scenes to shape policy, but she could never be sure whether she would be heeded.[27]

This marginal exercise of influence was not sufficient for Eleanor Roosevelt after she began, through trial, error, and incessant activity, to develop a public role within a framework of social feminism. If passion had evaporated from marriage, there remained duty, which called on her to make life useful and meaningful. Having broken the Victorian mold for women, she had discovered she liked public recognition for her own achievements. This seemed an impossible aspiration in view of the constraints placed on previous first ladies. She noted in her autobiography, "I had watched Mrs. Theodore Roosevelt and had seen what it meant to be the wife of the President, and I cannot say that I was pleased at the prospect."[28]

The night Roosevelt received word that he had won the Democratic nomination for president, Mrs. Roosevelt glared at a woman reporter among the well-wishers thronging the governor's mansion. This stony-faced stare constituted her sole reply when the woman gushed, "Mrs. Roosevelt, aren't you thrilled at the idea of being in the White House?" The look intrigued another reporter, Lorena A. Hickok of the Associated Press, who was among the crowd. She recognized that Eleanor Roosevelt was not the usual candidate's wife. Soon Hickok would become an intimate friend, advising Mrs. Roosevelt on ways of breaking down the barriers that had enclosed her White House predecessors.[29]

3

Lorena A. Hickok, Unlikely Mentor 1932–33

New York, Nov. 9 (AP)—"If I wanted to be selfish," said Mrs. Franklin D. Roosevelt today, "I could wish that he had not been elected."

The voters settled that matter yesterday, however, and on March 4 Mrs. Roosevelt will acquire the title bestowed upon her so often in the last few months by the toastmasters.

"I suppose they'll call me that," she said, "But there isn't going to be any 'First Lady of the land.' There is just going to be plain, ordinary Mrs. Roosevelt."

She smiled, but the expression in her eyes was serious.

"I never wanted it," she said softly, "even though people have said my ambition for myself drove him on—even that I had some idea in the back of my mind when I married him.

"I never wanted to be a President's wife, and I don't want it now. You don't quite believe me, do you? Very likely no one would—except possibly some woman who had had the job. Well, it's true, just the same.

"For him I am deeply and sincerely glad. I wouldn't have had it otherwise. And now I shall start to work out my own salvation."

—First of a three-part series on the new first lady
by Lorena A. Hickok, AP staff writer, 1932

On the surface Lorena Hickok seemed a peculiar friend for Eleanor Roosevelt, since their backgrounds and experiences were strikingly dissimilar. Yet it was Hickok who taught Mrs. Roosevelt to trust women reporters and to use them in constructing an acceptable public role as first lady. In time the pupil would far surpass the teacher, but initially Hickok appeared the superior in terms of personal and professional competence.

Few women made it to the top of the man's world of journalism in the 1920s and 1930s, but Lorena Hickok exhibited exceptional determination. Surmounting sex prejudice as she fought her way upward in journalism, she became one of New York's leading "front-page girls," the title given to outstanding women reporters. Although the census counted nearly 12,000 women reporters and editors in the United States in the 1930s, most were limited to women's pages, women's magazines, or excessively sentimental "sob sister" feature stories. Most were denied the opportunity of covering the same "hard news" as men, such as politics, crime, courts, public affairs, and other front-page topics. Even the exceptional women reporters were paid less than men and expected to make "few demands of their city editors," according to Ishbel Ross, herself a "front-page girl" for the *New York Herald-Tribune*. "The fact remains that they never were thoroughly welcome in the city room and they are not quite welcome now," she wrote in 1936.[1]

Four years before the 1932 campaign, Hickok encountered Mrs. Roosevelt while covering the Democratic National Committee headquarters in New York City, but she was not impressed. In retrospect she described Mrs. Roosevelt at that point as "very plain," with prominent front teeth and "light brown hair tightly tucked under a hair net that even covered part of her forehead." Hickok also was struck by Mrs. Roosevelt's height—approaching six feet—awkward appearance, and unbecoming clothes. When Hickok interviewed Mrs. Roosevelt in the governor's mansion, she considered her poor copy— "woman's page stuff"—and a standoffish individual who kept away from reporters.[2]

At the time they became acquainted Hickok had just accomplished a rare feat for a woman—obtaining a job with the Associated Press. Her life, noteworthy in its own right aside from her impact on Mrs. Roosevelt, illustrated the herculean efforts needed for a woman to succeed in journalism. Born in 1893 in East Troy, Wisconsin, she acquired an inner armor of resistance against the cruelty of her father, a traveling butter maker. In a fragmentary autobiography she wrote: "Never once did he whip me—and the whippings grew progressively more severe as I grew older—when I didn't mutter, inaudibly behind my gritted teeth: 'You wouldn't dare do this to me if I were as big as you are.'"[3]

At the age of fourteen Hickok was ordered by her stepmother to leave the family home, then in the dusty village of Bowdle, South

Dakota, where her mother had died the previous year. For two years the awkward teenager earned her living as a "hired girl," until a saloon keeper's kindhearted wife made arrangements for Hickok to live with her mother's cousin, Ella Ellie, in Battle Creek, Michigan. After completing high school there, Hickok spent an unhappy year at Lawrence College, in Appleton, Wisconsin, where sororities rejected her and she was taunted with the nickname "Fatty."[4]

Turning to newspaper work, Hickok began as a cub reporter in Battle Creek, meeting trains and collecting items for the personal columns, before moving on to the *Milwaukee Sentinel*. Sex-stereotyped as a society reporter, Hickok overcame this handicap by volunteering for night assignments to gain favor with the city editor. She also deliberately provoked a dowager into demanding she be fired, a tactic that resulted in her transfer to the regular reportorial staff.[5]

From the *Sentinel* she progressed to the *Minneapolis Tribune* in 1917, where she eventually attained unusual distinction for a woman. At the start of her career there, however, she left the paper briefly, hoping to go to Russia as a war correspondent. She got only as far as New York, where she was fired following a month's stint on the *New York Tribune*. Returning to Minneapolis, she enrolled at the University of Minnesota while working on the *Tribune* at night. When a dean of women tried to force her to live in a dormitory, she dropped out of college.[6]

At the Minneapolis paper Hickok starred as a protégée of Thomas J. Dillon, the managing editor, whom she affectionately called "The Old Man." She credited him with teaching her "the newspaper business, how to drink, and how to live," as well as giving her assignments, including political and sports stories, usually reserved for men. Acclaimed as a feature writer, she was named Sunday editor and made the paper's chief bylined reporter, but she felt keenly the disadvantage of being a woman.[7]

When a male journalism student interviewed her, he described her as being "good-natured, overweight, erratic and the cleverest interviewer in this section of the country." But she discussed herself and her women colleagues with self-loathing: "I always think of the woman journalist type as a sour individual, a kind of disillusioned being, with the 'Listen girlie' manner, and mannishly dressed. Something like myself, is the type, I guess, only I don't dress mannishly.

Then there's another sort of woman journalist—the office flirt variety. That sort is rather messy, coming into the office and disrupting all the organization of the reporting staff. On the whole, I like them better than the first type. The first is just awful." She also complained of the limitations placed on advancement by her sex: "The best job in a newspaper office is, of course, the managing editorship and you seldom see a woman getting a job like that."[8]

In 1927 Hickok tried again in New York. She had been stricken with diabetes the previous year and had left Minneapolis for San Francisco to regain her health while trying unsuccessfully to become a writer. New York journalism during the jazz age reeked of sex, sin, and sensationalism as reporters jousted for blazing tabloid headlines. Hickok fit right in.

After a year on the Hearst tabloid the *Daily Mirror*, she was hired by the Associated Press in 1928 for its new feature service. Her difficulties as a woman in a man's world did not abate. Writing to Bess Furman, her counterpart in AP's Washington bureau, she spewed out her anger: "The trouble is that, being a woman, I never should have gone into this business. My God, how tired I get of being a woman reporter!"[9] Knowing Furman would understand, she complained about discrimination in assignments, noting her seventeen years of reporting and "even with my handicap of sex, more varied experience, than any man here . . . below the rank of general Eastern editor." Yet, she continued, "the AP wouldn't let me handle a big story, not if there was a male cub, not yet dry behind the ears, within 50 miles of the place! Sometimes it hurts like hell. Sometimes I just get—savage."[10]

Eventually industry and competence, combined with her human interest, "sob sister" approach, brought Hickok recognition. When the baby son of aviator Charles A. Lindbergh was stolen from his nursery on March 1, 1932, Hickok joined the boisterous crew of reporters dispatched to the Lindbergh estate near Hopewell, New Jersey. Literally beating down bushes for clues, she searched an abandoned farmhouse, where she found muddy footprints. She also crawled up a mountain path at 2 A.M. to peer in the windows of the Lindbergh home to check out a false report that the baby had been returned. When his body later was found in a shallow grave near the farmhouse, Hickok suffered what she called a "delayed heartbreak" to realize how close she had come to breaking the phenomenal story. All she had been able to get on the wire were "bright little color stories" invented by "humming Brahms' 'Lullaby' to get myself worked up to the proper pitch," she noted years later.[11]

Such enterprise gave Hickok "standing with the AP that no other woman has matched," according to Ishbel Ross. At the time her path crossed Eleanor Roosevelt's, the gruff-voiced, genial Hickok was described as "hard-boiled and soft-hearted at the same time—a big girl in a casual raincoat with a wide tailored hat, translucent blue eyes and a mouth vivid with lipstick." She had finally broken into the male ranks of political reporting as the only woman assigned to cover Franklin Roosevelt when the 1932 campaign opened.[12]

After watching Mrs. Roosevelt's strange behavior on the night of the nomination, Hickok suggested to her editor that a reporter be assigned to the candidate's wife, although she did not want the job. It went to Katherine Beebe, another woman in the AP New York office, but Beebe soon resigned. Hickok inherited the assignment about a month before the election.[13]

Even before Beebe left the scene, Hickok had sought to make friends with Mrs. Roosevelt on the campaign train. Initially Hickok went out of her way to resume her acquaintance with Malvina Thompson, Mrs. Roosevelt's secretary, confiding memories of her painful childhood to Thompson, who apparently relayed them to Mrs. Roosevelt. Known for her kindness toward the unfortunate, Mrs. Roosevelt warmed up to "Hick," as everyone called her. Although cool toward full-time news coverage, she was persuaded by Howe to help the campaign by letting Hickok accompany her "whenever I do anything publicly."[14]

The close relationship between Thompson, known as Tommy, and Mrs. Roosevelt, whom Thompson always called "Mrs. R.," illustrated one aspect of Mrs. Roosevelt's dependence on women as a source of emotional, as well as practical, support. Unlike women who seek rewarding relationships only with the opposite sex, Mrs. Roosevelt developed close attachments with both men and women. Frances Perkins observed that Mrs. Roosevelt "was very much a woman's woman. She talked with another woman on the frankest, pleasantest terms." Yet she had intense friendships with men too, including the handsome Earl Miller, a state policeman assigned to the governor's mansion.[15]

Among the women with whom she had close ties were several thought to have lesbian relationships, including Dickerman and Cook. As Joseph Alsop, a Roosevelt cousin, explained, "There is no use pretending that the atmosphere that Eleanor Roosevelt lived in during the Twenties and the early Thirties was not a partly Lesbian atmosphere." While denying that she was a lesbian, Alsop concluded that independent, self-assertive women who functioned without men as dominant factors in their lives served as role models for the increasingly independent Mrs. Roosevelt.[16]

In addition, passionate female attachments may have been known to Eleanor Roosevelt as a teenager. A short novel titled *Olivia* appeared in 1948, chronicling a lesbian attachment that ended tragically within a girls' boarding school. Written by Dorothy Strachey-Bussy, who taught Eleanor Roosevelt English literature at Allenswood, the novel, a lesbian classic, depicted a passionate infatuation between an innocent pupil and a commanding figure modeled after Marie Souvestre. A girl named Laura is introduced as a minor character, described as dressing "dowdily" and having a face "almost plain," but "so frank, so candid, so glad and so intelligent." Although Laura is believed to be Eleanor Roosevelt herself, Mrs. Roosevelt never acknowledged it, nor commented on the book after being sent a copy.[17]

Of Hickok's own homosexual orientation there is considerable evidence. Obviously she developed a crush on Eleanor Roosevelt so intense that it caused Hickok to give up her hard-won career. To what degree the attachment was expressed in physical terms, however, remains unclear. Eleanor Roosevelt was a product of the Victorian era when friendship flourished on many levels between persons of the same sex. Intimate, loving friendships between women, married or unmarried, were not treated as deviations from the normal, as they were to be viewed later, but were seen as an acceptable form of social tie. To the degree the Roosevelt-Hickok relationship had sensual as well as platonic aspects, it fell into what one scholar has termed "the female world of love and ritual" of the nineteenth century.[18] But in the case of historical figures like Eleanor Roosevelt, the pertinent issue is not what physical manifestation occurred but the significance of the association to the individual's achievements.

The challenge of Mrs. Roosevelt's life as first lady was the creation of a public personality suitable for a woman of her station, embracing many of her personal experiences but still allowing her a private life. In this undertaking she could have found no better assistant than Hickok. Accepting Mrs. Roosevelt's claims that she did not like publicity, Hickok, to prove her loyalty and to keep a monopoly on her news source, initially advised Mrs. Roosevelt on ways of dealing with other journalists. "About those reporters and cameramen—If there are any at the station, I can probably get rid of them without any hard feelings if I tell them you'll see them when you get back from Cambridge. Would that be too awfully bad?" Hickok scrawled in a note to Mrs. Roosevelt on a Boston trip. "I know you hate it." [19]

During the campaign Hickok had little to report, since Franklin Roosevelt's advisors thought it would appear unseemly for his wife to be very active. Hickok's first story about Mrs. Roosevelt, an interview on her forty-eighth birthday, hinted at her forebodings over the prospect of becoming first lady. "I'm a middle-aged woman," Hickok quoted her as saying. "It's good to be middle-aged. Things don't matter so much. You don't take it so hard when things happen to you that you don't like." In September Beebe had written a glowing article, introducing Mrs. Roosevelt as "an aristocratic Democrat," and "a person of more than one paradox." Hickok later picked up on the theme of the contradictions in Mrs. Roosevelt's personality. [20]

Soon Hickok herself was figuring in the stories she filed—identifying herself as "a friend" or a "woman companion." One dispatch the week before the election described Mrs. Roosevelt inspecting the site of a water power project on the St. Lawrence River. It referred to her "striding swiftly down through a cow pasture, while the cows stared at her mistrustfully," and the "friend" stumbled along behind. [21]

When Mrs. Roosevelt went to visit her sons at the Groton school, she took Hickok along only on "the understanding I don't have to put out anything unless a really good story breaks," Hickok informed her editors. To head off orders to produce a "good story," Hickok enumerated the few unlikely possibilities she foresaw: an automobile accident, attempted kidnapping, or a comment if anything happened to a member of Mrs. Roosevelt's family. Hickok concluded, "No reporters are allowed at the school. In taking me with her, she is not telling them I am a reporter." [22]

As the sole reporter assigned to Mrs. Roosevelt before the election, Hickok turned out a stream of stories used primarily by the pro-

Roosevelt press to keep the candidate's name before women readers, although some of Hickok's voluminous detail was cut out. Roosevelt's opponent, Herbert Hoover, tried belatedly to meet this challenge. Bess Furman was summoned into Mrs. Hoover's private car for a single interview as the Hoover campaign train pulled through Ohio. Mrs. Hoover discussed her great-grandfather, who had founded Wooster, Ohio, but Furman was allowed to use the information only as if gleaned from a library. It provided a pale contrast to the stories on Mrs. Roosevelt that were punctuated with direct quotes.[23]

Hickok's best pieces about Mrs. Roosevelt ran immediately after Roosevelt's landslide election on November 7, 1932. They showed her as a career woman with a life of her own, and they finally portrayed her reluctance to become first lady, which Hickok had hinted at earlier. Hickok was the only reporter allowed to accompany Mrs. Roosevelt to her class at Todhunter school the day after the election. The beginning of Hickok's article read, "In a small classroom with blue-painted woodwork and walls decorated with charts and maps done by her pupils, the wife of the next President of the United States came back to her job this morning."[24]

The following day Hickok started the first in a three-part series with unusual news from a politician's wife: " 'If I wanted to be selfish,' said Mrs. Franklin D. Roosevelt today, 'I could wish that he had not been elected.' " Dramatic quotes continued, representing page-1 material, had they appeared before the election. They were constructed out of confidences entrusted to Hickok on the campaign train, but carefully saved until Roosevelt safely had won. "I trust you," Mrs. Roosevelt had told Hickok.[25]

Obviously Mrs. Roosevelt had become Hickok's closest friend, to be introduced to the nation in the best possible light via the Associated Press. In the series Hickok presented Mrs. Roosevelt as a traditional yet commendably independent woman, combining the feminine virtues of modesty, self-effacement and service to others with modern career interests. In the same story that described her reluctance to become first lady, Hickok included three other news items: Mrs. Roosevelt intended to dispense with Secret Service escorts; she planned to give up teaching at Todhunter; she intended to continue her journalistic activities. Hickok quoted Mrs. Roosevelt on her plans to edit a magazine called *Babies—Just Babies* so she could earn money to give "directly to people who need help." In the story Mrs. Roosevelt said, "The contract was signed months ago with my husband's permission."[26]

The second installment of the series, dispatched the next day, featured an interview with Mrs. Roosevelt as she recalled her life story while gazing out of a Pullman car window. The story emphasized Mrs. Roosevelt's development as a person, the recurring theme of the Eleanor Roosevelt legend. It included references to her unhappy girlhood, the liberating influence of Souvestre, her settlement-house work before marriage, the births of her children, her years in Albany and Washington, and her volunteer work during World War I. She credited war work with enlarging her interests, although she said she had to curtail her activities to nurse her husband through his polio ordeal.[27]

"The war," Hickok quoted her as saying, "was my emancipation and my education." It also was the period of her husband's affair with Lucy Mercer, but that, of course, was not mentioned. More surprising, neither was the often-told tale of her entry into politics to keep her husband's name before the public during his convalescence.[28]

The final article depicted Mrs. Roosevelt as a new kind of first lady who would refuse to give up her individuality in the White House, in spite of social convention. It began: "The prospective mistress of the White House thinks people are going to get used to her ways, even though she does edit *Babies—Just Babies*, wears $10 dresses, and drives her own car." It praised her "whirlwind" ability to get along "perfectly on five or six hours' sleep a night," and credited her with nearly superhuman self-control: "She is never hurried, apparently never harassed, and is seldom, her secretary says, even slightly irritable." This paragon also, it was said, "likes a truly Spartan life," and "has intimate friends among people of all ages and all circumstances of life." Her voice was called "gentle, beautifully modulated," a questionable description, since other observers referred to her high-pitched giggle.[29]

By this time Hickok clearly had become part of the Roosevelt publicity apparatus. In violation of professional standards, she cleared her stories in advance of publication with either Howe or Mrs. Roosevelt. This was an act, Hickok later confided to Malvina Thompson, "that probably no other reporter in the country would have done."[30]

Hickok, concerned that the cameras did not capture the warmth of Mrs. Roosevelt's personality, also tried to advise her on having her pictures taken. Mrs. Roosevelt merely shrugged and said, "My dear, if you haven't any chin and your front teeth stick out, it's going to show on a camera plate." She and Howe joked about their unflattering press photographs.[31]

Hickok's closeness to Mrs. Roosevelt did not escape the notice of her editors. The closeness helped Hickok obtain a quick, vivid account of Mrs. Roosevelt's reaction to the attempted assassination of her husband less than a month before the inauguration. But it brought Hickok into disfavor for failing to write a story giving Mrs. Roosevelt's reaction to criticism of a comment she had made on her paid radio series around the same time. Sponsored by Pond's, a cold-cream manufacturer, the series included a dozen programs on child-rearing and family relations. On one broadcast Mrs. Roosevelt remarked that the girl of today "faces the probability of learning, very young, how much she can drink of such things as whisky and gin, and sticking to the proper quantity." Apparently made sarcastically, the comment provoked outrage from Prohibitionists.[32]

Mrs. Roosevelt asked Hickok to ignore the incident, so she told her editors it was "doubtful" that she could get a story on it. Unfortunately for Hickok, Mrs. Roosevelt discussed the remark with a male reporter for the *New York Post*, thinking it was "off the record," and he wrote a story. "I was given Hell [by the editors] and my salary was cut as a disciplinary measure," Hickok recalled late in life to Thompson.[33]

The radio series generated newspaper criticism that the future first lady was using her name "for commercial purposes," and Mrs. Roosevelt announced that she intended to accept no more radio contracts. In a bylined story Hickok reported that Mrs. Roosevelt would "curtail somewhat her activities" after moving into the White House. She quoted her as saying, "I suppose I have made some mistakes."[34]

The election made it impossible for Hickok to keep Mrs. Roosevelt to herself as a news source, although both women tried to continue their unique relationship. On election eve Mrs. Roosevelt drove with Hickok in a small convertible from Poughkeepsie to New York, leaving behind a rival woman reporter who wanted to ride in the rumble seat. Mrs. Roosevelt also left women reporters idling around her office at the Democratic National Committee while she took off with Hickok, who then wrote exclusive stories about Mrs. Roosevelt's usual flurry of activity. When a persistent woman reporter tried to track Mrs. Roosevelt from Albany to Hickok's New York apartment, Mrs. Roosevelt refused to be followed and stayed in Grand Central Station until her pursuer gave up.[35]

As the Roosevelts left New York for Washington and the March 4, 1933, inauguration, Hickok rode down on their train for one last big story about Eleanor Roosevelt. Hickok had obtained permission from the president-elect to interview his wife following the inaugural ceremony, marking the first on-the-record interview by a first lady in the White House. The interview took place in a bathroom, the only spot Mrs. Roosevelt could find to avoid interruptions.[36]

Copyrighted by the AP, the story quoted Mrs. Roosevelt's concern over depression conditions, illustrated by the reaction to her husband's inaugural address: "The crowds were so tremendous and you felt that they would do anything—if only someone would tell them what to do." In spite of economic hardship, she called on women to "go about our daily task of home making," and she outlined her own housekeeping regime for the White House: trying out nutritious menus for families of depleted incomes, cutting back on expenses "twenty-five per cent," and simplifying social life. The interview also announced that she would serve as her crippled husband's "eyes and ears," seeing as many Americans as possible and reporting to him about their concerns.[37]

It constituted an announcement that she would play a more political role than any previous president's wife, but the interview did not receive prominent news display and this disappointed Hickok. The story landed on page 7 of the *New York Times* while a bright AP feature in the bated-breath style of Furman made page 1. It started, "The century-old White House wore a startled air today as its new mistress took over."[38]

By this time Hickok realized that she had ceased to think like a reporter, having passed up bigger stories than the interview. As Mrs. Roosevelt's closest friend, Hickok accompanied her the day before the inauguration to view the St.-Gaudens statue *Grief* in Rock Creek Cemetery and to hear Mrs. Roosevelt recount her sadness over the Mercer affair during her previous residence in Washington. That night she listened while Mrs. Roosevelt read aloud her husband's inaugural address, never even thinking about telephoning the gist of it to the AP and thereby gaining her "biggest scoop," she recalled thirty years later. Confessing guilt over neglecting her job to Howe, she received little comfort. "A reporter," he told her drily, "should never get too close to news sources."[39]

The night after the inauguration Hickok headed back to New York and never covered Mrs. Roosevelt again. In a letter marking the start of an exchange of correspondence that grew to 3,000 letters over a thirty-year period, Mrs. Roosevelt wrote, "Hick, my dearest, I cannot go to bed tonight without a word to you. I felt a little as though a part of me was leaving tonight, you have grown so much to be a part of my life that it is empty without you even though I'm busy every minute."[40]

No doubt the two women met emotional needs in each other. To the self-made Hickok, whose friends saw her as a diamond in the rough, Mrs. Roosevelt represented unattainable heights of aristocratic charm, warmth, and ladylike dignity. To Eleanor Roosevelt, Hickok offered a model of success in the man's world of journalism, which Mrs. Roosevelt admired. Furthermore, Hickok provided a pillar of emotional security at a time when Mrs. Roosevelt was perplexed and anxious over her move to the White House, fearing that convention would keep her from continuing to develop an independent career.

Equally important, Hickok possessed the professional skill to provide an extremely useful service for Mrs. Roosevelt. She was able to translate Mrs. Roosevelt's complex personal aspirations into an acceptable public image during the pivotal preinaugural period. Hickok's favorable articles helped Mrs. Roosevelt win acceptance as a different kind of first lady.

Hickok's aid did not end with her coverage of Mrs. Roosevelt. While she churned out preinauguration stories, down to the details on Mrs. Roosevelt's gown, of an unflattering blue-gray shade named "Eleanor blue," Hickok hit on a long-range plan for public relations. She proposed that Mrs. Roosevelt hold press conferences for the capital's women reporters. Hickok knew news, and she knew the frustrations experienced by women who tried to compete with men to get it. She was sure that a first lady who supplied news that men could not obtain would endear herself to women reporters.[41]

When Hickok suggested such conferences, Mrs. Roosevelt demurred, certain that neither her husband nor Howe would approve. But they did, as Hickok had expected, for they saw the publicity value involved. Over the years the conferences would become more than just a way of publicizing the New Deal. Hickok's inspiration would make Mrs. Roosevelt the focal point for a group of women journalists who would provide a lifelong network of support and friendship. They would help to make Eleanor Roosevelt into a symbol of womanly achievement that transcended partisan politics.[42]

4

The "Newspaper Girls" 1933

It will save my time enormously if I see you all together once a week and do not have to see three now and three later and so on. I feel that your position as I look upon it is to try to tell the women throughout the country what you think they should know. That, after all, is a newspaper woman's job, to make her impressions go to leading the women in the country to form a general attitude of mind and thought. Your job is an important one and if you want to see me once a week I feel I should be willing to see you, and anything that I can do through you toward this end I am willing to do. The idea largely is to make an understanding between the White House and general public. You are the interpreters to the women of the country as to what goes on politically in the legislative national life and also what the social and personal life is at the White House.

—Eleanor Roosevelt's statement to the newspaperwomen attending her first press conference, March 6, 1933

Like Hickok, many of the thirty-five women reporters who assembled for Mrs. Roosevelt's first press conference had struggled against the handicap of their sex to attain journalistic careers. They represented the heart of the women's press corps in the capital. Its origins dated back to 1850 when Jane Grey Swisshelm, a correspondent for Horace Greeley's *New York Tribune*, marched into the Capitol press galleries determined to claim equal privileges with men, but left after a brief stay. In 1933, nearly a century later, women journalists still were fighting for equality and suffering recurring defeats. Barred from membership in the National Press Club, where prominent figures made news-making appearances, the women had their own professional group, the Women's National Press Club, but they found it hard to gain equal access to news sources.[1]

The women, almost universally referred to as "newspaper girls," were routinely paid less than men. Relatively few tried to compete directly with male journalists by covering politics and government; most wrote features or were assigned to women's pages and society news. The depression made their situation particularly precarious, a fact that Hickok pointed out to Mrs. Roosevelt. In her autobiography Mrs. Roosevelt noted, "Unless the women reporters could find something new to write about, the chances were that some of them would hold their jobs a very short time. Miss Hickok pointed out many of these things to me, because she felt a sense of responsibility for the other women writers."[2]

In planning the conferences, Hickok enlisted the aid of her colleagues. Six weeks before the inauguration, Furman, known for her woman's-angle features, drove all night from Washington to New York to lunch with Mrs. Roosevelt at Hickok's suggestion. When Mrs. Roosevelt broached the subject of press conferences, "It was her belief that news of interest to women the country over was being bypassed," Furman noted in her diary.

A freckle-faced former teacher from Nebraska, Furman had worked her way through Kearney State Teacher's College before becoming a reporter in Omaha, where her talent at feature writing brought her a job offer from the Associated Press. Furman thought the press conference proposal a godsend to women reporters accustomed to being ignored by the White House. To get a "close-up" piece on Lou Henry Hoover, for example, Furman had resorted to disguising herself in a Girl Scout uniform and joining a scout group singing Christmas carols at the White House.[3]

Mrs. Roosevelt also mentioned the conference proposal to Marguerite Young of the *New York World-Telegram*, who informed Ruby A. Black, a feminist operating her own Washington news bureau. Young wrote Black that she viewed Mrs. Roosevelt as a refreshing change from the usual women's page subject: "She is slightly more than a clothes rack; although I, of course, disapprove of publicizing anybody, as someone else's appendage." Young welcomed the conferences, too, because she believed they would give reporters a chance to pin Mrs. Roosevelt down. At the Democratic convention in Chicago, Mrs. Roosevelt mysteriously had denied plans to attend the funeral of former President Calvin Coolidge, although she went to it, Young told Black.[4]

The plan delighted Black, who had been hired on a part-time basis by the United Press, in spite of its prejudice against women reporters, to compete with Hickok's coverage of Mrs. Roosevelt for the Associated Press. Black was the "third girl . . . that they've tried out on Mrs. R.," Hickok informed Furman, and Black intended to be the last. A resourceful individual like Furman, Black also had been determined to obtain news about the aloof Mrs. Hoover. To get details for an innocuous story titled "Mrs. Hoover's Day" in *Household* magazine, Black had bribed a male colleague for material gleaned by "snooping around among the Secret Service men."[5]

A prototype of the 1920s flapper with her slim figure and boyish haircut, Black was a Texas-born feminist who used her maiden name. Taking an independent path early in life, she had chopped cotton as a child and paid her own way through the University of Texas. She acquired experience as a reporter in Madison, Wisconsin, where she attended the University of Wisconsin, and in St. Louis. But she had been rebuffed when applying for a job with the United Press where her husband, Herbert Little, worked as a reporter. In rejecting her job application, a vice president wrote, "Very frankly, from the standpoint of effective management I regard one member of a family as quite enough in any one office." To this Black responded that women tired of fighting discrimination eventually would avoid marriage.[6]

With Mrs. Roosevelt planning to hold press conferences for women only, Black's hopes for a press association job soared. She eagerly discussed the conferences with Furman, Ruth Finney, a correspondent for Scripps-Howard newspapers who had staked out a career by covering public power issues being overlooked by men, and other women reporters. In a letter to Mrs. Roosevelt, Black suggested that Malvina Thompson meet with "an informally selected committee representing straight news reporters, feature writers and society editors to work out such eligibility rules as may be necessary and as you may desire." She listed three groups from which to draw the committee—an informal organization of White House society writers known as the "Green Room group," women members of the White House Correspondents Association, and the "more than twenty women" admitted to the congressional press galleries.[7]

Mrs. Roosevelt's willingness to have personal contact with reporters broke all precedents for a first lady's press relations. She was, for example, the first president's wife to attend the annual stunt party of the Women's National Press Club. Stunt parties included spoofs on public figures and politics and were the women's counterpart of all-male Gridiron dinners for leading political figures and journalists. Mrs. Hoover had refused to attend a stunt party, not even acknowledging the invitation. Her predecessor, Grace Coolidge, while personally liked by the women reporters, had been an equally uncooperative news source. Ordered by President Calvin Coolidge not to make statements to reporters, Mrs. Coolidge, once a teacher in a school for the deaf, had used sign language when pressed to speak at a luncheon for press women.[8]

By contrast, Mrs. Roosevelt's apparent openness promised exciting new opportunities for women reporters. When Mrs. Roosevelt expressed fears that she might not have anything to say at the conferences since political news "must come from my husband," Black reassured her in a letter that the newspaper women "are confident your wide interests will give us much interesting news." Black described establishment of a committee to plan the conferences with Howe. Members were Furman, Finney, Katharine Dayton of the Consolidated Press, Ruth E. Jones, society editor of the *Washington Herald*, and Black.[9]

Jones compiled a list of newspaper women who wanted to attend and submitted it to Stephen T. Early, Franklin Roosevelt's press secretary, with the understanding that only one woman from each of the Washington newspapers was to attend. Early then certified forty reporters representing Washington newspapers, press associations and Washington bureaus of metropolitan dailies. His role showed that the Roosevelt administration considered Mrs. Roosevelt's press conferences a part of its well-orchestrated program to communicate with the public.[10]

No previous administration had devoted as much attention to political communication. Presidential press conferences dated back to Theodore Roosevelt, who developed them as a strategy to feed the news-hungry press that gobbled up White House reports. Under Woodrow Wilson the informal press conferences of Theodore Roosevelt developed into an institutionalized channel of political information, sending a flow of news throughout the government and to the public as a whole. During his four terms, Franklin Roosevelt utilized all the technology of the day—radio, newsreels, photography—to reach the American people, but his most regular channel of communication remained the White House press corps. During his White House tenure, he held frequent press conferences, exchanging an estimated five million words with reporters in 998 conferences.[11]

Just where did press conferences by the first lady fit into this process? This question would be answered through a mutually rewarding relationship that started before the conferences began. Mrs. Roosevelt wanted to do a job within the administration. Fearful of having few meaningful tasks in the White House, she had asked her husband if she could help with his mail, only to be told that his secretary, Missy LeHand, would consider it interference with her job. Through press conferences Mrs. Roosevelt hoped to make her position of use to others and so to convince herself that her life had importance. As one who needed to feel needed, Mrs. Roosevelt could gain the satisfaction of knowing she was aiding other women to keep employed during the depression.[12]

In gratitude for her help, at least some women reporters tried to shield Mrs. Roosevelt from adverse publicity that might cause the press conference idea to be abandoned. In 1981 Dorothy Roe Lewis, a retired professor of journalism at the University of Missouri who in 1933 reported for Universal Service, the Hearst night wire service, recalled Mrs. Roosevelt rushing up to her and three other women reporters, Hickok, Black, and Dorothy Ducas. According to Lewis, Mrs. Roosevelt tried to leak the news that her husband had refused to sign a joint proclamation with Hoover to close the banks the day before the inauguration, but the four told her the story could start a "worldwide panic" and refused to print it.[13]

Ducas, the only other member of the group alive in 1981, recalled covering Mrs. Roosevelt for International News Service, the day wire service for Hearst newspapers. "The women always covered up for Mrs. Roosevelt. All kinds of things were said [by her] that shouldn't be said in print," she said. Ducas credited Hickok with guiding Mrs. Roosevelt in press relations: "I think Hickok helped her not to dissimulate—made her say the wise things, not the impulsive. Mrs. Roosevelt had a tendency to ramble on."[14]

Mrs. Roosevelt's single press conference between election and inauguration had proven more of an embarrassment than a success. Mrs. Roosevelt questioned the propriety of the inaugural ball because of the depression, but outbursts of protest came from the garment industry, florists, musicians, and others who stood to profit from it. Mrs. Roosevelt quickly changed her mind.[15]

Perhaps because of this, the prospect of regular conferences made news. Mary Hornaday announced their advent in the *Christian Science Monitor*. She noted, "The feminine contingent of the Washington press corps is anticipating more 'copy' than they have had for a long time." Furthermore, she added, "a number of newspaper women have already obtained additional contracts on the strength of announcements from Mrs. Roosevelt that she will hold meetings with women writers."[16]

Hornaday, described by a contemporary as "quiet" and "modest," was a Swarthmore graduate whose father was a Washington correspondent for the *Indianapolis News*. She had been hired by the *Monitor*'s dignified bureau chief, Cora Rigby, the first woman to head a Washington office for a major newspaper and a charter member of the Women's National Press Club, founded in 1919. At the time the press conferences started, Rigby had been dead three years, and Hornaday was the only woman in the *Monitor*'s Washington bureau as well as one of the few women regularly assigned to Congress. From their inception to their end twelve years later, Hornaday covered Mrs. Roosevelt's conferences regularly. Reflecting on them years later, she saw the guiding hand of Hickok. "I think Lorena Hickok persuaded Mrs. Roosevelt that everything she did was news," Hornaday commented.[17]

The first conference was held March 6, 1933, just two days after Roosevelt's inauguration and two days before he held his initial press conference. Mrs. Roosevelt detected disapproval from Ike Hoover, the chief White House usher, as she entered the Red Room where the "girls" were assembled. She thought that the White House staff considered a press meeting undignified for a first lady.[18]

Hornaday recalled Mrs. Roosevelt's agitation: "She was so nervous . . . that she grabbed up a box of [candied] grapefruit peel and passed it to her 'guests.'" Hornaday thought that Mrs. Roosevelt was uncertain whether she should act as a hostess. In her autobiography Mrs. Roosevelt remembered, "Most of the women facing me were total strangers . . . I only hope they did not know how terrified I was in entering this untried field." She added, "I knew, too, that many people around my husband were doubtful whether I could handle press conferences without getting myself and him into trouble."[19]

The first conference, intended as a get-acquainted session, yielded little news except Mrs. Roosevelt's reasons for the gatherings. She told the women it would save her time to see them in a group. In her autobiography she listed another practical purpose — to avoid the journalistic snooping of the Hoover years. Consequently, Mrs. Roosevelt wrote, she decided that "everything that was legitimate news should be given out by me."[20]

By this statement she showed an intuitive grasp of the advantages gained through holding press conferences. True, she might be disconcerted by embarrassing questions. But the conferences gave her the chance to influence directly her own portrayal. A press conference represents a staged event, starring a key figure. Daniel J. Boorstin has called it a "pseudo-event," an activity created to make a person, idea, or act seem important. To Boorstin the "pseudo-event" leads the public to confuse heroes with celebrities by elevating those who are known simply for "well-knownness."[21]

Journalists themselves have raised questions about manipulation of the news through press conferences. The one in control decides the ground rules—time, place, duration—often choosing in advance topics to bring up, and brushing off unwelcome questions. Integrity of the news-making process, however, concerned most of the women reporters covering Mrs. Roosevelt less than the opportunity to have direct access to the first lady.[22]

In managing the conferences, Mrs. Roosevelt, like President Roosevelt at his press conferences, put definite limitations on the use of direct quotations. The president stipulated that they could be used only when given out in writing by his press secretary. Mrs. Roosevelt initially required reporters to obtain permission from her and to check their notes for accuracy with her secretary, Malvina Thompson. The loyal and unobtrusive Thompson stationed herself on one side of Mrs. Roosevelt at the conferences and kept a shorthand record. Nearby sat Edith B. Helm, the discreet widow of an admiral, who was the White House social secretary. She advised on questions pertaining to the social calendar.[23]

Bolstering their self-esteem by referring to the journalists as "interpreters to the women of the country," Mrs. Roosevelt saw their importance as channels for communicating specifically to women. She saw the conferences, according to her autobiography, as a way of identifying news "of special interest and value to the women of the country and that the women reporters might write up better than the men." Her interest in a women's communication network was encouraged by Howe, one of the few male politicians of the era who did not discount women voters. Howe believed a woman could be elected president on grounds of feminine insight into humanitarian concerns linked to the depression.[24]

But Mrs. Roosevelt realized the need to tread carefully and not "trespass on my husband's prerogatives," as she expressed it. This may have accounted for her reply at the first conference when asked if she had a message for American women facing the depression. No, she replied, because the president had delivered his inaugural speech to all the American people and "American people include the women." She consented to be quoted only as saying, "The time is one that requires courage and common sense on everybody's part."[25]

That remark was compressed into a one-column headline, "All Alike in Crises," above a brief, nonbylined story on the conference in the *New York Times*. The reporter was fifty-four-year-old Winifred Mallon, who had chronicled capital affairs, both governmental and social, for thirty years, first for a news bureau and starting in 1929 for the *Times*, as its first woman political writer. A strong voice in the Women's National Press Club, Mallon believed the organization essential to combat "the conspiracy of men to keep women off the newspapers—or at least to reduce their number, wages and importance to a minimum."[26]

Mallon, unlike some of the other women at the first conference, did not always stay in Mrs. Roosevelt's good graces. Those present who soon formed Mrs. Roosevelt's inner circle included Furman, Black, Genevieve Forbes Herrick of the *Chicago Tribune*, Elizabeth May Craig, a correspondent for the Guy Gannett newspapers of Maine, Martha Strayer of the *Washington Daily News*, and Emma Bugbee of the *New York Herald-Tribune*. (Hickok never covered the conferences, but Mrs. Roosevelt kept her informed via letters and telephone calls.)

Genevieve Herrick, nicknamed Geno, was the only one in the group whom Hickok considered her equal. Known for her graceful writing, speed, and accuracy, Herrick had become a "front-page girl" for the *Chicago Tribune* after graduating in journalism from Northwestern University in 1916 and completing a master's degree in English at the University of Chicago the following year. Her journalistic feats included posing as an Irish immigrant and crossing the Atlantic in the steerage to expose the hardships of immigration. She also had treated readers to exclusive interviews with Al Capone and other gangland figures. Recognizing the tremendous prejudice against women, she advised novices that the newspaperwoman "should strive to write all the news she can better than as many men as she can."[27]

Unlike Herrick and most of the women reporters at the conferences, Elizabeth May Craig, a peppery, life-of-the-party type, disagreed with Mrs. Roosevelt on an important issue—the admission of men to the press conferences. As a young woman, Craig had attended George Washington University Nursing School. Becoming a journalist to help her husband, a Washington correspondent for the *New York Herald*, after his injury in an automobile accident in 1923, Craig had struggled hard to attain equality with male correspondents in news coverage. One of the first women political columnists, she produced "Inside in Washington" for Maine newspapers.[28]

Along with Black, Finney of Scripps-Howard, and a few other women, Craig was accredited to President Roosevelt's press conferences and thought it unfair to bar men from Mrs. Roosevelt's. Mrs. Roosevelt never agreed with this viewpoint, contending that the admission of men would "encroach on my husband's side of the news," a statement indicating she thought news topics could be divided along sex-role lines.[29]

Taking shorthand notes on the first conference—as she was to do at each conference she attended over the twelve-year period of their existence—was the industrious Martha Strayer. Shorthand had proven the key to her landing a job on the *Washington Daily News* and she customarily used it for all of her assignments. A native of Ohio, Strayer had not been able to afford college. Hired as a secretary when the *Daily News* opened its doors in 1921, she attained her goal of becoming a reporter two months later by walking twenty-five blocks through five-foot-deep snowdrifts to cover the collapse of a theater roof that killed ninety-eight moviegoers. The *Daily News*, where she was to spend her entire forty-three-year reportorial career, soon became her life.[30]

Expecting to return to New York, Emma Bugbee of the *New York Herald-Tribune*, a leading Republican newspaper, lingered after the first press conference to tell Mrs. Roosevelt good-bye. Described by a contemporary as a "shy girl with candid blue eyes and a New England conscience," Bugbee was a graduate of Barnard College. She already had spent twenty years as the paper's chief woman reporter and had covered Mrs. Roosevelt in New York. When Bugbee mentioned that she was "crazy to know what things were like upstairs [in the White House]," Mrs. Roosevelt quickly responded with an invitation to "come to lunch tomorrow and bring all the New York newspaper girls with you." The following day the first lady led a small group of wide-eyed reporters through the family living quarters, including the president's bedroom, and gave permission for feature stories about the chintz slipcovers and other homey furnishings preferred by the Roosevelts.[31]

Bugbee's editors were so impressed that they told her to remain in Washington as long as Mrs. Roosevelt was generating stories. Four months elapsed before Bugbee returned to New York. During this period Mrs. Roosevelt met with the reporters at least weekly, encouraged them to follow her on trips and entertained them at the White House.[32]

The resentment and contempt of male reporters surfaced after publication of a photograph taken at the second conference, March 13, 1933, in the family living room. It accompanied a story about curtailment of White House entertaining because of the depression. The picture showed Mrs. Roosevelt with women reporters clustered about her, some sitting on the floor at her feet. It disturbed Furman, who sent a copy back home to Nebraska, telling her family: "The girls . . . all crowded around to get in the picture —just like they were a bunch of tourists who never saw a President's wife before. . . . It is not my original idea of the way the picture should look and I was the one who asked for it."[33]

The pose prompted masculine competitors to dub the group "the incense burners," and gave them an excuse to scoff at the gatherings, which they initially had scorned. When Furman told Byron Price,

Associated Press bureau chief, about plans for the conferences, he predicted that they would last less than six months—"the only poor prediction I ever heard him make," Furman said. According to Hornaday, "Mostly the men preferred to ignore Mrs. Roosevelt and her views." [34]

At least one other woman reporter was dismayed at the sight of her colleagues on the floor gazing up at Mrs. Roosevelt. Mrs. George F. Richards, who wrote a column signed simply "Richards" for the *Worcester* (Massachusetts) *Gazette* and other New England papers, was appalled and refused to attend other conferences. Richards, described as the last woman in the press gallery to sport a tippet (a long fur stole), jet beads and a bonnet, was one of the few Republican women reporters not captivated by Mrs. Roosevelt along with their Democratic counterparts. [35]

Contact with the first lady affected the personal lives of many of the women. Black told readers of the *Matrix*, a magazine published by Theta Sigma Phi, a journalism sorority of which she was a past national president, that Mrs. Roosevelt had gone to Black's home to see Black's baby daughter, Cornelia Jane Little, the second Sunday after the inauguration. "Cornelia Jane's first party and her first movie were at the White House on March 25, when she went to 'Sistie' Dall's birthday party," Black bubbled on. (Sistie was Eleanor Dall, Mrs. Roosevelt's grandchild). [36]

Black's child was not the only one so favored. According to Dorothy Roe Lewis, the children of all members of the Washington press corps were invited to the White House to play with the Roosevelt grandchildren, and any reporter covering Mrs. Roosevelt's press conferences "received flowers from the White House greenhouse if she stayed home even a day with the sniffles." Every year, Lewis noted, her parents received a Christmas card signed by the Roosevelts and invitations to White House social events, even though they lived in southern Arkansas and it must have taken "exhaustive research" to locate them. The families of other reporters were similarly remembered. [37]

In a letter to her relatives in Nebraska, Furman praised Mrs. Roosevelt's kindness to her but, perhaps nervous at the prospect of losing reportorial objectivity, discounted any special treatment.

"Twice she had picked me up in her car, just to help me along my rushing way," Furman wrote. "And it isn't favoritism. She's just as nice to any of the press women assigned to cover her."[38]

The friendship between Mrs. Roosevelt and the women reporters stemmed from a natural rapport between like-minded persons, Rosamond Cole, once Ruby Black's assistant, recalled in 1979. Many of the women liked Mrs. Roosevelt "as a person," because they shared her liberal views, Cole said: "She stood for everything they stood for [believing] the New Deal was going to rescue us." Career benefits also figured in. Cole noted, "They were smart, intelligent women who were well established in journalism before Mrs. Roosevelt came along, but their friendship with her didn't hurt their standing with their editors." She remembered how Black and other women reporters were invited to visit Mrs. Roosevelt at Hyde Park and Campobello.[39]

Still this did not mean that the women were totally happy with the press conferences as news sources. Furman wrote in her diary that Mrs. Roosevelt would tell willingly "when she gets up in the morning and what she eats for breakfast . . . [but] she rules out all controversial subjects, and won't be queried on anything in the province of the President." Describing the conferences' meandering quality in the *Matrix*, Black stated that Mrs. Roosevelt would talk only in general terms about social concerns such as housing, married women working, education for peace, and not about pending legislation.[40]

Sharper criticism was voiced directly to Mrs. Roosevelt by Anne Hard, a *Tulsa Tribune* correspondent. In a letter dated March 27, 1933, she called for "thoughtful questions prepared in advance," to cut down on the "silly and useless—and possibly impertinent." She also recommended limiting the duration of the conference to conserve Mrs. Roosevelt's strength. This was a polite way of calling for shorter sessions. The few women who were busy political writers, like Ruth Finney, objected to spending up to an hour and a half in chitchat that might not produce solid stories.[41]

But the women's press corps wanted the conferences to continue. As Hard concluded, "So far as the purely selfish standpoint of the woman writer in Washington is concerned, the value of those conferences cannot be overestimated." The focus of the conferences remained troublesome for their duration, but the problem of news production was partially addressed. The White House press office made sure that Mrs. Roosevelt occasionally gave the newswomen a sensational announcement. More to the point, Mrs. Roosevelt and the reporters struggled together to keep the conferences a viable medium that benefited both the first lady and the journalists.[42]

Eleanor Roosevelt at Democratic State Committee headquarters in New York in 1929 with (left to right) Nancy Cook, Caroline O'Day, and Marion Dickerman. Forced to resign as editor of the *Women's Democratic News* when Franklin Roosevelt was elected governor, Mrs. Roosevelt continued to work behind the scenes. Franklin D. Roosevelt Library.

Kate Scott, first president of the American Newspaper Women's Club, served Eleanor Roosevelt tea at the first party given for her after President Roosevelt's first inauguration. Anna Roosevelt Dall, her daughter, shared the honors at the event held by special permission at the male-only National Press Club on March 6, 1933. American News Women's Club.

Eleanor Roosevelt's press conference in the Monroe Room of the White House on March 13, 1933. Martha Strayer is believed to be the woman in the back row behind Mrs. Roosevelt, wearing glasses and a hat with a white bow. Bess Furman is in the front row at the extreme left (seen in profile). Franklin D. Roosevelt Library, supplied by Historical Pictures Services, Inc.

"For gosh sakes, here comes Mrs. Roosevelt!"

Eleanor Roosevelt's wide-ranging travels kept her constantly in the public eye and inspired this *New Yorker* cartoon in 1933. Perhaps it was the cartoon that prompted her descent into a coal mine two years later. Drawing by Robt. Day; © 1933, 1961, The New Yorker Magazine Inc.

Governor Paul Pearson of the Virgin Islands as he escorted Lorena A. Hickok and Eleanor Roosevelt on a tour of St. Thomas, March 7, 1934. Franklin D. Roosevelt Library.

Reporters who accompanied Eleanor Roosevelt on her trip to the Caribbean in March 1934 gathered around her in Puerto Rico. Left to right: Emma Bugbee, Dorothy Ducas, Mrs. Roosevelt, Ruby Black, and Bess Furman. Franklin D. Roosevelt Library.

Eleanor Roosevelt and her secretary, Malvina Thompson (second from left), with two of Mrs. Roosevelt's close newspaper friends, Martha Strayer, left, and Bess Furman. This photograph is believed to have been taken in 1934. Franklin D. Roosevelt Library.

Members of the American Newspaper Women's Club (now the American News Women's Club) presented a skit, "Where Is Alice?" based on *Alice in Wonderland,* at the first Gridiron Widows party given by Eleanor Roosevelt at the White House, December 8, 1934. Left to right: Elisabeth Ellicott Poe as the Duchess with her pig; Lillian Arthur as the Mad Hatter; Kate Scott Brooks as the March Hare; Margaret Hart as the White Rabbit; Margaret Germond as the Dormouse; and Katherine M. Brooks as the Red Queen. The American News Women's Club.

'BUT IT WOULD MAKE SUCH A NICE SCOOP IF YOU'D ONLY TELL ME, FRANKLIN.'

Speculation over whether Franklin D. Roosevelt would run for a third term in 1940 lay behind this cartoon, which originally appeared in the *Augusta* (Georgia) *Chronicle* on April 28, 1940. It was a time when Eleanor Roosevelt's "My Day" column was carefully read by political observers eager to pick up hints of the president's plans. This drawing so amused Mrs. Roosevelt that she requested the artist's original. *Augusta Chronicle.*

Eleanor Roosevelt posed with Mayor Fiorello H. LaGuardia in his office in Washington after she was sworn in as assistant director of the Office of Civil Defense. The ceremony, marking the first time a president's wife had held an official appointment, took place on September 29, 1941. Library of Congress.

Just before the United States entered World War II, Eleanor Roosevelt interviewed Daniel Arnstein, a transportation expert who had recently returned from China, on her NBC broadcast of November 23, 1941. UPI Acme photo/Bettmann Archive.

Helen Essary, *Washington Times-Herald* columnist and president of the Women's National Press Club, sat between President and Mrs. Roosevelt at an off-the-record club luncheon in the president's honor at the Willard Hotel in 1941. Roosevelt was the first president to attend a meeting of the club. He was introduced as the "husband of Eleanor Roosevelt, columnist." National Press Club Archive, Women's National Press Club.

As part of her effort to prepare the nation's women for war, Eleanor Roosevelt joined Henrietta Nesbitt, White House housekeeper (left), and Harriet Elliott, associate administrator in charge of the consumer division of the Office of Price Administration, in taking the "Consumer Pledge for Total Defense" on November 3, 1941. Library of Congress.

5

Headlines and Friendships
1933–34

When it is legal to serve beer in any government house, it will
naturally be proper to do so for any one who desires it at the White House.

I hope very much that any change in legislation may tend to improve
the present conditions and lead to greater temperance. There has been a
great deal of bootlegging in beer and once it is legal this will be unprofitable
and I hope that a great many people who have used stronger things will be
content with legal beer so that the cause of temperance will be really served.

No matter what the legislation, I myself do not drink anything with
alcoholic content but that is purely an individual thing. I should not dream of
imposing my own conviction on other people as long as they live up to the
law of our land.

—Statement by Eleanor Roosevelt at her press conference,
April 3, 1933

As she developed close relationships with some of the reporters,
Mrs. Roosevelt received their affection along with advice on how
to conduct the conferences. Since the concept was so novel, a few
reporters volunteered to help the first lady create news that would
impress their male editors. Although professional standards called on
them to be impartial observers behind the scenes, a small group of
Mrs. Roosevelt's friends actively allied themselves with her in planning
for the success of the conferences. They planted questions, proposed
topics, and coached on the wording of statements. Sometimes Mrs.
Roosevelt accepted their advice; other times she did not. Often she
expressed appreciation by hospitable gestures, including trips to Hyde
Park. Through meeting with the women, both informally and at the
actual conferences, Eleanor Roosevelt enhanced her skill in dealing
with the press and overcame her initial nervousness. Howe and Hickok
remained her trusted confidants, but now she also consulted with her

intimates among the press women. Through a trial and error process, Mrs. Roosevelt soon became accustomed to making headlines.

The press conferences produced front-page news on April 3, 1933, when Mrs. Roosevelt announced that beer would be served at the White House as soon as it was legal to do so. This marked the first time the women reporters got a story that their male counterparts considered significant news. The announcement easily could have been made by President Roosevelt or his press secretary. But when the president was asked at his press conference about the return of beer as the first step in ending Prohibition, he referred reporters to his wife. From a political standpoint, it made excellent sense for the first lady to be the spokesperson on the use of alcoholic beverages. Known as a teetotaler, she could partially appease the Prohibitionists, still a potent political element, by referring to her personal abstinence.[1]

Alerted to the prospect of Mrs. Roosevelt making this controversial announcement at a press conference, her reporter friends hastened to offer assistance. After lunching at the White House to discuss ways of improving the conferences, the prim Martha Strayer, herself a teetotaler, advised Mrs. Roosevelt on the beer statement. She told her to prepare "a carefully thought-out statement . . . written in advance with enough copies so that everybody could have one." She also advocated a "carefully worded expression of hope that the change would contribute to temperance." Mrs. Roosevelt followed both suggestions, but ignored Strayer's admonition to confine the April 3 conference discussion to that statement only. Instead, Mrs. Roosevelt commented on topics ranging from Easter hats to sweatshops, perhaps to deemphasize the beer question.[2]

Strayer assured Mrs. Roosevelt that she was "a very grand person" and the conferences "a very grand idea" that Strayer wanted to promote. Stating that she worked closely with men who decided what made news, Strayer told Mrs. Roosevelt to emphasize her plans for the traditional White House Easter egg rolling because newspapers gave the event a lot of space. Egg-rolling trivia might be inserted among the messages "you really want to give out," Strayer commented. "That will help give them an air of unpremeditation, which I think most necessary." In this category, she put statements on relief and volunteer programs to bring renewed hope to poverty-stricken women.[3]

Black, an active member of the National Woman's party, urged

Mrs. Roosevelt to speak out on feminist issues. Black sought a press conference statement opposing an act of the Hoover administration aimed at the discharge of married women from the federal work force during budgetary cutbacks if their husbands also were government employees. Three days after Black's request Mrs. Roosevelt made a statement protesting dismissals of workers based on marital status. It marked the first of numerous occasions when the first lady broke her professed ban against involvement in political matters. The discriminatory provisions, however, were not repealed until 1937, four years later.[4]

The statement favoring retention of married women workers received relatively poor news display, compared to human interest items. Editors were more interested in Mrs. Roosevelt's activities than her pronouncements. Copious details of the egg rolling filled columns. Mrs. Roosevelt's tumble from a horse during her daily ride received even more attention from Bugbee and other reporters.[5]

Furman cannily sought personal ties with Mrs. Roosevelt that paid off in news stories. At first she used Hickok's name to develop rapport with the first lady. One time shortly after the inauguration Mrs. Roosevelt started to brush off Furman, who sought to accompany her on a walk, but Furman quickly mentioned Hickok, and Mrs. Roosevelt's mood changed. She wrote Hickok that she had been "almost rude to Miss Furman," until discovering that "she's nice though & likes you which melted my heart!" Within two months Mrs. Roosevelt accepted an invitation to tea at Furman's home. When the first lady admired a small ornament Furman was wearing, the reporter bought her an identical one.[6]

In return, Mrs. Roosevelt took Furman along on what Furman recounted in her diary as "a most glorious night of high adventure, flying with Mrs. R. and Amelia Earhart to Baltimore and back—in evening dresses!" The flight, a publicity stunt for Eastern Air Lines, yielded a byline for Furman. It came shortly after Furman received a letter from Mrs. Roosevelt confiding that she had been blacklisted for active membership in the Daughters of the American Revolution, although arrangements were being made to make her an honorary member. It would have been a big story but Furman kept it quiet.[7]

In June 1933, Furman continued to refer to Hickok in efforts to influence the press conferences. (By this time Hickok, caught between

53

devotion to Mrs. Roosevelt and duty to her editors, who pressed for intimate news on the Roosevelts and their family, had left the Associated Press. Mrs. Roosevelt had encouraged Hickok to resign, writing her, "When you haven't the feeling of responsibility to the AP, I know you have a happier time with me.") Proposing subjects for Mrs. Roosevelt to discuss, Furman complimented the first lady in a letter for expressing appreciation of Hickok's career at a luncheon for a select group of reporters that included Black, Bugbee and Herrick. "I just love the things you said and the way you said it," Furman wrote. "The entire occasion was one to be treasured always in memory—to be trotted out at the times when the going seems rough."[8]

The praise, however, did not prompt Mrs. Roosevelt to do what Furman wanted—comment publicly on divorce in view of the marital breakup of her son Elliott. But the first lady obediently brought up at a press conference two of the other subjects Furman mentioned— Franklin Jr.'s college graduation trip to Europe and plans for the Roosevelt grandchildren's Fourth of July. Human interest items of this type formed the basis for the social columns that Furman churned out among her other journalistic chores.[9]

A detested sideline for Furman, society writing represented the chief livelihood for many of the conference regulars. With Mrs. Roosevelt's hectic schedule of official entertaining and other activities announced at the start of each conference, these women received reams of material. But social reporters never became part of her inner circle, reflecting a split among Washington women journalists. Society reporters moved in different circles from those of journalists like Black and Furman, who competed directly with men.

The alienation of the two groups was institutionalized in 1932 when a group of women withdrew from the Women's National Press Club, which emphasized luncheons with serious speakers, and formed the Newspaper Women's Club (which remains in existence today as the American News Women's Club). Active membership initially was limited to women employed by newspapers, but associate status was available to prominent women who were helpful to social reporters, and honorary membership was given to women famous either in their own right or through their husbands. Led by cofounders Margaret Hart and Katharine M. Brooks, both society reporters for the *Wash-*

ington Star, the club staged parties and benefits for charity. On the day of Mrs. Roosevelt's first press conference, it entertained her and her daughter, Anna, at tea, and Mrs. Roosevelt received honorary membership.[10]

Relationships between Mrs. Roosevelt and the society writers were somewhat strained, according to two journalists who looked back on the conferences decades later. "I don't think the society reporters were very impressed," commented Dorothy Ducas, who covered Mrs. Roosevelt from 1933 to 1935. She said Mrs. Roosevelt showed too little social flair to add luster to the society pages. "Mrs. Roosevelt was unconventional in some ways but not others," Ducas said. "If she gave a tea it was absolutely conventional." To Rosamond Cole, Black's assistant, "Mrs. Roosevelt wasn't a society glamour girl . . . and she didn't help the society pages, so maybe society reporters felt she had let them down."[11]

The gulf may have widened because of varying attitudes toward personal appearance. Society writers placed a premium on the arts of makeup and dress. For them Mrs. Roosevelt presented an uncongenial model. "She had no pride in her physical appearance at all," remembered Ducas. "That was implicit in everything she did—she never played up her blue eyes, for example."[12]

Mrs. Roosevelt's appearance as a presidential candidate's wife had come as a shock to Kathleen McLaughlin, a *Chicago Tribune* reporter. McLaughlin saw Mrs. Roosevelt at the national Democratic convention in Chicago in 1932 "shrinking to the back rail of this elevated rostrum" overshadowed by her husband. "My God," McLaughlin first thought. "She was so long and so tall and she was wearing black cotton stockings and a very simple, unchic, straight-line dress, black, with red floral sprigs; and a very large hat, rather flat-crowned; black gloves and a pedestrian handbag."[13]

In the White House Mrs. Roosevelt sought to improve her wardrobe. She arranged with Arnold Constable, a New York store, to obtain fashionable clothing at reduced rates in return for being photographed in outfits identified with the store's name. But Mrs. Roosevelt did not relish the role of model. According to Anne Wassell Arnall, who photographed Mrs. Roosevelt for Arnold Constable, the first lady hurried through the photography and "never bothered to look at herself before her picture was taken." Still the fashion photographs made news, especially for women's pages, which promoted department store advertising.[14]

Questions about Mrs. Roosevelt's wardrobe came up repeatedly at her press conferences. In her answers, she displayed an adroit defensiveness. Asked what she would wear for a series of balls on the president's birthday to raise money for the fight against infantile paralysis, for example, she answered, "A perfectly plain cream-colored tricot silk" and a white fur evening coat, "the only one I have, and probably the only one I will have for many years." It was a wise reponse for the depression years, which saw an estimated one-third of the population ill-housed, ill-clothed, and ill-fed. When Mrs. Roosevelt was selected to head the list of the best-dressed American women of 1934, the reporters wanted to know her reaction. "Was I? I didn't know it," she merely replied.[15]

Hope Ridings Miller, society editor of the *Washington Post* during the Roosevelt administration, believed that Mrs. Roosevelt's own emotional needs propelled her away from those reporters who were concerned with fashion and society. For many of the frantically busy "hard news" women, matters of style and grooming held little personal appeal. For instance, Black was described as having hair "usually in the same dishevelled state as a little boy's." Plainness predominated among the regulars, according to Ducas, whose heart-shaped face and carefully groomed dark hair made her an exception.[16]

"Mrs. Roosevelt's closest friends were very homely girls and Lorena Hickok was one of them," Miller recalled. "Mrs. Roosevelt was homely herself and felt comfortable with them. She felt she could do something for them—build up their ego." This was not to say that society writers were overtly hostile toward the first lady, Miller continued. "She gave us plenty to write about; usually when press people write mean things they don't have anything else to write."[17]

The style and format of the press conferences were set within the first few weeks. Obviously Mrs. Roosevelt's reports on her activities conveyed a not-so-subtle political message. On May 16, 1933, she described her visit to a camp set up by unemployed World War I veterans seeking soldiers' bonuses. President Hoover had ordered a previous makeshift encampment, believed to be led by communists, burned down, but the Roosevelt administration took a politic tack.

Accompanied only by Howe, Mrs. Roosevelt drove to the site, returning to tell the reporters of a "remarkably clean and orderly camp," according to Strayer. She noted that Mrs. Roosevelt spoke "in a matter-of-fact manner, no doubt intended to quiet all future fears of bonus marchers." [18]

The press conferences soon served to float trial balloons for specific New Deal programs. A week after her visit to the bonus marchers' camp, Mrs. Roosevelt promoted forest work camps for unemployed women. Following complaints that women would be taken from the home, Mrs. Roosevelt and Secretary of Labor Perkins announced jointly that the first camp, at Bear Mountain, New York, would be for single women only. [19]

Whether consciously or unconsciously done, New Deal image making through identification with the past entered into the press conferences, too. At the end of May 1933 Mrs. Roosevelt invited the press women to join her on a tour of two Virginia shrines: Stratford, ancestral home of the Robert E. Lee family, and Monticello, Thomas Jefferson's home. The trip had symbolic value, linking the Roosevelt administration to traditional values at a time of experimentation with unprecedented governmental activity. Mrs. Roosevelt also pressed history into service for hints to the housewife, using her press conference to pass out frugal recipes for dishes that former presidents' wives had served their husbands. [20]

At the same time, Mrs. Roosevelt was confiding to Hickok that her public actions masked her true emotional state. "Monticello was lovely, and everyone is kind, but my zest in life is rather gone for the time being," Mrs. Roosevelt wrote Hickok following the Virginia pilgrimage. "If anyone looks at me, I want to weep . . . my mind goes round and round like a squirrel in a cage. I want to run and I can't, and I despise myself." [21]

Determined to be useful as an antidote to her recurring bouts of depression, Mrs. Roosevelt assumed the role of an instructor for American women on various social topics during the press conferences. This contributed to sudden shifts of subject. On June 15, 1933, for instance, she told the group how women should read a newspaper —"First the headlines, then the first paragraph"—and insisted that the average woman should read three daily newspapers with opposing points of view in order to reach her own conclusions. The same day she attributed unemployment among Arizona copper miners, which she had observed on a recent trip, to competition from underpaid workers in Africa and South America. "They couldn't compete with South Africa savage labor, nor with South America," she said. The remark, with its overtones of racist sentiment, would have caused intense controversy thirty years later, but at the time it did not, probably because the reporters themselves, in line with contemporary biases, did not think it newsworthy.[22]

What did make headlines was Mrs. Roosevelt's denial at a press conference two days earlier that she had insulted Texas Governor Miriam Amanda (Ma) Ferguson on a stopover while returning from Arizona. The first lady had been criticized when photographers were unable to pose the two women together. Mrs. Roosevelt explained that she had decided to eat breakfast before being photographed, and the governor had declined to wait. Since "Ma" Ferguson was a firm supporter of the New Deal, it is unlikely that Mrs. Roosevelt intended to slight her. More important than the incident was Mrs. Roosevelt's use of the public opportunity to defuse criticism; over the years the press conferences became her personal tools for defending herself and her family.[23]

Their rambling nature, however, made them of little value to the very top women reporters, who did not attend regularly. While Franklin Roosevelt's press conferences did not exceed twenty-five minutes, Mrs. Roosevelt's lasted three to four times as long. Anne O'Hare McCormick of the *New York Times*, the first woman to win a Pulitzer prize for reporting, interviewed President Roosevelt but paid no attention to Mrs. Roosevelt's conferences, although Mrs. Roosevelt told Hickok that she had made the arrangements for McCormick to see the president.[24]

With time out for summer vacations with Hickok, which reporters were told were off-the-record, Mrs. Roosevelt held twenty-nine press conferences in 1933 and thirty-eight in 1934, the record number for a single year while she was in the White House. As the first term progressed, Mrs. Roosevelt turned the conferences into a platform for prominent women in the New Deal: Secretary of Labor Perkins; Nellie Tayloe Ross, director of the mint; Hilda Smith, who had charge of women's camps; Ellen S. Woodward, director of women's relief work in the Federal Emergency Relief Administration;

and Dr. Louise Stanley, chief of the Bureau of Home Economics, Department of Agriculture. Guests came from outside the administration, too—Ishbel MacDonald, daughter of the British prime minister; Dame Rachel Crowdy of the League of Nations; and Rose Schneiderman, an old friend and president of the National Women's Trade Union League.[25]

By presenting these women, Mrs. Roosevelt established herself at the center of a network of those involved in women's causes, but effective action did not necessarily result from publicizing their concerns through the press conferences. In December 1933 Mrs. Roosevelt pointed out that women on relief were paid less for skilled work in sewing, nursing, and teaching than men doing unskilled labor in relief projects. This led reporters to question Harry L. Hopkins, federal relief administrator, about women's pay. He replied, "Yes, I know it's lower. We think that's right." Women's pay was not raised.[26]

New Deal women invited to the conferences pushed causes as diverse as Stanley's effort to promote the use of dried skim milk and Woodward's attempt to reassure women that they would get a fair share of relief jobs. Strayer told Mrs. Roosevelt that the guests were not as effective as the first lady herself. "Frankly, Mrs. Roosevelt, I don't believe you can delegate your own ability to publicize practically anything you may choose to mention," Strayer commented after hearing a faltering attempt by Mary Harriman Rumsey to interest the reporters in her "buy now" campaign. Rumsey, who directed the consumers' division of the National Recovery Administration, had little success in persuading housewives to consume more to aid the economy.[27]

To help publicize the "buy now" campaign, Mrs. Roosevelt proposed that Strayer and Furman be hired part-time by the NRA. The first lady's friendship with the two reporters had led to discussions of their personal finances. Both women needed extra money. Furman's husband, Robert Armstrong, had lost his job with the *Los Angeles Times* after his father was dismissed as Washington bureau chief for that paper. When the senior Armstrong's investments evaporated in the depression, Furman had to support her in-laws as well as her husband. Strayer was unmarried but wanted to assist depression-stricken relatives. Mrs. Roosevelt offered the publicity job after trying to loan money to Furman, whose savings of $625 were wiped out in a bank failure. Furman declined with a sentimental note: "Someday, I myself am going to have the pleasure of putting down in printer's ink just what a swell person you are."[28]

For Strayer, described as a pleasant woman with a "gentle, rather wistful expression," the offer created conflict between professional ethics and a wish to earn more, coupled with eagerness to aid the New Deal. "I take a great deal of pride in the fact that I do an honest job, that I've never done a line of publicity or taken the simplest kind of favor in return for anything I've written," she wrote Mrs. Roosevelt. In rejecting the proposal for herself and Furman, however, Strayer was apologetic: "We're so sincerely anxious to do anything we can for the NRA and the whole New Deal, that it seems perfectly awful to say we've decided we're a little afraid of the proposal to work with Mrs. Rumsey." Furman had good reason to be afraid, since she had signed an oath not to accept government money while on the AP payroll.[29]

It was not surprising that Mrs. Roosevelt failed to understand the line between publicity and reportorial work, since the reporters themselves seemed to cross it in providing her guidance with press relations. Even as she turned down the job offer, Strayer suggested several planted questions to make the conferences more newsworthy. She urged Mrs. Roosevelt to "allow us" to ask questions about her plans for a winter wardrobe as part of the "buy now" campaign. Strayer also proposed the women raise queries so Mrs. Roosevelt could refute criticism of the Bear Mountain camp for unemployed women and describe her book, *It's Up to the Women*: "Something direct from you would make a much better story than just a plain outline of the book itself," Strayer advised.[30]

Possibly in return for such assistance, Mrs. Roosevelt encouraged Strayer to ask as many questions as she liked at the conferences, although other newswomen resented her wandering inquiries. Mrs. Roosevelt's secretary, Malvina Thompson, "sometimes looks as if she was about to explode, and the restlessness among the reporters as a whole often becomes extremely marked," noted Frances Parkinson Keyes, a magazine writer who became a best-selling novelist. Keyes remarked that Strayer's intimacy with Mrs. Roosevelt approached, but did not equal, that of Furman, Black, and Herrick.[31]

Mrs. Roosevelt kept an eye on the women's news stories to see whether New Deal programs were receiving favorable mention. In the summer of 1933, she wrote to Hickok, "Geno Herrick wrote two nice things about HP [Hyde Park, where she had been a guest] and Camp Tera [the Bear Mountain camp for unemployed women]. She is so much better than Emma." The difference may have been due to editorial direction. By this time both Herrick and her husband, John, also a journalist, had left their jobs with the Republican *Chicago Tribune* because they did not want to write articles unfavorable to the Roosevelt administration. Geno Herrick changed to a newspaper syndicate and her husband took an administration public relations job at the Department of the Interior. In contrast, Bugbee represented the Republican *New York Herald-Tribune*, which did not encourage fulsome praise of Democratic programs.[32]

But at her press conferences, Mrs. Roosevelt played down her own political involvement, maintaining the conventional fiction that a president's wife should remain aloof from politics, even though she obviously violated this dictum. On January 16, 1934, Mary W. (Molly) Dewson, director of women's activities for the Democratic National Committee, appeared at a press conference to announce the "reporter" plan for party women. This called for a pyramidal organization extending from the national level down to the local level with women designated as "reporters" in each county who were to inform themselves and others about New Deal programs. Ruby Black tried, unsuccessfully, to get Dewson to admit that Mrs. Roosevelt was behind the plan. According to Black, "Mrs. Roosevelt gave me a humorously reproving look for my impudence." Black reported in *Editor and Publisher*, the newspaper trade journal, that all of the women knew Mrs. Roosevelt was responsible.[33]

As the correspondent for Maine's only liberal newspaper, Black once supplied Mrs. Roosevelt with information about a Republican-dominated combination of waterpower and banking interests allied with Guy Gannett, the owner of a rival newspaper. Mrs. Roosevelt passed the material on to President Roosevelt, who commented at his press conference, "Ruby Black brought Mrs. Roosevelt some clippings about the Gannett [interests] in Maine. . . ." The incident brought an uncharacteristically sharp note from Black to Mrs. Roosevelt: "Can't you persuade your husband to be more discreet? Was my face red."[34]

Perhaps to compensate for Black's annoyance, Mrs. Roosevelt

arranged for Black to get an exclusive story. In a copyrighted article in November 1933 Black scooped her competitors with the news that plans for a national theater would be laid before President Roosevelt as the result of discussions between Mrs. Roosevelt and actress Eva Le Gallienne. Eventually the idea became part of the Federal Theater Project.[35]

The news value of the conferences soared in early 1934. The first big story was another announcement about alcoholic beverages —a statement that wines would be served in the White House after the repeal of Prohibition. This time, Mrs. Roosevelt and the press women orchestrated the release of the story themselves, an indication of their rapport. Mrs. Roosevelt had offered to hold a special press conference as soon as the repeal bill was signed, but the president rejected this suggestion, preferring not to draw extra attention to the announcement.[36]

Instead, when the women arrived for the regular conference on January 29, 1934, a White House usher passed out a five-line statement saying that wine, preferably American, would be served in the White House but not distilled liquor. Mrs. Roosevelt took pains to ensure that the representatives of the leading wire services, Furman and Black, were not scooped: after a society reporter raced to a telephone to break the story, contrary to Mrs. Roosevelt's wishes, the first lady let Furman and Black use the telephones in her private quarters.[37]

At this point frequent contact with the press had sharpened Mrs. Roosevelt's zest for news, as shown by her actions when Meggie, her Scottish terrier, bit Furman while she was riding in Mrs. Roosevelt's car. The first lady rushed Furman to a hospital, held her hand while the wound was stitched up, and insisted on calling the Associated Press. She even offered to write the story, but an astonished editor rejected the suggestion. A *Washington Post* reporter, who saw Furman and Mrs. Roosevelt leave the hospital, broke the story, so the AP was forced to follow suit.[38]

In the spring of 1934 the press conferences became a forum for Mrs. Roosevelt to answer criticism of her involvement in the resettlement of unemployed West Virginia miners at Arthurdale, a planned community for subsistence farming and factory work. First she denounced charges by Dr. William A. Wirt, school superintendent of Gary, Indiana, who claimed that the project was communistic. Two weeks later she responded to accusations by Senator Tom Schall, a Republican from Minnesota. Schall alleged that Mrs. Roosevelt was wasting $25 million in tax funds to set up a furniture factory in West Virginia. Mrs. Roosevelt notified the senator that she would like to see him before her conference with "the girls." When he did not appear, she proceeded with a lengthy refutation: no $25 million furniture factory had been proposed for Arthurdale, she said, only a small factory to make post office boxes, which was being opposed by a company already in existence.[39]

By furnishing ammunition for public controversy, the conferences soared in news value to the delight of "hard news" reporters like Furman. On Easter Monday, Mrs. Roosevelt read a parody of Wirt's communist-hunting activity at a press conference, after presiding over an Easter egg rolling and inspecting a school kitchen for the underprivileged. Furman ecstatically noted in her diary that she had received bylines on several stories that day but the "Wirt story was best of all." According to her entries, that day far surpassed a "blue Monday" two months before when the conference produced only one story—"about a Negro to sing at the White House." When the Schall charges were answered, Furman jotted down, "And Mrs. R. made the third swell news story of the month."[40]

The Arthurdale project, which continued to make headlines embarrassing to the New Deal, marked the most conspicuous of Mrs. Roosevelt's ventures into administration programs. Because Louis Howe ordered flimsy prefabricated houses that had to be rebuilt for the project, the homesteaders were not able to move in on schedule. Strayer recommended a public disclosure of the housing fiasco and Mrs. Roosevelt replied, "Entirely off the record, I tried to get Colonel Howe and the Secretary [Harold L. Ickes] to make a statement saying that these houses had been an experiment, that they had not worked out." Previously Howe had been her advisor. Now she was his in effective political communication. Since Mrs. Roosevelt's first hesitant press conference, where she had squelched her own anxiety by passing out candy, she had become wise enough in the ways of the press to realize that the best defense may sometimes be the offense.[41]

Mrs. Roosevelt's interest in West Virginia stemmed from her friendship with Hickok. After leaving the Associated Press, Hickok took a job, which Mrs. Roosevelt arranged for her, as chief investigator for Harry L. Hopkins, head of the Federal Emergency Relief Administration. Her mission was to travel throughout the nation to observe relief operations, a task that took her to thirty-two states from 1933 until 1936. Her findings were sent to Hopkins in confidential reports and to Mrs. Roosevelt in daily letters and both shared them with President Roosevelt. It was after receiving Hickok's description of the unparalleled destitution near Morgantown, West Virginia, in August 1933 that Mrs. Roosevelt drove there alone to tour the area. Her shock led to the creation of Arthurdale, Mrs. Roosevelt's chief humanitarian project.[42]

In March 1934 Hickok accompanied Mrs. Roosevelt on a mission to inspect depression conditions in Puerto Rico and the Virgin Islands. Obtaining Mrs. Roosevelt's permission to go along were Furman, Bugbee, Black, Ducas, and a male photographer, Sammy Schulman. Black strongly favored the trip, which boosted her influence as Washington correspondent for the Puerto Rican paper, *La Democracia. Time* magazine viewed it as a boondoggle for Hickok, referring to her as a "rotund lady with a husky voice, a preemptory manner, [and] baggy clothes" who has "gone around a lot with the first lady." It labeled her a has-been reporter — "in her day one of the country's best female newshawks." But Hickok's former colleagues barely mentioned her presence on the 6,000-mile trip, which coincided with her forty-first birthday.[43]

In their stories the women depicted Mrs. Roosevelt as a human whirlwind who thrived on a frantic pace that exhausted them. Mrs. Roosevelt seemed totally at ease with the press, calling out to the photographer as she passed by a pool of flies and filth on the street, "Saammee! You can take this." Ducas, dispatched from New York only occasionally to cover Mrs. Roosevelt, saw the first lady in a new light as "one of the girls," frolicking in the surf with a jump rope. Striving for feature angles, the women compressed words to avoid cable charges, which led Ducas to produce a memorable passage: "Ducas onstepped pig running street eliciting squeal pigward remark Eleanor quote poor thing unquote."[44]

Mrs. Roosevelt described the trip in her autobiography as a serious, fact-finding mission for her husband, the first of many to follow. If she saw it as part of her "job" as first lady, it must have stood out as a pleasant interlude. Comparing the task of being first lady with Hickok's position as Hopkins's chief investigator, she told Hickok, "Your job is more stimulating than mine."[45]

It was difficult to determine what Mrs. Roosevelt saw as her "job" because she worked behind the scenes via questions and requests to various officials. Some press women, however, credited her with considerable influence. "Surplus farm products are being fed to the hungry instead of being destroyed because she asked a government official a question," Black trumpeted in *Editor and Publisher*. Hornaday of the *Christian Science Monitor* found it hard to get Mrs. Roosevelt to admit responsibility. After reporters discovered that the first lady had telephoned government officials to ask why surplus pigs could not be fed to the needy, they inquired whether the Federal Surplus Relief Corporation was her idea. According to Hornaday, Mrs. Roosevelt sidestepped a direct answer but said she was "enormously interested" in the agency.[46]

During the summer break of 1934, Mrs. Roosevelt maintained contact with her press conference intimates. Black, who was suffering from exhaustion, took her small daughter to Campobello and recuperated there, indebting the newswoman still further to Mrs. Roosevelt. Black told Mrs. Roosevelt that she had written a United Press story about Campobello and added that she hoped "I said nothing unwise." Like Herrick and her husband, Furman and her husband paid a vacation visit to Hyde Park. Mrs. Roosevelt extended a similar invitation to Strayer and her sister, but Strayer, convalescing from an infected leg, declined. Earlier, in a letter to Hickok, Mrs. Roosevelt had called Strayer "poor thing," and added, "I begin to be sorry for her as I see her at one [news event] after another. At least she has little time to think of the man she didn't marry [a reference to Strayer's confiding in Mrs. Roosevelt about a broken engagement]."[47]

During the first term, Mrs. Roosevelt grew increasingly fond of Furman, whose diary details twenty-seven visits to the White House during one four-month period alone. The usual reason was to cover press conferences and other events, but she was invited three times for lunch, twice with her husband for dinner, including once to the Roosevelts' famous Sunday night scrambled-egg suppers, and twice for tea. With Herrick and Black, she helped plan the first of Mrs. Roosevelt's annual Gridiron Widows' parties for newswomen and wives who were excluded from the all-male Gridiron dinner held by elite journalists to poke fun at honored guests, including the president.[48]

Clearly Furman benefited from the relationship. In her autobiography she describes herself "swinging on a star," by covering Mrs. Roosevelt for the 1,400 newspapers belonging to the Associated Press. In 1979 Kathleen McLaughlin, who moved from the *Chicago Tribune* to the *New York Times*, where Furman eventually worked, remembered her as "a petite, brown-eyed, auburn-haired girl with an infectious giggle, indefatigable in gathering news and in writing it." To her, Furman seemed "always unflappable," and "utterly reliable," and she concluded, "of us all, I tend to think that Mrs. Roosevelt cherished her most."[49]

Undoubtedly, the friendship was a two-way street, but Furman kept her eye on the main objective: to get news. Less than a month after opening Mrs. Roosevelt's 1933 Christmas present of "a cute little black velvet evening jacket," Furman complained in her diary about a press conference that yielded "the most meager results yet." Three days later she wrote: "Dear Diary, Please don't send me anymore ghastly and devilish days like this. . . . Scooped by Martha [Strayer] on Mrs. R.(!)"[50]

There were times when Mrs. Roosevelt wanted freedom from press coverage and her press conference friends obliged. To Hickok Mrs. Roosevelt alluded to concealing plans for an off-the-record weekend from the women reporters, "They smelled a rat but were kind and didn't press me!" she exclaimed. When Hickok and Mrs. Roosevelt vacationed together in the West in July 1934, they successfully avoided the press.[51]

Without doubt some of the women felt compassion for the first lady. Ducas remembered Mrs. Roosevelt as somewhat gullible — "easily led by people she felt were her friends"—and not a profound thinker. "Mrs. Roosevelt once told me," Ducas recalled, "'I don't think I'm very bright but I've been exposed to so many bright people I can pick their brains. That's why I've learned things.'" Ducas saw her as a woman searching for warmth and love while motivated to "do good" under a somewhat "prissy" exterior.[52]

These qualities were conveyed in her press conferences, which differed greatly from her husband's. At Franklin Roosevelt's conferences, he cultivated an informal camaraderie with the press corps but remained the star performer. Mrs. Roosevelt, on the other hand, reverted to the manner of her Todhunter days, holding forth like a schoolteacher. In an AP feature, written after sitting in on the president's conferences, Furman captured the dissimilarity: "At the President's press conference, all the world's a stage, at Mrs. Roosevelt's, all the world's a school. . . . Give Mrs. Roosevelt a roomful of newspaper women, and she conducts classes on scores of subjects, always seeing beyond her immediate hearers to the 'women of the country.' "[53]

As in any well-managed classroom, interaction occurred between the teacher and pupils. It was a measure of women's position in the 1930s that both parties accepted their places. As "classes" for women, the press conferences fell within the framework of women's traditional sphere of teaching. Thus, the conferences allowed Mrs. Roosevelt to perform the traditionally feminine duty of instructing other women while at the same time enlarging the concept of the first lady's position. With some reporters almost pathetically grateful to Mrs. Roosevelt for their jobs, the women raised no objections to being pictured as students, who would in turn pass on knowledge to others, although they were helping to educate their teacher.

6

Building a Career
1933–35

I do not like to think that my name is entirely responsible for my receiving these offers, although I realize it must be a part of it, as I cannot very well divorce myself from my name. I honestly try to do every job to the best of my ability.

—Eleanor Roosevelt to Aron Mathieu,
a *Writer's Digest* staff member,
May 9, 1933

I want you to tell me about the particular problems which puzzle or sadden you, but I also want you to write me about what has brought joy into your life, and how you are adjusting yourself to the new conditions in this amazing changing world. . . .

We all know that no human being is infallible, and on this page I am not setting myself up as an oracle. But it may be that in the varied life I have had there have been certain experiences which other people will find useful, and it may be that out of the letters which come to me I shall learn of experiences which will prove helpful to others.

—"I Want You to Write to Me,"
"Mrs. Franklin D. Roosevelt's Page,"
Woman's Home Companion, August 1933.

I think you are entirely right that no one is worth $500 a minute. . . . I do not feel that this money is paid to me as an individual, but that it is paid to the President's wife.

—Eleanor Roosevelt to Edward G. Ekdahl,
May 21, 1934, in the *New York Times*

In the opinion of her family, Eleanor Roosevelt wanted and needed a career to justify her own self-worth. Her son Elliott attributed it to a need for "power and influence, provided it was in her own right and her own name." Her son-in-law, Dr. James A. Halsted,

68

thought pursuit of a career allowed her to handle "wisely and intelligently" the emotional problems resulting from disclosure of her husband's infidelity with Lucy Mercer. Her grandson John R. Boettiger saw it as a part of Mrs. Roosevelt's struggle "to be as full a human being as she was."[1]

Her reservations about becoming first lady, so often expressed to Hickok, centered on fears that she would be forced to limit her endeavors because of her duties as an official hostess. Having reluctantly given up teaching at Todhunter, Mrs. Roosevelt was determined to continue writing. She contributed a column to the *Women's Democratic News* from February 1933 until December 1935, when the *News* merged with the *Democratic Digest*. Titled "Passing Thoughts of Mrs. Franklin D. Roosevelt," the column focused on details of her ceremonial activities as first lady. Even so it was one of the ways in which she used writing to express her own individuality. In a revealing article titled "What I Hope to Leave Behind!," printed in *Pictorial Review* in April 1933, she supported nondomestic careers "if holding a job will make a woman more of a person so that her charm, her intelligence and her experience will be of great value to the other lives around her."[2]

But her editorship of the magazine *Babies—Just Babies* soon ended, following disagreements with Bernard MacFadden, the publisher. Presumably because of her position, Mrs. Roosevelt declined to make the magazine a forum for controversy instead of a collection of baby pictures and light pieces on the joys of motherhood. When the topic of birth control was proposed in a memo on possible articles, she penciled "no." Her reporter friends poked fun at the publication, with one of the songs at a Women's National Press Club party beginning, "Where did you come from, babies dear? Out of the ballot-box into the here."[3]

After she exercised her option to withdraw, she was asked to rewrite the editorial announcing her resignation. As she explained to Hickok, MacFadden representatives "thought the one I sent before said I was giving up the magazine too emphatically." Without the prestige of her name, *Babies—Just Babies* ceased publication.[4]

The lure of a first lady's byline prompted the *Woman's Home Companion*, a leading woman's magazine, to offer her a monthly column featured as "Mrs. Franklin D. Roosevelt's Page." Her contract called for her to receive $1,000 per month and her daughter, Anna, $325 for handling letters addressed to Mrs. Roosevelt in care of the magazine. News of the financial arrangement, which the magazine editors had expected to keep confidential, appeared in the *New York Herald-Tribune*, apparently told by Mrs. Roosevelt to Bugbee.[5]

Soon letters criticizing Mrs. Roosevelt for capitalizing on her position arrived at the *Companion*. The editor, Gertrude B. Lane, advised Mrs. Roosevelt to reply by insisting that the modern role of a president's wife was to maintain contact "between the White House and the public." Lane also urged Mrs. Roosevelt to endorse a proposed constitutional amendment outlawing child labor. While Mrs. Roosevelt agreed to favor the amendment, she did not follow Lane's direction in responding to criticism for commercializing her name.[6]

Instead, she wrote to a *Writer's Digest* staff member who raised the issue that she hoped her "name" was not the sole reason for journalistic offers made to her. Clearly she wanted to establish herself as an independent writer, not just as her husband's mouthpiece or as a tool for editors. She rejected any addition to her column by a *Companion* staff member "who felt that this was exactly what you would have said."[7]

Responding to Mrs. Roosevelt's personal appeal to "write me," readers besieged her with letters, many describing economic hardship. At times she commented on the correspondence in her column, which generally addressed noncontroversial subjects: inexpensive vacations, better working conditions for household servants, reverence for American holidays, need for improved prenatal care, gardening. Often she praised New Deal programs, such as those to ensure mortgages for owners of inexpensive homes. One of her most outspoken columns upheld the right of married women to work: "The right to work seems to me as vital a part of our freedom as any right which we may have." Even so, she hedged her position, noting that during the depression it might be necessary for either men or women to give up their jobs to needier persons.[8]

A well-paying newspaper contract came her way too. In April 1933 she launched a monthly column for the North American Newspaper Alliance, agreeing to a series of 750-word articles for $500 each to be written "from one woman to another." The first article told how White House household expenses had been pared to meet the 25 percent cut in the expenses of all government departments ordered by President Roosevelt, while the second laboriously recited the president's daily schedule.[9]

Pronouncing "our membership most enthusiastic," the syndicate editor passed on suggested subjects from member newspapers, indicating what newspapers considered appropriate topics for women's pages: food for state functions, White House china, servant problems, Washington society, fan mail, whether women members of Congress represented their constituencies "as well and as conscientiously as the men," and "your greatest pleasure in being the wife of the President." Mrs. Roosevelt responded with a column saying "truthfully" her greatest joy lay in "having all the flowers that I want around me and being able to send them . . . to friends."[10]

In her articles Mrs. Roosevelt attempted an informality in contrast to the reserve of previous presidents' wives, although she often fell into generalities. A typical example occurred in a column on the White House: "One should use one's imagination and one's experience and do what one feels is the desire of the public."[11]

On other occasions she gave vivid details. Describing her vacation with Hickok, she ridiculed her efforts to escape recognition: "My hair was tied down with a bandeau and I looked like an African Bushman." Her account of the impression made by her Buick convertible coupe on fishermen of the Gaspé peninsula gave a glimpse of male prejudice. She found the "male population . . . patting it and even the old curé . . . seemed awed at the idea that any woman should own anything so expensive and beautiful," she wrote.[12]

Perhaps benefiting from the practiced hand of Hickok, the piece brought praise from the syndicate. The editor told her it added "so much interest to your contributions when you discuss specific matters in a specific way." But the most specific of all was left out—Hickok's presence on the trip. Mrs. Roosevelt used the pronoun "we" but never explained who "we" were. Apparently the syndicate never asked, accepting Mrs. Roosevelt's right to privacy.[13]

After six months she moved to the McNaught Syndicate, which promised to handle her columns "on a dignified plane," without using "such ballyhoo as might be considered objectionable." The editors politely cautioned her against platitudes: "Of course, the plainer the speaking, the more effective the article." They suggested that she enlarge on a theme she had mentioned in a speech—that if the wealthy did not feed the unemployed, "unpleasant times may come." [14]

But her McNaught articles never approached this level of controversy. With few subscribers, the series drew little attention and Mrs. Roosevelt gave a year's notice in 1934 of intent to cancel her contract. Although her first topics included relatively lively subjects such as the right of women to work, the series bogged down with articles on the work of federal agencies. Background information was funneled to Mrs. Roosevelt by George Allen, a syndicate representative, who questioned the project: "There is so little of the esthetic in the work of the Bureau of Animal Industry that the whole subject is difficult of treatment in a popular article," he advised. [15]

Sales of the column were hampered, to the syndicate's displeasure, by rival marketing of condensations of material from Mrs. Roosevelt's book, *It's Up to the Women*. Rushed into print in November 1933, the book contained a compilation of Mrs. Roosevelt's speeches and articles urging women to sacrifice, volunteer and become politically active to make the best of hard times. In a chapter on women in public life, Mrs. Roosevelt acknowledged the importance of role models presented in the media: "In this country women are placed where the newspapers recognize their positions and this will mean undoubtedly increased interest in the opportunities for public service amongst girls and women," she wrote. [16]

In 1934 Mrs. Roosevelt resumed commercial broadcasting. Going off the record at her news conference, she expressed her determination to, as Furman put it in her diary, "get the money for a good cause and take the gaff." She broadcast first for a roofing company, which paid her $500 per minute, the same amount earned by the highest-paid radio stars. Next, the Simmons Mattress Company sponsored her at the same price for five commentaries on highlights of the week's news. [17]

When a Brooklyn man wrote to complain that she was not worth $3,000 for a six-minute broadcast, she agreed in her reply that the pay was based on her position as the president's wife. Her answer contrasted with her broadcast comments about the role of women in public life in which she stated, "No woman can really reach a place of recognition unless she has actually earned that place." A woman must be able to "deliver the goods," she emphasized. [18]

Mrs. Roosevelt did deliver listeners for her sponsors, becoming a popular attraction. Her commentary for Simmons, although scorned by intellectuals, appealed to the average person. She described her visit to the World's Fair in Chicago, parents' attempts to clean up movies seen by children, attendance at an all-star baseball game and the humorous aspect of New Deal programs and personalities. For instance, she told how complicated it was for the president to change his vacation plans, since "the ship upon which he is to sail is kept in a constant tizzy-wizzy of shining buttons and brass."[19]

After the Simmons contract ended, she presented six fifteen-minute talks on education for the American typewriter industry. In 1935 the Selby Shoe Company sponsored her broadcasts, which fed the public's irrepressible appetite for first-person White House vignettes. With a mixture of guilelessness and cunning, she defended herself against charges of neglecting her husband. On a radio program she read a letter asking, "Why do you take so many trips; think of your poor husband sitting at home alone in the evening with no one to keep him company by the fireside?" Her answer was that her critic lacked "the remotest idea" of White House life, and, moreover, that her husband was too busy to miss her.[20]

A broadcast in March 1935 was a staged press conference at which Mrs. Roosevelt was interviewed by Strayer, Black, Herrick, Marie Manning Gasch, who, as Beatrice Fairfax, wrote an advice to the lovelorn column, and Alice Hughes, fashion editor of Hearst newspapers. The program served chiefly as White House public relations. A query by Strayer let Mrs. Roosevelt deny use of a ghostwriter as she declared, "I dictate, or sometimes write in long hand, every word of every article or speech which I make." In response to Hughes, she minimized interest in her new Easter wardrobe, saying, "I have ordered a blue suit, Miss Hughes, but it is so long since I ordered it, I have forgotten what it really is like."[21]

A question by Herrick on a work relief bill before Congress brought Mrs. Roosevelt's usual "I cannot comment specifically on that legislation because it is still pending." But a follow-up query by Black urged her to say "what has been done for women," and Mrs. Roosevelt quickly enumerated New Deal relief jobs. They fell into sex-stereotyped categories: sewing, canning and preserving, serving school lunches, working in nurseries, schools, libraries, and playgrounds, doing clerical work for local governments, and census taking.[22]

Mrs. Roosevelt justified her commercial contracts on grounds of earning money for charity. She announced that payments for her radio broadcasts would go directly to the American Friends Service Committee, a Quaker social service organization, chiefly to benefit Arthurdale. It was never made clear exactly how much she turned over to the group. In United Press stories, Black gave the total variously as $66,000 and $72,000 for an eighteen-month period in 1934–35.[23]

In fact, Mrs. Roosevelt conveyed the misleading impression that she donated all the proceeds to charity, when this was not quite the case: of $4,000 per broadcast from the shoe company, for example, her agent received $1,000. Representative Hamilton Fish, Sr., a Republican who represented the Roosevelts' Hyde Park district and never hesitated to embarrass the administration, charged that giving the money directly to charity created tax irregularities. Since 15 percent of income was the maximum permissible tax deduction for charitable contributions, the first lady, regardless of intent, was actually withholding tax revenue from the government, Fish contended.[24]

Mrs. Roosevelt never accounted publicly for her entire earnings from her books, magazine articles, and newspaper work, although Black reported that the first lady received $15,000 in 1934 from the *Woman's Home Companion* alone. When questioned at a press conference, Mrs. Roosevelt admitted that she did not give all the proceeds to charity but she did not provide a specific breakdown. Criticism of commercializing her position did not unduly concern the president's advisors, who may have thought it good politics to reach a large audience of women voters. When a manufacturer of mattresses complained that the prestige of her name would lead listeners to flock to the Simmons product, Mrs. Roosevelt answered ingeniously by replying that broadcasting for one sponsor was no more unfair to competition than writing for a single magazine.[25]

Admirers accepted the triteness of her comments, both written and spoken, as her way of identifying with ordinary people. *Radio Guide* extolled her as a performer in spite of her high-pitched voice. Neither originality nor distinction of expression marked much of her speaking and writing. Instead, there were clichés, platitudes and non sequiturs (as in this example: "It looks to me as though we cannot relax in the study of the general problems which face us all, for there is the nut which must be cracked."). But many perceived in Mrs. Roosevelt qualities that transcended quibbles over rhetoric.[26]

Supporters, including some members of her press conference group, saw Mrs. Roosevelt as a larger-than-life figure. Ducas called her "the only true person I've ever known in my life . . . . an honest do-gooder." She received 300,000 pieces of mail during her first year at the White House, some of which saluted her as almost a deity: "Our dear First Lady of America," "Esteemed One," or "First Mother of the land." Heywood Broun, a popular columnist, compared Mrs. Roosevelt to Nora, the heroine of Ibsen's play, *A Doll's House*, who sought to be a human being rather than a plastic creation of her husband. He contended, "Neither marriage nor the last national election can obliterate the fact that Eleanor Roosevelt is an individual."[27]

Nevertheless her detractors comprised a sizable segment of the population. A woman correspondent not among her coterie accused the first lady of seeking the limelight: "Mrs. Roosevelt doesn't hide her light under any bushel; if she had a bushel she'd burn it to add to the light." Some journalists were constrained by anti-Roosevelt editors to curtail their own enthusiasm for her. Mildred Gilman, who covered Mrs. Roosevelt's activities in 1934 for Hearst's *Washington Herald*, remembered a half-century later that "too friendly stories were often cut, and I envied the reporters who could go all out in their admiration of her."[28]

It was not an era of vigorous investigative reporting of financial or personal affairs. The women journalists accepted what Mrs. Roosevelt chose to tell of her financial arrangements just as they ignored hints of past strains in her marriage. "All during the Roosevelt administration there were rumors that the Roosevelts had once been on the verge of divorce," but the full story was not known to the journalists, Hornaday recalled in 1979. "Probably only Walter Winchell [a gossip columnist] would have printed it, if it had been known."[29]

Reporters like Black and Furman, who combined marriage with a career, were delighted with Mrs. Roosevelt's example. To Black, money-making represented the crux of Mrs. Roosevelt's personal contribution to feminism: "For, if the wife of the President of the United States cannot live on her husband's prestige and money, what other wife can?" Black asked rhetorically. "Mrs. Franklin D. Roosevelt, only working First Lady this country ever had, is earning for charity by radio talks and writing, at least as much as the government pays her husband for being President," Black began a United Press feature.[30]

Black paid a price for being considered Mrs. Roosevelt's apologist. In an *American Mercury* article in 1935, Eugene A. Kelly said, "Even the women reporters in Washington today are amazed at the extremes of Ruby's idolatrous attitude toward the First Lady." The criticism came at a bad time for Black, then seeking new clients for her news bureau and trying to collect back pay from the foundering *Portland Evening News*.[31]

Furman, indefatigably writing feature material, asked Mrs. Roosevelt to explain her concept of money as part of a "First Lady's Lexicon" that publicized her personal definitions of various words. Money, Mrs. Roosevelt said, was "a token which represents real things. . . . real work of some kind must attend the honest making of money." (This contrasted in terseness with the expansiveness of some of Mrs. Roosevelt's other definitions: "Politician—A public servant unselfishly giving his time to carry out the wishes of a majority of the people and devoting to that task all his education and experience.") To Mrs. Roosevelt, money represented a tangible payment for socially valued achievement.[32]

Her pursuit of monetary reward, even if she had not been first lady, made her an exception among married American women during the 1930s. The majority of married women remained at home, although overall the percentage of working women increased in the decade (from 24.3 percent to 25.4 percent), with a growing number of married women seeking jobs because of reduced family income. Public opinion overwhelmingly opposed this trend: A 1936 poll showed 82 percent of the population against wives working if their husbands also were employed, on the theory that women were taking work away from men.[33]

At a press conference reporters pressed Mrs. Roosevelt to define the role of modern women, asking if she agreed with Henry Noble MacCracken, president of Vassar College, who declared that "ladies" no longer existed in America. Indeed not, she said, defining a contemporary "lady" as one with "kindliness of a spirit and a type of naturalness which isn't dependent on birth or circumstances," but on "inner assurance . . . you're doing what you consider is the right and kind thing." Strayer thought that perhaps Mrs. Roosevelt intended it as a self-definition.[34]

Lorena Hickok continued to play an important part in Mrs. Roosevelt's personal life and journalistic education, offering both repeated encouragement and concrete advice on writing style. Mrs. R. wrote to Hickok in the fall of 1934, "I am terribly grateful for all the work you did on that article [on illiteracy]." Fighting off one of her recurring bouts of depression, Mrs. Roosevelt told Hickok, "I will try, dear, to do better work as long as it matters to you." Referring to herself as having failed in "a woman's real duty," Mrs. Roosevelt added, "I might at least do these other things to the best of my ability, which, however, is far more mediocre I fear than you imagine." In the context of her life, her meaning seemed clear: lacking a physical relationship with her husband, she sought other outlets for fulfillment.[35]

At times the two women plotted to slip away from the reporters covering Mrs. Roosevelt. When Hickok made plans to join Mrs. Roosevelt on a trip to Ohio that included the first lady's celebrated visit to a coal mine, Mrs. Roosevelt warned her that the "girls" might be on hand. "I told Tommy [Malvina Thompson] to discourage hard but [she] said she feared they or at least Ruby Black said she had been ordered [to go along]. I'll take a compartment, however, and order our breakfast there!" Mrs. Roosevelt wrote.[36]

As a trusted confidante, Hickok saw no possibility of ever returning to journalism herself, even though she realized Hopkins had little need for her reports after 1935. She feared editors would demand the same kind of intimate revelations about the Roosevelt family that had caused her to leave the Associated Press. Mrs. Roosevelt urged, "Forget you ever knew us, tell them [potential employers] you never saw me and can't find out anything." But Hickok exclaimed, "Gosh, I'm not prepared to give you up entirely!"[37]

In 1935 the *Woman's Home Companion* dropped Mrs. Roosevelt's column on the apparent pretense that "two years was about as long a time as we should continue a special feature of this type." A more logical explanation was the approach of the 1936 election and the magazine's desire not to appear to endorse the administration. Perhaps the advent of the election also accounted for discontinuation of her radio broadcasts after the Selby series ended.[38]

But the first lady did not stop her magazine efforts. In the summer of 1935, Mrs. Roosevelt acquired as her agent George T. Bye, a well-regarded figure in New York literary circles, replacing Nannine Joseph, who in turn had replaced Louis Howe. Bye strove to place her pieces in the *Saturday Evening Post*, one of the biggest and best-paying magazines, keeping in mind her aspiration to sell an article a month for $2,500, an ambition not easily attained. Before he sold her article "In Defense of Curiosity" to the *Post*, Mrs. Roosevelt told Bye that she hoped "they will like it and that it will not shock them too much so that they will not be willing to continue with me." [39]

Scouting for ideas to interest editors, Bye proposed several possibilities: skills involved in giving parties, the costs of public education, the art of courtesy. Mrs. Roosevelt ruled out meatier topics. "I am very sorry that I cannot write on birth control as long as my husband is President because I feel that as long as it offends the religious belief of a large group of citizens, I have no right to express my own opinion publicly," she wrote Bye. An article on divorce would be "unwise" too, she said, because of the divorces of her children. [40]

When the *Post* returned her second submission, Mrs. Roosevelt turned to Hickok for "detailed criticism," noting that editor George H. Lorimer thought she had "written things like it before." She told Hickok not to be afraid of hurting her because she wanted to be judged as a writer, not as a celebrity: "I'm glad to have it back because it shows they are wanting something besides name. If I can't do this after giving it a good try then I must do something else. . . . One can only find out by trying." [41]

So Mrs. Roosevelt persevered in trying to master a craft, after she had passed her fiftieth birthday and attained more prominence than any other woman of her day. She accepted Hickok's suggestions gratefully: "I think I know what you mean about structure," she wrote naively. "It [structural defect] comes from not thinking through from the start and building up step by step and I think I can do that better." Referring to Hickok's "perfectionistic" standards, Mrs. Roosevelt wrote, "I've been working on an article today and thinking of you and trying to make myself really work on it." She also noted time spent on the *Women's Democratic News*, which ran her column under a standing headline, "Passing Thoughts of Mrs. Franklin D. Roosevelt." [42]

Mrs. Roosevelt had no intention of settling for a ghostwriter, although she agreed to her publisher's demand that a "juvenile doctor" be hired to revise portions of her tourist guide for children, "Bobby and Betty Go to Washington." The results displeased her and she complained to Bye. "I wish they had let me do a little work on my own manuscript. . . . I look upon it as a piece of educational work."[43]

Frequently Mrs. Roosevelt depended on Hickok more as a sounding board than an actual colleague. Although she asked Hickok to critique an article titled, "Can a Woman Be Elected President of the United States?," Mrs. Roosevelt sent the piece on to meet a deadline at *Cosmopolitan* before Hickok could respond. Her answer to the question, given as her husband prepared to seek a second term in 1936, was negative — a woman would not be elected for the foreseeable future. "The feminists will be down on me and a lot of people will say it is camouflaged political partisan material and in a way it is!" she told Hickok.[44]

Having herself been mentioned facetiously as a presidential candidate, she disavowed the idea. Reviewing the presidents since George Washington, she held that men were better trained "by custom and experience" for the office. "A vast majority of women have not as yet attained the power to be objective about their work, and impersonal in their business contact," she said, presenting women stereotypically as emotional, rather than rational, creatures.[45]

She apparently considered herself one of the "majority of women" lacking the power for the "objective" reasoning that she assigned to men. Her correspondence with Hickok portrayed her as an uncertain individual emotionally distant from her husband. Upset with her husband's treatment of their oldest son, James, then an aide to his father, she burst out in a letter to Hickok: "I know I've got to stick. I know I'll never make an open break and I never tell FDR how I feel. . . . I blow off to you but never to F! . . . I'm never likely to fight with F. I always 'shut up.' " It was the martyrdom of the Victorian wife, suppressing herself and suffering in silence, but with a new twist. Mrs. Roosevelt's career interests helped to compensate for her frustrations.[46]

As a president's wife, Mrs. Roosevelt faced limitations on her ability to write freely, although her career depended on her position. She gave up on attempts to sell articles to the *Post*, returning one to

Bye doubting "if Mr. Lorimer will take it under any circumstances." Lorimer suggested an article on peace, but Mrs. Roosevelt decided that she "could write nothing new" on the subject in view of congressional passage of the Neutrality Act of 1935. This legislation, unwillingly signed by President Roosevelt after Italy's attack on Ethiopia, tied the United States to a policy of isolationism.[47]

Unable to explore the issue in the *Post*, she raised the peace question at a press conference, calling on American women to think of ways to settle international disputes short of actual war. The statement came only after she had concluded not to market her ideas to a magazine. She informed Bye, "If you see a report in the paper that I made a statement to my press conference, you will understand that I made it because I had fully decided not to do the article."[48]

Not surprisingly, editors of intellectual periodicals dismissed Mrs. Roosevelt's efforts as New Deal propaganda. Her secretary, Malvina Thompson, advised Bye to forget about trying to place an article on education by Mrs. Roosevelt in *Harper's Magazine*. She referred to a letter from the editor "saying he would be glad to take anything from her if it were not complimentary to the administration but that they could not take anything which was favorable."[49]

As her agent, Bye worked diligently to convince editors that Mrs. Roosevelt was a professional writer who merited substantial payment. When she gave an article on "Christmas Reading at the White House" to a struggling little magazine called *Driftwood* published near her Hyde Park home, Bye asked the editor to let him see the piece. He noted acidly: "Some of the editors who are paying Mrs. Roosevelt high prices might think that the public would be of the opinion that it was no great novelty to get an article by Mrs. Roosevelt since she even wrote for non-paying magazines." He managed, however, to turn the incident into favorable publicity for both Mrs. Roosevelt and the magazine by release of the article to the Associated Press.[50]

Much of Mrs. Roosevelt's journalistic career during her White House years fell into the category of promotion for the Roosevelt administration. This was acceptable to the American public, which perceived Mrs. Roosevelt as a wife aiding her husband. The majority accepted her right to receive payment because she assured the public that her earnings went to worthy causes. She found a congenial market in women's magazines where her opinions, usually conventional, fit the publications' ideology of categorizing women primarily as wives and mothers. The 1930s were a period when many women were forced to make extra contributions to the family unit, but their basic role remained that of wife and mother.[51]

Mrs. Roosevelt herself was seen as a larger-than-life version of a woman "helping out" and "making do." But in her case the family unit was broadened to include the entire nation. Far from yielding to the constraints of the White House, she enlarged the concept of the role of first lady to include a right, if not a duty, to speak out on issues. She asserted her right to earn money. She developed her own circle of journalistic admirers, whose reverence for her both as an individual and as a news source ensured her favorable treatment in news reports transmitted throughout the nation. Yet she did not move beyond areas acceptable for women. In line with social feminist philosophy, she did not challenge a male-oriented political system in which only a minority of exceptional women were able to function independently. What was revolutionary about Mrs. Roosevelt was not what she said or even what she did, since her causes, like the Arthurdale project, fell into the range of philanthropic activity considered appropriate for upper-class women.

What was unique lay in Mrs. Roosevelt's ability as first lady to inspire the public with a message that reinforced traditional values at the same time that it enlarged them. Lauding those humanitarian concerns believed to be the special province of women, she credited women with the intelligence and motivation to solve social ills. To the masses of American women, Mrs. Roosevelt stood alone as a symbol of unattainable prestige, as well as a benevolent advocate and counselor who was readily accessible through the media.

7

"My Day" 1936

They say that women cannot laugh at themselves as men do. . . .
Women find it difficult to get away from the habit of a lifetime which
requires that they smooth out things for others, and oil the wheels of existence as they go their daily rounds, or perhaps we have a subtler way of
expressing our humor. Who knows?

> —Eleanor Roosevelt, "My Day," sample column
> submitted to prospective purchasers by
> United Features Syndicate, December 1935

As the election year of 1936 opened, Mrs. Roosevelt's journalistic
career entered a new phase. She became a daily syndicated columnist,
offering to newspapers "My Day," described as a diary of her activities. It was intended to be livelier and more personal than her weekly
column, which, by Mrs. Roosevelt's own admission, had become a
"very dull affair." At this point the weekly column was marketed by
the Columbia Syndicate, which had been formed by George Allen on
the strength of her agreement to sell the column through it after
she left McNaught. When the Columbia Syndicate was absorbed by
United Features in the fall of 1935, it cleared the way for Mrs. Roosevelt to sign a five-year contract for publication of the "diary."[1]

United Features had asked Mrs. Roosevelt to do a daily column
shortly after she moved into the White House, apparently at the
suggestion of Gretta Palmer, the women's page editor of the *New
York World-Telegram*. At the time Mrs. Roosevelt rejected the idea,
because of her other writing commitments. Now she plunged into
the venture, writing to Hickok about the decisive factor: "I've started
with the syndicate —400 words every day, rather a lot but I need the
money!"[2]

A series of sample columns, circulated to editors to attract subscribers, proved easier to write than she had expected. Fearing that a
daily column would be "the most dreadful chore," she surprised herself by quickly turning out the preview pieces. She told Hickok:
"The writing is easy so far, they just want one incident out of the
day and so far I've had no trouble." Her initial effort featured an
innocuous account of herself falling over "gentlemen" waiting to see
the president in a dark White House hall. This made the White
House analogous to the typical American home where misadventures
often occurred, and set the tone for subsequent entries. The gentlemen, however, were not identified, which was either a deficiency in
reportorial skill or a deliberate exercise in discretion.[3]

Monte F. Bourjaily, general manager of United Features, had
his own doubts about her ability to perform. Fearing that she might
lack ideas, he sent her a long list: the "high spot" of her day; what the
individuals she met "have on their minds"; "things of interest to
women in their homes as reflected in White House housekeeping";
her personal concerns; "real life stories" taken from her mail or her
own experiences; tips on etiquette; "pieces of inspiration"; the "trend
of thought in the country" as revealed in her mail, and "most important of all, the day-to-day experiences, interests and observations in
which you may share that part of your life which you are willing to
make public with newspaper readers."[4]

Bourjaily's reference to that "part of your life which you are
willing to make public" indicates the difference between attitudes
toward public disclosure of personal affairs in the 1930s and today.
Bourjaily recognized that a sizable segment of the public would be
interested in almost everything Mrs. Roosevelt wrote because it was
so unusual for the wife of a famous man, let alone a president, to
reveal anything of herself as a person. In four pages of instructions,
Bourjaily pointed to the extraordinary public interest in Mrs. Roosevelt's activities. He mentioned that Drew Pearson and Robert Allen
had attempted to include a daily item on her in their "Washington
Merry-Go-Round" column but had discovered that her fast pace outran the column's deadline of five days preceding publication. Bourjaily
noted that Mrs. Roosevelt's "diary" would be sent daily to subscribing
newspapers by telegraph wire to keep the news fresh.[5]

Uncertain she would develop a suitable format, Bourjaily enclosed a model—the popular column by Franklin P. Adams titled "Diary of Our Own Samuel Pepys," which appeared in the *New York Herald-Tribune.* Fearful that copy might not flow continuously, Bourjaily proposed that Mrs. Roosevelt's secretary, Malvina Thompson, play a "Boswellian role" and jot down comments that the first lady made each day to be used if "the regular column fails to reach us on time."[6]

Specific tips on writing were included from two syndicate executives, George A. Carlin, business manager, and Frank L. Brady, promotion manager. Carlin wanted the column "glittering with names," adding "whether the names are important or not doesn't matter." Brady proposed "pleasant and personal news of events and people, particularly people, which no one would be so able to reveal as Mrs. Roosevelt." Bourjaily urged "printing the pieces each day as if they were letters written to a dear friend."[7]

He had no way of knowing about Mrs. Roosevelt's considerable practice in this regard. One feature of Mrs. Roosevelt's daily letters to Hickok was a detailed listing of her engagements, which the first lady called "my diary," in contrast to the intimate tone of the rest of the letters. In 1933 she had turned down Emma Bugbee's proposal to write her biography, telling Bugbee that she was sending Hickok an account of her "daily doings" for inclusion in a book that she and Hickok might write. But by late 1935, Mrs. Roosevelt's friendship with Hickok was waning in emotional intensity as Hickok's desire for an exclusive relationship conflicted with Mrs. Roosevelt's broad interests and affections for others. "My Day" may have seemed to Mrs. Roosevelt a better way to capitalize on the kind of material she was accustomed to jotting down than saving it for some vague future project.[8]

The name "My Day" originated with the syndicate, which promoted the column heavily. Bourjaily expressed delight over Mrs. Roosevelt's eighteen sample articles with their mixture of vignettes from mail sent to the White House and glimpses of the Roosevelt family celebrating Christmas. The first published column was hastily released for December 30, 1935, to compete with another novel entry in the Washington field. This was a column by Mrs. Roosevelt's tart-tongued anti–New Deal cousin, Alice Roosevelt Longworth, whose famed wit failed to entertain as much in print as in person. Offered by McNaught, Mrs. Roosevelt's former syndicate, the Longworth column soon faded from the scene. "My Day" was to go on for nearly thirty years, until Mrs. Roosevelt's death in 1962.[9]

Criticized as shallow and trivial, "My Day" nevertheless captured the spirit of a remarkable woman's reaction to her times. Following her editor's instructions, she paraded the names of many famous persons through "My Day," especially those of women connected with the New Deal. Frances Perkins, Mary W. (Molly) Dewson, Representative Caroline O'Day, and Representative Mary T. Norton all appeared in "My Day," making it a kind of newsletter reporting on women in politics.[10]

Like Mrs. Roosevelt, most of these women, married or single, personified vigor and independence and were unconcerned with displaying the overt femininity that marked the media image of women in the 1950s and early 1960s. Still, they upheld a traditional framework. They exhorted women to enter politics on grounds of bettering family life, not on grounds of challenging its institutional base. Indeed, in "My Day," Mrs. Roosevelt pictured herself in a comfortable role as a matriarch.[11]

"I wonder if anyone else glories in cold and snow without, an open fire within, and the luxury of a tray of food all by one's self in one's own room?" Mrs. Roosevelt began her first column. She introduced the reader to domestic yuletide scenes in the White House. "The house was full of young people, my husband had a cold and was in bed having milk-toast for his supper," she reported, so she retired to her room, lit a fire, and read reports on the problems of youth. Family life remained the backdrop for her movements as pictured in her column.[12]

Mrs. Roosevelt's tendency to leave out vital information brought forth a delicate admonition from Bourjaily within the first three weeks of the column. After she praised the work of a Works Progress administrator in Arkansas who had been killed in a plane crash, but failed to mention his name, Bourjaily chided gently: "I may be entirely mistaken but it seems to me that such a beautiful tribute would have been heightened and everyone concerned would have been highly pleased if you had mentioned the name of the WPA administrator involved." When she told of fruitless attempts to obtain a Chuddar shawl for Louis Howe, then dying in a hospital, without explaining what a Chuddar shawl was, the syndicate added an editorial note defining Chuddar shawls as large sheets worn by women in India.[13]

From the first, "My Day" proved to be a success, but it did not hit the target mark of 100 newspapers. The syndicate kept the price low to compete with the Longworth column, offering "My Day" on a sliding scale based on circulation. Small dailies could obtain it at a bargain rate of less than a dollar a week. Six months after "My Day" began, Bourjaily reported it had fifty-one clients, the same number as it had started with, although several large papers had dropped it and small ones had picked it up. Among impressive initial subscribers were the Scripps-Howard newspaper chain and other important outlets: the *Atlanta Constitution*, the *Kansas City Star*, the *Milwaukee Journal*, the *Providence Journal*, and the *St. Louis Post-Dispatch*.[14]

Five of the better-paying papers dropped the column: the *Minneapolis Journal* at $25 a week; the *Boston Herald* at $42.50; the *St. Louis Post-Dispatch* at $90; the *Nashville Banner* at $12.50; and the *Providence Journal* at $20. Those picking it up, generally to pair with the Longworth column, were the *Orlando* (Florida) *Sentinel* and *Scranton* (Pennsylvania) *Republican*, each at $3 a week; the *Reading* (Pennsylvania) *Times* and *Waco* (Texas) *News Tribune*, each at $5; and the *Minneapolis Star* at $10.33.[15]

The syndicate predicted to Mrs. Roosevelt that she would receive about $1,000 a month from the column, but she kept the amount quiet. Asked at a press conference, "Can you tell us how much money it will earn for you?" she hedged: "In the first place, I have no idea what I will get, because it is simply on their regular basis; whatever their contracts are with other people. I have the same contract they make with anyone else. So I have no idea what I will get." She told the women the money would go straight to her so it would be taxed, adding, "I do think that is what you want to know." She said she planned to use it partly for charity and partly for herself: "There are a great many calls on you here for a great many personal things."[16]

The answer was not challenged by the group of reporters, whose tendency not to press Mrs. Roosevelt stemmed from their loyalty, according to Hope Ridings Miller. "The men were always prying around trying to get something nasty about her, and we did protect her," she recalled. In Miller's opinion, Mrs. Roosevelt deserved the journalists' protection because "she did the best she could for the country and herself with the gifts she had." This protection damaged Mrs. Roosevelt's value as a news source but saved her from embarrassment, Ishbel Ross wrote in the first history of women journalists, published in 1936.[17]

A few of the newspaperwomen, however, would feed juicy tidbits from press conferences to the male reporters, even when Mrs. Roosevelt talked off-the-record, sometimes at the prompting of solicitous reporter friends. At the conference on January 16, 1936, when she dodged the question on her earnings from "My Day," reporters asked if she had received appeals to oppose the sentence of capital punishment given to Richard Hauptman, who had been convicted of kidnapping and murdering the Lindbergh baby. Perhaps misunderstanding or failing to think quickly enough about the most judicious response, Mrs. Roosevelt first said "Yes," but then retracted her reply, saying only, "I have had communications from a number of people." Realizing how she had blundered, she declined permission to be quoted, but this did not prevent leaks from occurring.[18]

Within two weeks Stephen T. Early, White House press secretary, told Mrs. Roosevelt to reprimand offending reporters. He urged her to remind the "ladies attending the next conference that it is not fair to those who obey the rules of the conference and refrain from direct quotation . . . for others to repeat conference proceedings, so that absentee writers get them indirectly and quote directly."[19]

Violations of Mrs. Roosevelt's off-the-record remarks incensed Black, who wrote a column on the situation, claiming that it was "destroying the illusions of veteran newspaperwomen, brought up by city desks to hold firmly to the tradition that anything learned in confidence is inviolate." As an example, she pointed to a story told by Mrs. Roosevelt about her son Franklin picking up a hitchhiker. According to Mrs. Roosevelt, the car radio was tuned to Walter Winchell, who was rebuking the Roosevelt sons for alleged reckless driving. The hitchhiker agreed vigorously, while Franklin, Jr., meekly defended them and drove on carefully, not revealing his name until the hitchhiker got out. Black said the story ended up, word for word, in a syndicated column, although Mrs. Roosevelt had asked the women not to repeat it and instead had provided a watered-down version for publication.[20]

Black said Mrs. Roosevelt had told the original tale after Black

had asked her whether her sons were heeding a safe-driving campaign advocated by President Roosevelt. She was willing for the story
to be used until a protective woman reporter advised sweetly: "Mrs.
Roosevelt, I don't think you ought to say anything about that. It
might embarrass the boys." Mrs. Roosevelt, with the reporter's help,
then changed her on-the-record reply so that "it was not nearly as
good a story," Black argued curiously, both defending Mrs. Roosevelt's
use of off-the-record comments and criticizing reporters who urged
her to make them.[21]

The incident, trivial in itself, illustrated the collaboration of some
of the press women with Mrs. Roosevelt's desire to avoid embarrassing
news. As Early recognized in his recommendation, the majority of the
press conference members could be held in line by pressure to go
along with the group, a fact that Mrs. Roosevelt clearly recognized.
For instance, during the height of her relationship with Hickok, Mrs.
Roosevelt assured her friend of rapport with the newspaperwomen
that would ensure almost no attention to Roosevelt-Hickok meetings:
"I rather think Lorena often 'girls' are [illegible] pretty good chaper-
ones: There have been one or two miserable stories and I spoke about
them that morning and I [illegible] found the majority were with
me."[22]

"My Day" gave Mrs. Roosevelt even firmer control over the
image that she presented to the public, by offering charming glimpses
of her family that made the column a low-keyed, but effective,
political weapon for the 1936 election. She wrote about her younger
sons inviting two of their Harvard professors who were critical of the
New Deal to a White House dinner so they might debate the president on the philosophy of government. When the Supreme Court
invalidated the Agricultural Adjustment Administration, a key New
Deal agency, she pictured her husband accepting the decision with
good grace, swimming as usual, and turning aside from the present to
good-naturedly argue at the dinner table over the dates of the Holy
Roman Empire. Claiming a self-effacing role for herself at a press
conference at which Hallie Flanagan, director of the Federal Theater
Project, spoke, she wrote, "When I have a guest at these conferences.
. . . I can sit back and listen with the knowledge that the girls will
take something with them of real interest."[23]

The column pictured her as the prototype of a wife and mother, a role that she handled well in public under sometimes trying circumstances. For example, it was Mrs. Roosevelt who confirmed reports in 1934 of the impending divorce of her daughter, Anna, from Curtis Dall. Mildred Gilman, who covered the story for Hearst newspapers, remembered years later the sadness with which Mrs. Roosevelt approached the subject. With divorce a frequent occurrence among her children, Mrs. Roosevelt's pleasant sketches in "My Day" helped to disarm critics of her family.[24]

According to Elliott Roosevelt, his mother concealed her personality in the column, picturing herself as "a calm, contented woman deeply concerned with the world and her family. . . . not the detached, harried, fault-finding wife and parent we knew." Yet there existed hints of deep-seated emotions that she kept to herself. Not surprisingly, these cropped up in observations on women. Referring to Nazi attempts to relegate women to childbearing only, she expressed support for the concept of work as a human right: "There are three fundamentals for human happiness—work which will produce at least a minimum of material security, love and faith. These things must be made possible for all human beings, men and women alike."[25]

The first lady sometimes alluded to a vague sisterhood of sex in remarks such as: "There are practical little things in housekeeping which no man really understands." She took little jabs at men: when she attacked a claim that there would never be great women playwrights because women were intellectually inferior, she wrote, "Women know not only what men know, but much that men will never know. For, how many men really know the heart and soul of a woman?"[26]

Like those who keep diaries to account to themselves for the way they spend their lives, Mrs. Roosevelt used "My Day" for a kind of personal accounting, but one made to the public. Historically, the diary format has been important to women, since it has corresponded with their lives: "Emotional, fragmentary, interrupted, modest, not to be taken seriously, private, restricted, daily, trivial, formless, concerned with self, as endless as their tasks," as one scholar put it. Except for the category of "private," Mrs. Roosevelt's column met these criteria almost exactly. But because it was public it assumed an unusual importance. Perhaps she wanted to match her husband's accounting to the public, as chief executive, with a parallel explanation of her performance as the chief executive's wife, subconsciously trying to make her role somewhat comparable to his.[27]

"My Day" chronicled innumerable official dinners and entertainments with Mrs. Roosevelt performing the traditional duties of the first lady. An undertone of alienation from her official responsibilities occasionally crept in: "It may be most difficult to keep the world from knowing where you dine and what you eat and wear, [but] so much interest is focused on these somewhat unimportant things, that you are really left completely free to live your own inner life as you wish." The more "you live in a 'goldfish bowl,'" the less people really know about you," she wrote. At the same time she complained to Hickok, "I must dress for the diplomatic dinner, a cozy party of 98! Gee, I'm sick of it!"[28]

Some readers found the simplicity of the column disappointing. After glancing over "an unusually large batch of letters" stimulated by the column, Bourjaily told Mrs. Roosevelt, "There is a recurring insistence that you treat more serious subjects." He recommended that she "present a fuller picture of you and your mind." Yet he expressed pleasure because "so many readers tell you they get joy and inspiration from it."[29]

The reason seems easy to understand. Readers may have been diverted from daily cares by an "inside" look at the celebrities who marched through the column. But the true star, capable of energizing all but the most woebegone, was Mrs. Roosevelt herself. To women past their youth, she presented herself as a "superwoman" of heroic proportions, a grandmother devoted to family, friends, and worthy causes, while presiding at the White House and flying around the country to give speeches. The column also showed her finding time to read popular books, attend the theater and keep up on cultural affairs. If her critiques were not sophisticated, at least they could be easily understood. She advised that *Gone With the Wind* was "a book you would like to read straight through. . . . I can assure you you will find Scarlet O'Hara an interesting character . . . circumstances mold even the little animal she seems to be."[30]

Columns were popular features of depression-era journalism, in part because local newspapers were hurt by loss of advertising and competition from radio. From 1931 to 1939, nearly 400 newspapers merged or suspended publication, and one-third of their salaried employees lost their jobs. In some cases it cost publishers less to subscribe to columns than to hire reporters to report local news. When small dailies could offer a personal chat with Mrs. Roosevelt for a few dollars a week, it is scarcely surprising that some of them seized the opportunity, although the column never ran in more than a small fraction of the nation's 1800 daily newspapers.[31]

That did not minimize its importance. By 1938, for example, it appeared in sixty-two newspapers, with a total circulation of 4,034,552, which gave Mrs. Roosevelt exposure to more readers than popular political pundits like David Lawrence and Raymond Clapper and the genial Heywood Broun. She lagged behind the scholarly Walter Lippmann, who reached eight million readers in 160 news-papers, and Dorothy Thompson, chief among the few serious women columnists, who reached seven and one-half million in 1940.[32]

While the awkward phraseology of "My Day" made it appear to be an indifferently executed venture, this was not the case. Mrs. Roosevelt and the syndicate took it seriously, from both business and professional standpoints. Editors took pains to save her from embar-rassing mistakes but let her know of their efforts. "I know that nobody enjoys a laugh on herself better than yourself, therefore pour le sport I am taking the liberty of enclosing copy of an editorial memoran-dum," wrote George Carlin, who succeeded Bourjaily as syndicate head. He enclosed a note from an editor who had corrected some of Mrs. Roosevelt's work: "I note with sorrow that the First Lady has turned cannibal. Her lead sentence in her story is 'We had a lunch of some 50-odd ladies yesterday. . . .' and a little further down she goes on with the fearful orgy as evidenced by: 'We returned in time for lunch and had a very distinguished group of doctors. . . .' I have carefully changed these two sentences lest we lose our vegetarian readers." In response Mrs. Roosevelt exclaimed, "I am afraid that my desire to eat them all crept into print."[33]

Stylistic problems in "My Day" resulted partly from the circum-stances under which Mrs. Roosevelt wrote the column. Frequently she dictated "My Day," which was published six days a week, to Thompson, wherever they happened to be: on picnic lunches, in auto-mobiles, trains, planes, or ships, or in hotel rooms so cramped that the bed was the only place for a typewriter. Sometimes she faced difficulties in filing the copy, carefully marked "Press Rates Collect," to meet the evening deadline. Sharing these experiences with her readers, she told them when telegraph offices were closed, transmission lines down and deadlines barely made. She never ran out of ideas, so Thompson did not need to assume a "Boswellian role."[34]

In the spring of 1936 Mrs. Roosevelt signed a contract for a lecture tour under the management of W. Colston Leigh, after radio offers were not forthcoming. The contract called for her to make two lecture tours annually for $1,000 per lecture, a handsome sum at the time. The tours also served to promote the column. As she prepared for a circuit through the Middle West, Bourjaily advised her to publicize it in "My Day": "Include as many instances and names as possible. . . . [since] the feature is published in Toledo and Cleveland and the editors there will be very pleased to have this particular attention paid to their cities and people."[35]

Encountering renewed criticism for commercializing the role of first lady as a paid speaker, Mrs. Roosevelt brushed it off. Her success enriched her self-esteem by providing tangible proof of her own competence. When Hickok returned a manuscript after criticizing the writing, Mrs. Roosevelt answered, "I'll just have to see if it can be improved, if not it can be scrapped. You know, dear, I may lecture better for my daily bread and apple sauce. Who knows?" After the first lecture tour, she reported to Hickok: "Back in New York with no fuss and feathers and $3,000 to my credit! It has to go out at once in income tax however!"[36]

From the viewpoint of the reelection campaign, both the lecture tour and the column contributed to the effort. Mrs. Roosevelt offered audiences a choice of five topics, all of which were often touched on in "My Day" and befitted the dignity of a first lady: "Relationship of the Individual to the Community," "Problems of Youth," "The Mail of a President's Wife," "Peace," and "A Typical Day at the White House." Her cultivated, upper-class diction contributed to a gracious, yet authoritative, stage presence, although her wavering, high-pitched voice eventually led her to consult an elocution teacher. In her lectures, she spoke as an educator, calling on the moral authority of religious belief and humanitarian precepts, which also undergirded her column.[37]

In her autobiography, Mrs. Roosevelt reported that her husband was "entirely agreeable" to her writing "My Day." Perhaps he saw it as a partial antidote to newspaper opposition. Franklin Roosevelt claimed that the owners of the press were overwhelmingly against him, charging that 85 percent of the nation's newspapers were antagonistic toward the New Deal in 1936. While this exaggerated the situation, its factual foundation lay in the Republican leanings of the majority of the nation's publishers. Statistics collected by *Editor and Publisher* showed that 36 percent of the nation's newspapers supported Roosevelt in 1936 while 57 percent backed his Republican rival, Governor Alfred M. Landon of Kansas.[38]

The Longworth column, with which "My Day" was often paired, campaigned vigorously for Landon, whose nomination Alice Roosevelt Longworth had seconded at the Republican national convention. Charging that Roosevelt's program of government-insured security reflected the president's physical handicap, Longworth contrasted his "mollycoddle" philosophy with her father's advocacy of the strenuous life. She claimed that Franklin Roosevelt wanted the nation to live with the depression, not fight and overcome it. In "My Day," Eleanor Roosevelt retorted: "No man who has brought himself back from what might have been an entire life of invalidism to physical, mental and spiritual strength and activity can ever be accused of preaching or exemplifying a mollycoddle philosophy." Thus readers were treated to glimpses of a family feud with the two women arguing over the merits of male relatives as political leaders.[39]

In other ways "My Day" also served as an extraordinary campaign vehicle in the 1936 campaign. It provided the logical place to scotch a silly rumor that the president's mother charged the government rent for the time Roosevelt spent at the family estate at Hyde Park. Simply by enumerating her activities, Mrs. Roosevelt called attention to the Democratic party, since she participated in its numerous functions. Her reminders of party affiliation were not subtle: "The Democratic Women's Division Dinner . . . last night was very successful."[40]

Without doubt Franklin Roosevelt and his wife conferred on some of the contents of the column. Shortly before the Democratic national convention in 1936, the president directed Mrs. Roosevelt to include a report on steel industry automation, which had caused unemployment that he wanted blamed on Republican industrialists, not the New Deal. The report appeared as though Mrs. Roosevelt had written it herself but the actual author was Hickok. Mrs. Roosevelt apologized to her in a letter: "If you mind I'm terribly sorry. I wanted to wait for your consent but Franklin won't let me. I think he wants me to be whipping boy and tho' he can't bring the question out he wants it out."[41]

When the figures cited by Hickok on the number of technologically unemployed steel workers in Youngstown turned out to be incorrect, Hickok's self-esteem, already at a low point, plummeted. Mrs. Roosevelt tried to bolster it. "The fact of the whole business is all that matters and both F. and I looked on your letter only as an example to illustrate a subject vividly which needed to be discussed," she reassured Hickok.[42]

Perhaps forgetting about the incident, she denied to her press conference in 1939 that her husband ever influenced the content of the column: "He has never called me in and said he wished I hadn't said anything, as far as I know. He has never called me in and said he wished I had said this or that or the other thing."[43]

As the 1936 election approached, she employed anecdotes to support her husband's campaign. Bourjaily encouraged her: "I thought the story of the cab driver human and amusing and your comment trenchant and humorous," he wrote. He bestowed this praise on a column about a taxi driver who, after discovering her identity, announced, "Will you tell your husband he has my vote in November and I guess he has the vote of every plain man, at least any plain man who has any sense." Her "trenchant" observation was "how my husband would chuckle at the inference that at least a part of his opposition is made up of people lacking in sense."[44]

Pathetic tales crept in of victims of the depression who were worried about Roosevelt's prospects. One concerned a ninety-year-old Bronx man, "hanging on to life," determined to vote for "Mr. Roosevelt before he dies." Another featured a three-year-old praying to "Dod" to let the president be fat so "he won't never be hungry the way we were before he helped Dadday get a job." These intensified the general sentimentality of the column. Stylists objected to repeated use of clichés and the "persistently sweet tone," marked by monotonous reference to events as "interesting," "lovely" or "momentous."[45]

Family vignettes, showing a high-spirited, closely knit group of

·likable individuals, abounded. In the same column that recounted the taxi driver incident, Mrs. Roosevelt portrayed the president as a fun-loving fellow who liked to elude his guards on land or sea. Referring to a cruise taken by "my husband and the boys," she noted, "I can imagine how much they enjoyed dodging around among the islands and giving the slip to their escort. . . . Nothing pleased my husband more, in Hyde Park or in Warm Springs, than to lose the Secret Service car which always follows him when he drives his own little car."[46]

Mrs. Roosevelt's human-interest stories fit somewhat within the framework of documentary literature of the 1930s that emphasized case histories and first-person accounts. Her vignettes might be treacly and their sources questionable, yet they articulated a philosophy of family life. "My Day" showed Mrs. Roosevelt as a doting grandmother pretending to be a growling lion for a grandson, and as a loyal mother pushing her daughter Anna's book, *Scamper, The Bunny Who Went to the White House.* Sophisticated supporters shuddered, although some, like Oswald Garrison Villard, discounted "the banality and intellectual poverty of her diary" because she sympathized with worthy causes.[47]

Shrewdly, Mrs. Roosevelt made complaints regarding anecdotes the subject of a column. She used a letter from a woman complaining of "inane chatter about your family affairs" and urging Mrs. Roosevelt not to "waste your valuable time and the space in the paper with something so worthless . . . when you could so easily write something which might have marvelous results." Mrs. Roosevelt ingenuously answered, "You must occasionally have something lighter to relieve you." Then she thanked the "many people" who had written to say that they enjoyed reading "about the little things." But taken in total, the trivia amounted to a substantial family portrait.[48]

The surface simplicity of "My Day" obscured the complex reality of Mrs. Roosevelt's personality. A psychologist who purported to analyze the first lady on the basis of her column pronounced her an extrovert whose "endocrine glands function very effectively." He found her "too much alive to be morbid, too many-sided to allow discouragement or criticism to dethrone her wholesome philosophy of life." But Hickok saw another side — Mrs. Roosevelt's loneliness and resentment of her husband's associates. Despite her involvement in the 1936 campaign, she told Hickok that she was "so indifferent" to the outcome. In her response, Hickok, who frequently stayed in the White House when she was between assignments for Hopkins, verbalized some of Mrs. Roosevelt's feelings: "A daily dose of Mac [Marvin H. McIntyre, the president's appointments secretary] and Missy [LeHand, the president's personal secretary], along with all the fuss and pomp and adulation the man receives will distract anyone's view."[49]

Advising Mrs. Roosevelt to get a firm grasp on her emotions, Hickok told her to remember "the kind of people you, of all people, are supposed to care about. The poor and the lowly." Mrs. Roosevelt despondently argued, "I don't flatter myself that it matters if I care or don't care about any people!" Just before the election, she wrote Hickok: "Dear I realize more & more that FDR is a great man & he is nice to me but as a person I'm a stranger & I don't want to be anything else."[50]

Thus, it would appear that Mrs. Roosevelt held onto her column as one way of exhibiting her independence, even though she was willing to use it for campaign purposes. When she became ill in September 1936 her husband offered to write it for her, but she declined his offer. She told her readers, "We refused, courteously and rapidly, knowing that if it once became the President's column we would lose our readers and that would be very sad."[51]

In public Franklin Roosevelt minimized the column, as Mrs. Roosevelt noted at a press conference. "I have heard him say to other people several times that he thought it was impossible to write a column where you were thinking up something worthwhile to say every day, but that he did think it possible to write a diary in the way I was doing, without . . . [writing] something really worthwhile," she said. The president's distinction between a "worthwhile" column and "My Day" was first made at a press conference when Roosevelt disparaged columnists in general. Reminded that his wife also wrote a column, he remarked, "She is in an entirely different category; she simply writes a daily diary."[52]

Initially the women reporters considered the column just one among Mrs. Roosevelt's precedent-breaking activities as first lady. At the annual stunt party of the Women's National Press Club in March 1936 they treated it lightly. In one skit a prospective presidential candidate's wife was interviewed to see whether she would be equal to the task of being first lady. "Can you write a newspaper column with one hand and shake 500 hands with the other?" the neophyte was asked.[53]

Privately the journalists considered "My Day" an amateurish venture based on position, not competence. "It was very naive," Ducas said. Over the years women reporters came to view it with less tolerance, especially after Mrs. Roosevelt used the column rather than her press conferences to break news stories. "Mrs. Roosevelt was always looking for ways to earn money," Hornaday recalled. "We resented that when she wrote her column competing with us." But the press women did not perceive the column as a threat when it began.[54]

A few important newspapers, including the *Milwaukee Journal* and the *Minneapolis Star*, canceled "My Day" after the 1936 election, assuming interest had faded following the campaign. But the journalistic fraternity as well as the public continued to read it, partly as a barometer of life in the White House. A brief mention of President Roosevelt's dissatisfaction with his meals was reprinted in newspaper stories and featured in radio broadcasts, coinciding rather unfortunately with the public outcry over his plan to "pack" the Supreme Court by sponsoring legislation that would increase the number of justices. Mrs. Roosevelt had thought the item "amusing and human," but the president's advisors were furious because of the inference that the chief executive was upset by the response to his proposal. She wrote to her daughter that when she apologized, "Pa answered irritably that it had been very hard on him & he would certainly say nothing more to me on any subject."[55]

The incident, which caused Mrs. Roosevelt to grieve over "my poor judgement," was ironic because she was using "My Day" to support the court plan. In one column she quoted a letter purporting to be from a reader who favored the proposal. Like other letters that appeared from time to time, it might have been written by Mrs. Roosevelt herself, since it contained her customary rhetorical flourishes, including references to the New Testament.[56]

In Mrs. Roosevelt's moral code, as expressed in her column, "hard times were not in vain," because they enabled individuals and societies to find within themselves the strength to rise above difficulty. In the surmounting of adversity, however, she was inconsistent on the issue of governmental power. On the one hand, she insisted upon individual action and courageous stands, fearing even late in life that she herself was not being as brave as her father had wanted her to be. She saw life in terms of the single human being, applauding individual craftsmanship, as evidenced by her support of the Val-Kill furniture factory.[57]

On the other hand, she wanted to graft the complex branches of an industrial society onto the democratic tree of pioneer virtues. This led her to call for collective action on either a voluntary or governmental basis. Drawing on analogies from the past, she compared the heroism of frontier days with efforts to unionize workers to insure they would "live decently in New York City."[58]

The column reflected an eclectic approach to political philosophy. It contained favorable notice of Mussolini's restructuring of the Italian economy "to allow women to enter any profession or business" and to pay married women equally with men. Although always opposed to Hitler, Mrs. Roosevelt urged Americans to examine innovations instituted by the Nazis. In 1938 "My Day" hailed "a very interesting departure in government" in Germany, "whereby every able-bodied man and woman will be obligated for short-term service to the nation to accomplish nationally urgent tasks." She suggested similar service here on a voluntary basis.[59]

But "My Day" was not intended to be an exposition of political thought. More important, the column articulated, however hazily, questions regarding the position of women in society. Mixing naivete and shrewdness, Mrs. Roosevelt's candor brought up issues that are still unresolved today.

As she described her hectic schedule, which combined ceremonial, political, and family responsibilities with her career interests, she personified the problem of fragmented lives faced by many women on a lesser scale. When she wrote, "I wish I could be three people, [one] holding teas, luncheons . . . [one sitting] . . . at a desk eight hours a day. . . . [one] a wife, mother, grandmother and friend," she surely hit a responsive note. In one sense, "My Day" can be viewed as a journalistic way station on the road to women's liberation. In another, it can be seen as a portrait of a woman seeking a personal liberation through circumstances so unusual they offered an irrelevant guide for others. It is impossible to say what millions of readers saw in "My Day," but the column's durability testified that substance lay behind its bland exterior.[60]

8

Successful Image Making 1936–39

Are the American voters ready to have the wife of their President assume semi-official duties or do they prefer her to keep in the background as have Presidents' wives in the past?
—Mary Hornaday, "Mrs. Roosevelt—a Campaign Issue,"
Christian Science Monitor, June 24, 1936

To a degree, Roosevelt's overwhelming victory in the election of 1936 represented an endorsement of Mrs. Roosevelt's conduct as first lady. Some of Roosevelt's strategists—but not the president himself—wanted to keep Mrs. Roosevelt in the background during the campaign. The Republican party, trying to make an issue of Mrs. Roosevelt's performance as first lady, pledged that Mrs. Alfred M. Landon would not travel but would "spend her time in the White House" if she became first lady. A *Boston Globe* editor queried Ruby Black about a rumor that Mrs. Roosevelt was giving up press conferences because of the campaign. Indeed not, Black replied, pointing out that Mrs. Roosevelt always ceased holding conferences in the summer. But then Black added defensively: "I am willing to let the idea go abroad that she herself has chosen to remain quiet during the campaign, inasmuch as she will not let her friends push her forward. But she has not been 'shut up.' "[1]

Nevertheless, the number of Mrs. Roosevelt's press conferences declined in 1936. The total fell from a high of thirty-eight in 1934 to thirty in 1935 and declined further to twenty-four in 1936. The low point of twenty-one came in 1938. During World War II the number increased, but it did not reach the depression peak. After the advent of "My Day," Mrs. Roosevelt used the column for some news items that otherwise would have been presented at the conferences.[2]

One source of controversy behind attempts to keep Mrs. Roosevelt in the background during the 1936 campaign was her advocacy of better treatment for black citizens. In some of her activities, Mrs. Roosevelt served as the administration's envoy to the nation's black population, incurring racist wrath. But if bigots resented her goodwill toward blacks, the majority of Americans responded to a personality who genuinely seemed to care about others. Crowds cheered as wildly for her as for her husband when the Democratic campaign train pulled across the country in the fall of 1936.[3]

In 1935 Mrs. Roosevelt had urged appointment of the black educator Mary McLeod Bethune to the national advisory committee of the National Youth Administration. Later Mrs. Roosevelt supported her as director of the agency's Negro affairs. Thus the first lady enlisted for the administration a recognized black leader who served both the white power structure and the black community, interpreting each to the other in favorable terms.[4]

In May 1936 Mrs. Roosevelt astounded her press conference group by announcing plans to hold a White House garden party for inmates of the National Training School for Girls, a dilapidated District of Columbia reformatory housing sixty young women, most of whom were black. Reporting to the journalists on an inspection visit there after a new superintendent, Dr. Carrie Smith, took over, Mrs. Roosevelt said, "Twenty-six of the girls had syphilis and almost every girl had gonorrhea. . . . Most of these girls are still school age." No vocational program existed except one to teach laundry work, although "there was no hot running water," Mrs. Roosevelt continued. "They eat in the kitchen. They wash in the kitchen. They do the laundry in the kitchen. At times they eat with the laundry drying over their heads. You know what that smells like." When reporters asked why she was giving the party, she replied, "As every young person enjoys an occasional good time, these youngsters should have an occasional good time."[5]

The party, which reporters were not permitted to attend, proceeded smoothly. The delinquents and their attendants were "served like other White House guests by meticulously uniformed White House butlers," Strayer noted. Nearly fifty years later, Frances M. Lide, who in 1935 had become the first woman to be hired to report city news, rather than social activities, for the *Washington Star*, remembered the event "as a great shocker for those days" and said it had posed unusual problems in coverage. With other members of the press conference group, she found herself peering through the iron fence surrounding the White House grounds to watch the gathering from afar. Lide, who credited her employment to her paper's need for a woman to attend the conferences, cited the incident as a symbol of the way Mrs. Roosevelt sometimes kept a distance between herself and the reporters.[6]

As a concession to local custom, the black guests at the garden party were served in a separate tent, although this failed to mollify segregationists, including two of the president's advisors, Stephen T. Early and Marvin McIntyre, who disliked Mrs. Roosevelt's liberal views. Spurred by Mrs. Roosevelt's interest, Congress soon appropriated $100,000 for renovation of the training school, but white supremacists denounced the first lady for her efforts. At a South Carolina Democratic convention, speakers were warned not to praise Mrs. Roosevelt because she had entertained "a bunch of 'nigger whores' at the White House." A group of Southern superpatriots circulated a crude drawing of Mrs. Roosevelt dancing with a black titled "Nigger Lover—Eleanor."[7]

During the 1936 campaign, reactionary groups joined with bigots to attack the administration. Vicious jokes and doggerel circulated as part of the hate tactics directed at both Roosevelts. One bit of verse, purporting to be an order from Franklin Roosevelt to his wife, began, "You kiss the Negroes, I'll kiss the Jews, We'll stay in the White House as long as we choose."[8]

Financed by the DuPonts and other industrialists, the ultraconservative American Liberty League spearheaded opposition to the New Deal. Consequently a rumor before the election that Franklin D. Roosevelt, Jr., was engaged to Ethel DuPont created embarrassment for the administration. Black tried to ignore it, but finally informed Mrs. Roosevelt: "I could not stall off the UP any longer on writing a story about the possibility of [the] engagement." Mrs. Roosevelt understood: "I realize you girls have to write such things," she remarked.[9]

Mrs. Roosevelt's travels were another target for critics. Hornaday estimated in the *Christian Science Monitor* that the trips totaled about 100,000 miles during the first term—a distance equal to about four times around the world. Anti-Roosevelt journalists, like Malcolm Bingay of the *Detroit Free Press*, seized on the word "ubiquitous," which sounded worse than its actual meaning, to attack the first lady. In an editorial against her, he pleaded with the Almighty that Mrs. Roosevelt "light somewhere and keep quiet."[10]

When the Republicans tried to garner votes on the basis that Mrs. Landon would be a stay-at-home housewife, the controversy over Mrs. Roosevelt's activities broadened into a public debate over the political influence of the first lady. Women journalists continued to play up Mrs. Roosevelt's political importance. According to Hornaday's article, it was easy to "trace Mrs. Roosevelt's hand in public affairs." She was credited with pushing the appointment of Frances Perkins as well as the selection of Ruth Bryan Owens, a close friend of Bess Furman, as minister to Denmark. Hornaday quoted Aubrey Williams, head of the National Youth Administration, as saying that Mrs. Roosevelt had "as much to do with getting that program started as any individual." This account, like others, may have attributed to Mrs. Roosevelt far more than her actual power. Perkins repeatedly denied she was indebted to Mrs. Roosevelt for the cabinet post, and Williams's comment to NYA directors was susceptible to varying interpretations.[11]

In the *New York Times*, Kathleen McLaughlin pointed out a way in which Mrs. Roosevelt might have influenced her husband: she "habitually" left memoranda and reports in a small basket on a table by his bedside. After the election, Black wrote United Press stories giving Mrs. Roosevelt credit for changes in National Recovery Administration codes to give women doing substantially the same work as men the same minimum pay. Convinced of Mrs. Roosevelt's ability to shape policy, Black urged her to meet with Luis Muñoz Marin, the leader of the Puerto Rican Liberal party, to advance the island's claim to independence. In eventually declining to do so, Mrs. Roosevelt told Black that she was "not in any position to represent [the president]."[12]

Mrs. Roosevelt had access to her husband's ear, but to what degree he acted on her advice remains a subject of speculation. She used the tactics of wives since time immemorial to exercise power indirectly. She brought individuals to meet the president and steered the conversation into fields of her own interest. She offered suggestions to officials, some of whom were more willing than others to do her bidding. With stronger convictions than her husband on the need for humanitarian measures, she advocated social welfare programs.[13]

To the women reporters covering the White House, Mrs. Roosevelt appeared a model wife helping a crippled husband, and so they pictured her. In a letter to Mrs. Roosevelt, Black proposed that she write a book about the Roosevelt marriage to be titled, "The Union Became Perfect." She said she was inspired by a story the president told, beginning, "Did I tell you the swell thing the Missus did for me?" It was a suggestion Mrs. Roosevelt ignored.[14]

In her *New York Times* preelection story, McLaughlin called attention to the president's disability, observing that it was difficult for him to move freely, and praising Mrs. Roosevelt as his "eyes and ears." Roosevelt was fond of quoting "my Missus" in cabinet meetings, saying, "You know my Missus gets around a lot," when he reported on what she had found. According to Hope Ridings Miller, "We [the women reporters] all felt that she was absolutely marvelous to look after him so well." The women tacitly assumed the president was incapable of a normal marital relationship and applauded his wife for her devotion.[15]

Yet it was evident to the reporters that cleavages existed between some members of Roosevelt's staff and the first lady. "We were aware that Mrs. Roosevelt was a little jealous of Missy [LeHand, the president's secretary]," recalled Miller. After Doris Fleeson of the *New York Daily News* wrote an article on LeHand for the *Saturday Evening Post*, Mrs. Roosevelt told the "girls" she wished "somebody would write a piece equally interesting about my secretary, Malvina Thompson, who is equally important to me," Miller noted.[16]

These personal strains fell into the category of items that the women journalists did not report. There were others too. Furman recorded in her diary subjects that were brought up off-the-record at the press conferences prior to the 1936 election: birth control, a *McCall's* magazine article attacking Mrs. Roosevelt for her role in the Arthurdale project, and radical comments by the historian Mary Beard, who charged that women had been robbed of their history by men, who had crushed women's curiosity. "With all her friendliness, Mrs. Roosevelt made it plain that there were certain subjects on which she did not wish to chat, [even off-the-record]," McLaughlin wrote in the *New York Times*.[17]

Still, access to the first lady yielded news, as well as glimpses of arresting personalities. Amelia Earhart was found "curled up on the corner of a couch" at one press session. When Mrs. Roosevelt supported teaching the definition of "communism" in the public schools, while not advocating it, Furman had what she called a "swell and profitable" story, which she wrote in three versions for various cycles of the Associated Press wire.[18]

There were fringe benefits, too, including the drama of arriving at the front door of the White House on Monday mornings and entering the Green Room, where the women smoked cigarettes and talked while "being gaped at by tourists," as Black put it. At first the women had gone up the formal stairway into the family "sitting room, full of comfortable sofas and deep chairs, and fragrant with fresh flowers," according to *Newsweek*. But after some of them wrote about the family's personal belongings and guests glimpsed en route to the conferences, the meetings were moved to the Monroe Room, "furnished with straight-backed chairs, blue davenport, and grand piano," *Newsweek* noted. Black observed that "Mrs. Roosevelt, without ever mentioning it, put an end to this 'girls at Mrs. Roosevelt's feet' crack of the columnists, by giving orders that chairs be provided for all attending." [19]

Socializing with Mrs. Roosevelt proved gratifying, even if the price paid was to keep material off-the-record. Furman commented in her 1936 diary on a dinner for herself and Martha Strayer at Malvina Thompson's apartment where "Mrs. Roosevelt, lovely in a pink lingerie-like gown. . . . read to us—two stories from *Hillsboro People* by Dorothy Canfield—and Martha told her fortune and Tommy's [Thompson's] fortune in the cards." When Geno Herrick returned to her suburban Washington home after being critically injured in an automobile accident in New Mexico, a White House chauffeur took Strayer, Bugbee, Black, and Furman, along with Mrs. Roosevelt and Thompson, for a surprise call on "the sweet dear," Furman wrote in her diary. She added that the group held "a kind of swell party right around her bed." [20]

The 1936 campaign interrupted the press conferences, with Mrs.

Roosevelt away from Washington on the campaign trail. Only one reporter, Bess Furman, accompanied her; and she was hard-pressed to get stories, since Mrs. Roosevelt kept silent. Bowing to the wishes of Roosevelt's advisors that she stay in the background, Mrs. Roosevelt only smiled and waved. Furman reported to the Women's National Press Club that Mrs. Roosevelt "simply won't say anything, even when crowds and the President of the United States ask her to."[21]

Thomas Stokes, a columnist who was riding the campaign train, watched how the faces of women "would blossom in smiles" as they raised their hands to salute Mrs. Roosevelt. This made Stokes wonder whether the influence of Mrs. Roosevelt "might not outweigh that of her husband" in the long run. Yet it was impossible to pinpoint exactly what the influence was. Certainly Mrs. Roosevelt displayed a ceaseless yearning for activity, personal growth, and self-assertion, coupled with a disarming charm, warmth, and modesty, and this is no doubt what her supporters responded to. She had launched forth on an uncharted course for a first lady at a time when American women in general were propelled into a sea of social change, forced, some-what like Mrs. Roosevelt herself, into making the best of trying circumstances.[22]

After Roosevelt's triumphant 1936 reelection, in which he carried all but two states, Mrs. Roosevelt set off on a lecture trip. She complained to Hickok of being scheduled in an auditorium so large that "at best only F.D.R. would fill [it]. I dread it! Why will they take these huge places which no woman can fill?" Fortunately 16,000 showed up for her address, which proved a woman could equal a man in drawing power.[23]

Comparison of herself to her husband—usually to her disadvantage—appeared in "My Day." After the 1937 inaugural she reported: "Last night we saw a newsreel of the Inauguration and I must say I marvel at how well the President looks in all the pictures. I am correspondingly appalled at how funny I look." Previously she had complained to readers about posing in her inaugural gown: "My only consolation was that there would never be another Inauguration and this was really the last time here, and I hope forever, the last posed picture I will have to have taken." Obviously she did not foresee two more elections. Momentarily depressed, she wrote Hickok, "Why can't someone have this job who'd like it & do something worthwhile with it? . . . I've got to use my opportunities & I am weary just thinking about it."[24]

It was a difficult period for Hickok too. Once she had been a top journalist. Now she was forty-three and viewed only as a political hanger-on in Hopkins's office. Occasionally when Mrs. Roosevelt's recurring depression afflicted her, she compared herself unfavorably to Hickok. "Someone else could do equally well what I do. . . . You have gifts and can really get somewhere," she told Hickok, but her confidante at this point lacked the will to believe in herself.[25]

Having enlisted Mrs. Roosevelt's aid in finding a new job, Hickok accepted a public relations post at the New York World's Fair. The job was suggested by Malvina Thompson, who correctly surmised that Grover Whalen, the president of the fair, would be eager for close ties with the White House. But before starting with Whalen, Hickok began to edit a book based on her reports for Hopkins.[26]

Mrs. Roosevelt sent her to see Bye, who found Hickok's manner appalling. "Good Lord," he said, Hickok reported to Mrs. Roosevelt, "are you always so humble and unsure of yourself in anything you do?" "No," she assured him, "I was a darned good reporter and knew I was." Now she was the recipient of Mrs. Roosevelt's cast-off wardrobe, trying to joke as she expressed her thanks, "From now on I shall probably take a rather ghoulish interest in your clothes." She was unable to publish her book.[27]

An editor of the *American* magazine dangled the prospect of an $18,000-a-year job before her, but Hickok decided that "all he can think of getting out of me is some 'dirt' on Harry and WPA which, of course, I'd never give him," she told Mrs. Roosevelt. A few days before the 1937 inauguration she mentioned, "Adela Rogers St. John, Hearst's No. 1 woman feature writer, . . . called me up today. She has to do a ten-minute broadcast about you on Inauguration Day and she wants some dope. Specific stuff that I certainly wouldn't want to give her without your consent."[28]

Journalists far less close than Hickok to Mrs. Roosevelt also made sure they did not offend her. Emma Bugbee did a radio script describing Mrs. Roosevelt's role in the 1937 inauguration—how she "sacrificed her own comfort for that of others" by distributing lap robes and rugs in the rain to other members of the inaugural party.

Bugbee sent it to the first lady, noting, "I thought you ought to see it and be reassured I wouldn't say anything behind your back that I wouldn't put in print!"[29]

During Roosevelt's second term, Mrs. Roosevelt continued friendly gestures toward reporters. In April 1937 *Newsweek* emphasized the cozy, "intimate" atmosphere of the press conferences, commenting, "Mrs. Roosevelt treats the reporters as welcome guests, calling many by their first names and often inviting them to return to tea that afternoon." She enjoyed entertaining the women at the annual Gridiron Widows' party. After the 1936 election, she sent her audience "into gales of laughter" with an off-the-record skit, which Furman described in her diary. She noted that Mrs. Roosevelt "rode Cal Coolidge's old exercise horse, besides impersonating herself as a shrinking somebody having to be instructed in White House ways."[30]

In return, the women satirized her with sketches that showed their affection at the Women's National Press Club stunt parties. In 1935 Black, Bugbee, and Furman pretended to be inmates of the Eleanor Roosevelt Home for Broken Down Newspaper Women exhausted from keeping up with the first lady. Two years later, in the wake of sit-down strikes in industry, the main skit pictured a paralysis of women's activities throughout the country as Mrs. Roosevelt demanded "Union Hours for First Ladies" and one day's rest in forty.[31]

There were thoughtful acts that the women never forgot. Furman resigned from the Associated Press in December 1936 owing to pregnancy, at the age of forty-one, but Mrs. Roosevelt kept her on the guest list for scrambled-egg suppers at the White House. She also knitted her a baby blanket. When twins arrived on April 4, 1937, Mrs. Roosevelt made them the chief subject at her press conference and wired Furman, who had gone back to Nebraska to give birth, "Will have to provide another blanket." At the twins' christening, Mrs. Roosevelt served as their godmother. Two years before, she had visited Dorothy Ducas Herzog at the hospital to view her baby son. Unimpressed with her own status, Mrs. Roosevelt had admonished the nurses not to bend their rules to allow her in the nursery, although they wanted to, just "as if my germs weren't the same as everybody else's," she told Ducas.[32]

But providing news remained the principal reason for Mrs. Roosevelt's contacts with the women reporters. Her conferences publicized her causes and enabled society reporters to fill their columns with formidable lists of her social engagements, which the first lady read off from a well-worn black notebook. Often Mrs. Roosevelt was "clever" in staging events to help her husband, according to *Newsweek*. Katherine Lenroot, chief of the U.S. Children's Bureau, for example, spoke to the women at the start of President Roosevelt's unsuccessful campaign to "pack" the Supreme Court by a legislative expansion of the number of justices. When Lenroot pointed out it had taken thirteen years to get twenty-six child-labor amendments through twenty-six states, she presented a handy example of the length of time necessary to reorganize the Supreme Court through constitutional amendment.[33]

To some of the journalists, the first lady remained painfully insecure. Mary Hornaday saw relatively little growth in Mrs. Roosevelt as a leader during the White House years, adding "That came later, at the United Nations." The women felt sorry for Mrs. Roosevelt, with "that nervous little laugh," Hornaday recalled. Mrs. Roosevelt's uncertainty struck the English novelist Rebecca West, who attended a press conference in 1937 and discovered Mrs. Roosevelt betraying "quite a number of secrets from her early life." West found Mrs. Roosevelt "always a little timid and tense," lacking "the peace of relaxation." In West's eyes Mrs. Roosevelt gushed "amiable enthusiasm" linked to duty, which she manifested by shaking hands with each of the newspaper women. "Every time she grasps a new hand her face lights up with a resolute effort to feel sincere, not to leave this a mere empty gesture. . . . she means to catch up with life," as if lacking the knowledge that no one ever does, West wrote.[34] Gilman remembered years later the way Mrs. Roosevelt's head hung in front of her body, perhaps because she was usually leaning forward in a hurry.[35]

As the year 1937 unfolded, millions became acquainted with some of the sorrows of Mrs. Roosevelt's childhood. Partly to keep occupied when not smiling and waving on the 1936 campaign train, she had begun dictating recollections of her girlhood. Sending installments for Hickok's critique, she sought reassurance: "You may think I dwell too long on the 'little girl' period. I've been honest so far about everything & I dread the grownup years."[36]

Could she tell the truth about her marriage and her husband's affair with Lucy Mercer? Obviously not. But Mrs. Roosevelt laid bare the story of her unhappy early life, her father's alcoholism, her mother's disparaging remarks about young Eleanor's lack of looks, the bizarre side of life in her grandmother's household, and the strain of residing with her domineering mother-in-law. Bye sold the autobiography to the *Ladies' Home Journal* for $75,000, an enormous sum for the times. Bruce Gould, who coedited the magazine with his wife, Beatrice, wanted more about the relationship between the president and Mrs. Roosevelt but was not able to persuade her to give details. She went into the early stages, "when she first met him, how happy she was," Gould recalled in an oral history interview. "Then suddenly, like an iron gate clanging shut, there was no more about them personally. This struck me as odd."[37]

The Goulds soon understood that Mrs. Roosevelt hungered for recognition apart from her husband. After a party to launch the serialized publication of the autobiography, titled *This Is My Story*, Mrs. Roosevelt, smartly attired in a black suit, white satin blouse, and sable fur piece, lingered on and said to the editors, "I can't tell you how happy this makes me, to receive all this attention for something I have done by myself and not because of Franklin." The $75,000 payment was equal to her husband's yearly salary as president, and Mrs. Roosevelt closed her eyes to the connection between his position and the price paid for her work. Her comment to the Goulds revealed her emotional need for monetary reward as evidence of her individual achievement. In a sense it summarized the reason behind her entire career.[38]

When the first installment of the autobiography appeared in April 1937, readers swept 250,000 copies of the *Ladies' Home Journal* "right off the newsstands," Gould recalled. *This Is My Story* helped to rejuvenate the magazine's faltering circulation and prestige and allowed the *Journal* to overtake its rivals. This feat astounded editors, who had not realized the widespread public interest in the first lady. Critics acclaimed *This Is My Story* for its frankness, charm, and literary style, which far surpassed Mrs. Roosevelt's earlier endeavors. She had needed no help from Hickok, who clearly recognized Mrs. Roosevelt's growth as a writer. Published as a book in the fall of 1937, *This Is My Story* might have been purchased simply because of the author's name, but after two pages, the reader was "well on the way to forgetting that fact," exclaimed a *New York Times* reviewer. The book was praised because it showed the evolution of a woman who broke away from "America's old and formal social traditions."[39]

"Mrs. Roosevelt has written outspokenly and directly about herself and at the same time has kept the dignity of reticence," another reviewer marveled. "I can see nothing in these pages which could embarrass her family and friends or those with whom their lives have been involved." This discretion might have made the book suspect as a biography, but it enhanced its value as a myth-making vehicle. It pictured Mrs. Roosevelt, in the words of the *Times*, as a woman lacking in "vanity, self-complacence or pettiness." It was a portrait, perhaps not of a flesh-and-blood woman, but of one whom the *New York Herald-Tribune* called "a great lady in a democracy."[40]

Possibly the era in which she wrote influenced Mrs. Roosevelt to describe her own youth as bleaker than it actually was. Identifying with young people in the depression who were facing a perilous economic future, she may have looked back on her "poor little rich girl" childhood as an illustration of the difficulties of growing up. She depicted her girlhood in contradictory terms, sometimes referring to the rigidity of discipline in her grandmother's home and other times to long summer days of reading and tree-climbing when she forgot to appear at meals but no one disturbed her. Speaking to its times, the autobiography told of an orphaned girl and shy young wife who surmounted personal travail without losing the traditional virtues of femininity. It was the story that Frances Perkins said Mrs. Roosevelt seemed compelled to tell, and she told it well.[41]

The inoffensiveness of the autobiography, which struck reviewers, stemmed from the care that Mrs. Roosevelt took in writing the book. She stated her aims: to picture "the world in which I grew up and which seems to me today to be changed in many ways," and "to give as truthful a picture as possible of a human being." Yet she never lost sight of political realities. After showing the manuscript to her husband, she altered a portion to give his version of why he had not gone into uniformed military service in World War I. She also deleted a mention of his delirium at the onset of polio, as well as a reference to infidelity in connection with her brother's divorce.[42]

Thus she strove to create an autobiography that offered no fresh ammunition for political enemies—not an easy achievement considering the hatred for the Roosevelts in reactionary quarters. When *This Is My Story* was brought out in book form by Harper, enmity toward the Roosevelts led some bookstore owners to hide it from view. Bye was informed that pressure from customers had made the booksellers "reluctant to give too great display to *This Is My Story. . . .* it is very often under the counter." The publisher promised, however, to promote the book extensively, especially to women, on the grounds that the story was "one to inspire faith in themselves and belief in American ideas."[43]

This Is My Story presented Mrs. Roosevelt as a woman to whom life was a process of self-education as she moved outside the narrow world of her upbringing into a broader arena. Supporters saw her as a woman who had groped her own way—just as they were groping theirs—through changing times. Opponents viewed her as a threat to the double standard that restricted the behavior of women. The Women's National Association for the Preservation of the White House, an anti-Roosevelt group, for example, maligned her as the first cigarette-smoking wife of a president because she toyed with an occasional cigarette so women who smoked would be comfortable with her.[44]

Male journalists continued to charge that Mrs. Roosevelt's press conference group made sure she was presented to the public favorably. A 1938 "Washington Merry-Go-Round" column sniped at the "loving protectiveness" of the women reporters, alleging that the group toned down Mrs. Roosevelt's frank remarks "that would blaze headlines across the nation." According to the column, when Mrs. Roosevelt commented "That is ridiculous" about some incident, "her loyal devotees immediately caution: 'You mean "regrettable," don't you Mrs. Roosevelt?' 'Yes, thank you, I think that would be better,' she replies, beaming gracefully." Hornaday recalled that sometimes Strayer or Corinne Frazier-Gillette, a public information officer for the WPA, gave a warning to Mrs. Roosevelt, who would then change her wording.[45]

Yet other reporters who looked back on the press conferences decades later denied that they gave Mrs. Roosevelt special treatment. Beth Campbell Short, who succeeded Furman in covering Mrs. Roosevelt for the Associated Press, said the first lady merited the coverage she received. "I admired her but I wasn't sentimental,"

Campbell said. "I was fair." In her opinion the conference members upheld standards of professional objectivity. "I don't think those women wrote puff pieces just because she was nice to them," she said.[46]

While *Newsweek* noted in 1937 that Mrs. Roosevelt gave the press women "few worries" as a professional competitor, this became less true when Mrs. Roosevelt resumed sponsored radio broadcasts in the spring of that year. The announcement came in "My Day," not at a press conference. Mrs. Roosevelt did not report the amount that the sponsor, Pond's cosmetics firm, had agreed to pay—$3,000 for each of thirteen broadcasts. But she incorrectly implied that all of the money would go directly to the American Friends Service Committee, and did not explain that $500 per broadcast was to be used for expenses and her agent's fees. The first program featured her being interviewed by Geno Herrick on a now well-worn topic, "A Typical Day in the White House."[47]

When she made plans to broadcast from Wilmington, Delaware, immediately after the elaborate wedding of her son Franklin, Jr., to Ethel DuPont on June 30, 1937, the women began to see her as a rival. After they complained to Stephen Early, he informed Mrs. Roosevelt, "They are afraid that you will 'scoop' them." He added he was sure "you will not and have told them so," but tactfully advised her to stay away from "a descriptive account of the wedding."[48]

Professional rivalries eventually arose over Mrs. Roosevelt's efforts to publicize conditions at District of Columbia institutions. When she inspected the district jail in 1937, she reported her findings in "My Day." She lauded the "able administration," but discovered overcrowding and termed the prison "a danger to the community." "My Day" also contained her report on a visit to the district's overcrowded House of Detention for Women. There she discovered that "a woman with a criminal record may sleep beside a little girl of twenty who has never been in prison before." Comparing Congress to a parent, she urged it in her column to take more responsibility for the capital city and to turn it into a model "child" for the rest of the country.[49]

After visits to other facilities, she seemed uncertain whether to use "My Day" or her press conferences as a forum for her findings. Following a trip in 1938 to Freedmen's Hospital, a part of Howard

University Medical School, Mrs. Roosevelt hinted in "My Day" of grave deficiencies at the predominantly black institution. "I feel I could write a rather lurid book on what I saw this morning, but I am going to get more accurate information and think it over before I decide what I think really needs to be told," she noted. Subsequently she told her press conference about the hospital's need for equipment, emphasizing that Howard was one of only two "adequate training schools for Negro doctors and nurses" in the nation. She expressed dismay over lack of facilities for treatment of tuberculosis, then the single largest cause of death among blacks. The publicity given her comments helped secure funds for a $700,000 tuberculosis annex.[50]

Mrs. Roosevelt's exposé of conditions at the district's Gallinger Municipal Hospital the next year dismayed the women reporters because it first appeared in "My Day," and at a press conference a *Washington Times* reporter voiced her city editor's complaint about the matter. As an apology, Mrs. Roosevelt answered, "Unfortunately, I couldn't take the press with me, because I wouldn't be able to see the things I did see." She described children housed in the "psychiatric building" for lack of other space, and the "totally inadequate" care provided by overworked student nurses, then recommended a visit by a congressional committee. Her explanation sidestepped the issue of the reporters' concern, however, because she easily could have made the trip and told the women what she saw.[51]

Overseeing the material and spiritual condition of the unfortunate was in harmony with Mrs. Roosevelt's conception of civic "housekeeping," which she viewed as a woman's responsibility. The first lady followed the Victorian tradition of visiting the poorhouse when, accompanied by Elinor Morgenthau, whose husband was secretary of the treasury, she drove in a chauffeured limousine on a snowy January day in 1940 to the district Home for the Aged and Indigent. The problem of publicizing the visit added a new, twentieth-century dimension to the "lady bountiful" tradition. In past times, charity constituted a private act, but by the New Deal era, attempts to remedy deprivation involved bringing conditions to public attention for governmental redress.

The publicity issue was discussed in an article in the *Democratic Digest*, one of a series by Bess Furman and her sister Lucile urging party workers to follow Mrs. Roosevelt's example by investigating institutions in their localities. The series was part of their free-lance writing and publicity business, set up when Bess Furman needed money for household expenses after leaving the Associated Press. According to the article, Mrs. Roosevelt took along one "trusted newspaper reporter" on her visit to the home for the aged in an outlying area of the capital called Blue Plains. As the Furmans explained, Mrs. Roosevelt "intended to report her findings in her own column, and she felt it wasn't fair to scoop the rest of the press. Yet she also felt a large press following would defeat her purpose."[52]

So she compromised by taking along "a newspaper woman especially qualified by her ability to take shorthand, . . . [to] fully inform all the newspapers," the article continued. The "qualified" journalist was Martha Strayer, faithful in dealings with both Mrs. Roosevelt and other reporters. She was the kind of person Bess Furman called "a swell sport," recounting in her diary how Strayer had once driven Ruby Black's car "so that selfish little somebody could get a scoop from Mrs. Roosevelt" when the women were covering a youth conference at Hyde Park. (Although Furman did not give details, the incident seemingly referred to Strayer assisting Black to get a story on the United Press wire before Strayer could send it back to her newspaper.)[53]

The article written by the Furmans quoted from Strayer's notes, which told how Mrs. Roosevelt had walked into a ramshackle wooden building and found 700 helpless residents packed into dingy rooms, sleeping on flimsy cots, receiving little medical care, and barely avoiding starvation on meager meals for which only 63 cents per day per resident were spent. What Strayer reported to her colleagues made a shocking story and was the subject of numerous questions at Mrs. Roosevelt's press conference. Asked what should be done, Mrs. Roosevelt answered cautiously: "Someone should make a very careful survey of the needs and then try to find out how the appropriations should be made. You couldn't do everything at once, but over a period of six years."[54]

Clearly Mrs. Roosevelt realized the need to move carefully where congressional action was involved, since Congress controlled the purse strings for district institutions. Nevertheless, she continued her efforts. Less than a week after the Blue Plains trip, she took Strayer with her to visit the Children's Receiving Home, where de-

linquent and deserted children alike were thrown together. The first
lady called it "the type of place from which boys and girls eventually
graduate to prison." In follow-up comments at a press conference,
she told the women that it was even more pressing to improve institutions for youth than for the aged.[55]

Her inspection visits caused her to become the first president's
wife to testify before a congressional investigative committee. On
February 10, 1940, Mrs. Roosevelt took the witness chair before a
House subcommittee examining district institutions. She looked, in
Black's words, "like something out of the latest fashion book in a
hunter green velvet dress edged at the neck and the cuffs with narrow
ruffles of creamy lace glistening with tiny pearl beads, on her head a
dashing hat with a curled and trailing green ostrich plume." As a
long-range solution to district problems, she advocated voting rights
for Washington residents, then disenfranchised, to ensure their interest in civic reforms.[56]

Mrs. Roosevelt did not challenge the leadership of the district
government. If she had done so, she would have confronted the board
of commissioners, appointed by her husband, which apparently had
not managed city institutions properly. As a columnist for the *Washington Times-Herald* pointed out, suffrage was not necessarily related to
the question of getting "better beds for the poor old people down at
Blue Plains." In her investigation of welfare facilities, Mrs. Roosevelt
had followed the example of Victorian ladies who attempted to relieve suffering but did not question the root causes.[57]

Of course, Mrs. Roosevelt was far more than a lady bountiful in
her approach to aiding the poor. As a settlement worker before her
marriage and later as a social feminist involved in reform in New
York State, she had moved beyond the concept of simply bestowing
token gifts. She saw the need for broad legislative programs aimed
at alleviating distress. But as the president's wife she had to move
cautiously, control her remarkable ingenuousness and cultivate a certain shrewdness to ensure she did not jeopardize her husband's administration. The fact that she met that challenge and still remained a
humane, caring person testified to her intuitive grasp of situations and
ability to use the media. In her public appearances she presented the
image of a lady adapted to a modern media world.

Occasionally Mrs. Roosevelt gave Congress direct advice; for example, she advocated the amendment of the administration's wage and hour bill to guarantee equal pay to women who did equal work with men, and she also recommended extending the Social Security Act to include protection for domestic servants and farm workers. For the most part, however, she believed the nation was not ready to accept a woman's ideas. In 1937, after Lillian D. Rock, the secretary of the feminist National Association of Women Lawyers, predicted that a woman president would be elected within Rock's life span, Mrs. Roosevelt disagreed, explaining that she did not believe "the majority of our people would feel satisfied to follow the leadership and trust the judgment of a woman as President." [58]

The press delighted in her comments. Headline writers enjoyed making jokes: "Women Up Chins at President's Job," for example. The Associated Press story tried to be cute, beginning, "The market for a woman President went down so far it has almost disappeared under the bearish influence of Mrs. Franklin D. Roosevelt." In a radio broadcast a month later, Mrs. Roosevelt urged more women to seek careers in public office, but she differentiated between the roles of men and women, contending that women's "humanistic" viewpoint should supplement men's "materialistic" concerns. Thus she assigned women to an indefinite subordinate status while paying homage to a "separate but equal" doctrine. [59]

Women needed to be ornamental, in Mrs. Roosevelt's opinion. She saw nothing degrading in using a mild form of sex appeal to promote a meritorious cause. For example, she advised the district's chapter of the League of Women Voters to send "young and pretty girls" to Capitol Hill to persuade congressmen to appropriate more money for welfare institutions. She thought women, including herself, ought to present an attractive appearance. In 1938 she started to use lipstick, telling her press conference, "My daughter says I have grown too old to go without lipstick. . . . She says I'll grow better at [using] it as time goes on." "My Day" is replete with references to her own appearance, often derogatory, as when she mentioned a portrait of herself and implied her own "set of features . . . might better be forgotten." [60]

In Mrs. Roosevelt's opinion, only a few women were emotionally and intellectually prepared to tackle the important questions of the day. Asked at a 1938 press conference about a League of Women

Voters report that stated that the number of women legislators had dropped from 149 in thirty-eight states to 130 in twenty-eight states in the last decade and from nine to five in Congress, Mrs. Roosevelt blamed women themselves for the loss. "Women as a whole do not back women's running . . . and are not really trying to get them to represent the woman's point of view," she said, although she did not spell out what this might be.[61]

Mrs. Roosevelt implied a future when women would no longer have to use "indirect methods" of dealing with men, but until then she assumed women would have to employ conventional feminine wiles to circumvent masculine authority. "I think we will probably have something jolting us into waking up some day," she told the press women. She seemed to be saying that women of her era lacked the self-awareness to play an equal role in society.[62]

For her own part, Mrs. Roosevelt wrote Hickok, "I am not unhappy. Life may be somewhat negative with me, but that is nothing new." She expressed concern over her husband's growing conflict with the Washington press corps, which had become increasingly distrustful of the New Deal publicity apparatus. "He [Roosevelt] is always looking for flaws & wanting to get back at them [the reporters]. The old attitude of friendliness is gone & instead of indifference which I could understand is this resentful feeling which I regret," Mrs. Roosevelt told Hickok.[63]

Mrs. Roosevelt exhibited a far different attitude toward her press corps. When her reporter friends experienced tribulations, she offered comfort and passed on tickets to shows and entertainment. Furman, whose financial woes were compounded by her husband's bout with alcoholism, found solace at White House luncheons. "A twenty-minute interview with ER gave me courage and help enough to last at least another year," Furman confided to her diary. Trying to support her family through public relations work, Furman thought it was "absolutely unreal . . . that after twenty years of it I am out of the newspaper game and as forgotten as tho I never was." Her spirits lifted momentarily when she joined her old associates in October 1938 for their annual birthday tribute to Mrs. Roosevelt at a country inn with "a most elaborate menu." Strayer played hostess for the group, which also included Bugbee, Herrick, Thompson, and Black.[64]

By the end of the second term, Mrs. Roosevelt had established herself firmly in the public eye as the outstanding woman of her day. In contrast to her success, however, some of the reporters who had helped her were experiencing career difficulties. The late 1930s saw the decline of Black's news bureau, although she continued to cover Mrs. Roosevelt part-time for the United Press and to act as Washington correspondent for *La Democracia*. "My bureau is now making $30 a month—not enough to pay my cook's salary, much less to pay that and her upkeep, too," Black confided to Mrs. Roosevelt in 1938. Subsequently the first lady helped Herbert Little, Black's husband, obtain a job as regional director for the National Youth Administration.[65]

When Black's bureau totally collapsed, Mrs. Roosevelt wrote her, "I do feel badly that you have to give up your bureau on which you have worked so hard and it is strange that your slump should come now." Black's partisanship toward the first lady appeared to be a factor in her failure. An editor of the *Appleton* (Wisconsin) *Post-Crescent* complained to Black about "Eleanor Roosevelt puff" and a "seemingly constant flavor of favor," in response to her irritation over a "reduced rate of payment." As the number of her clients waned, she depended increasingly on Mrs. Roosevelt as a news source, asking her for an "exclusive story" to keep the bureau afloat. Mrs. Roosevelt gently declined, saying, "I am afraid there isn't any exclusive story in connection with me which I could give you and I cannot think of any other source."[66]

According to Delbert Clark, the *New York Times* Washington bureau chief, the professional stature of women as newspaper writers was retarded, rather than advanced, by Mrs. Roosevelt. He claimed that she "coddled" the press conference group by supplying them with "chit-chat" masquerading as news. "The impression cannot be avoided of a great and good lady taking a bevy of forlorn little ones by the hand and saying: There now, don't you fret. You just let those men be reporters if they want to—we can play at newspapers, too!" he asserted.[67]

The women quarreled with this interpretation. Hornaday saw the press conference group as a brave band of women struggling "in the highest house in the land" to develop themselves and to survive economically. To her the sessions were "a school to elevate women's consciousness," and not just a platform for Mrs. Roosevelt. By 1939, however, it was obvious that close ties with the first lady did not necessarily aid the reporters professionally. Furman, once the Associated Press star, now attended the conferences as a struggling freelance writer; Herrick had failed to regain either her health or professional status; and Black was starting to drink heavily. Bugbee and Strayer, however, continued to be workhorses of their newspapers and Furman would eventually return to reporting.[68]

The conferences kept on furnishing headlines, particularly when Mrs. Roosevelt took a stand on specific items of legislation. She advocated admission of German refugee children to the United States in 1939. That same year, she expressed strong opposition to bills pending in twenty states to prohibit married women from working: "We like many other nations today are facing a possible change in the status of women. It is of great moment to us not to let this happen."[69]

The women faithfully reported her views, which they saw as an ever dependable source of news. "I just wrote what she said," Campbell recalled. "My job was to get what she said and to get it right," Lide noted. In the name of objectivity, the guiding journalistic precept for that era, reporters tended to stick to what was presented and to make little effort at interpretation.[70]

Investigative reporters of a later era might have made much out of Mrs. Roosevelt's agreement to serve as a director of her son James's insurance company, which did business with corporations that held federal contracts. But the members of her press conference reported without comment Mrs. Roosevelt's argument that a president's family should not be compelled to give up normal business ventures. Besides, Mrs. Roosevelt explained, she would receive no money for her services on the board but merely act as her son's representative.[71]

According to Furman's notes, Mrs. Roosevelt expounded to the group: "What kind of people does this country want in the White House? Does it want children who won't earn their living? Women who give up everything?" If so, Mrs. Roosevelt maintained, "some women might say, 'I won't live in the White House at that price.'" In her own case, she said it would be a hardship to give up her interests "and suddenly turn to her husband and be wrapped up in him alone." It was a strong response, although it did not actually address the issue of a potential conflict of interest.[72]

At this point Mrs. Roosevelt had reached a pinnacle of public acclaim. The Gallup poll asked Americans in January 1939, "Do you approve . . . of the way Mrs. Roosevelt has conducted herself as First Lady?" An overwhelming majority, 67 percent, said "yes," while 33 percent said "no." On the related question of her service on the board of the insurance company board, 44 percent answered affirmatively, while 56 percent disapproved. Americans as a whole found it questionable for a president's wife to sit on the board of a company that had commercial ties to the federal government, but they still admired Mrs. Roosevelt. Indeed, the poll showed her to be even more popular than her husband. While 67 percent of the public approved of her performance, only 58 percent approved of her husband's actions as president. She was more popular with women overall than with the well-to-do. Yet a majority of persons in all categories liked her performance.[73]

In 1939 Mrs. Roosevelt was featured on the cover of *Time* magazine. The accompanying story called her "an oracle to millions of housewives" and "the world's foremost female political force," attributing her power not to her husband's influence but to her own hold "on public opinion." In *Time*'s view, this stemmed from "thousands of small activities," including "My Day." It reflected the triumph of an exceptional personality, a woman who projected a unique image of achievement through the mass media. Eleanor Roosevelt had risen far above the reporters who originally had guided her, and become the dominant American woman of her times.[74]

9

Self-Assertion through the Media 1939–41

The jibes are long dead—the ones about Mrs. Roosevelt down in the coal mine, or about "My Day." From the elegant clubs where the old walruses sit and rumble-bumble, to those same coal mines, Mrs. Roosevelt is liked, respected and admired. Even when she goes off the deep end for some completely discredited mob such as the Communists in the American Youth Congress, nobody that we know of seriously complains. It is understood as being just Mrs. Roosevelt's way. The heart of gold is merely throbbing again; the integrity merely showing its full face and unafraid.

> —"Okay, Eleanor," editorial,
> *Collier's*, March 23, 1940

For most of us, it seems imperative that we meet physical force with physical force.

> —Eleanor Roosevelt, "My Day,"
> November 12, 1940

As Franklin Roosevelt's second term ended, Mrs. Roosevelt expressed herself with increasing freedom on public issues, although she spoke circumspectly. In 1939 she announced in "My Day" that she was resigning from an organization because she disagreed with its policies, but she named neither the organization nor specified the policies. Questioned at her press conference, she answered indirectly, "I can say no more than what I said in my column. . . . if I decided a certain action was one of which I did not approve I would be constrained to resign." Yet there was no doubt to what she referred— her resignation from the Daughters of the American Revolution. The announcement came one day after she had sent a telegram to a group of 1,500 persons expressing her regret that Marian Anderson, a black singer, had been denied permission to sing in Constitution Hall, which was owned by the DAR. Mrs. Roosevelt had joined the organization in 1934 after being offered an honorary membership.[1]

In refusing to name the DAR, Mrs. Roosevelt acted to minimize the incident. At that time legal segregation prevailed in Washington and Anderson had been barred from a white high-school auditorium as well as Constitution Hall. Subsequently she performed before 75,000 in an open-air concert at the Lincoln Memorial but Mrs. Roosevelt thought it wise not to attend. Her resignation from the DAR, however, symbolized Mrs. Roosevelt's political stance as being to the left of her husband's. If he was bound to the Southern Democratic leadership in Congress, she was free to uphold liberalism, although her gestures were not translated into public policy.[2]

As World War II loomed, Mrs. Roosevelt spoke out on issues of war and peace by identifying what she considered a woman's viewpoint. In February 1939 she expressed distaste at her press conference for the "vindictiveness" of the peace terms imposed by General Francisco Franco on the defeated loyalist forces in the Spanish Civil War. Since the United States was officially neutral, her comments perturbed the State Department. Months earlier in "My Day" Mrs. Roosevelt, sickened after seeing movies of the bombing of Barcelona, had written: "Why the women in every nation do not rise up and refuse to bring children into a world of this kind is beyond my understanding."[3]

In September 1939 she told her press conference that she favored amending the Neutrality Act (legislation designed to keep the United States out of war) to lift an embargo on selling munitions to warring nations. The purpose of the amendment was to allow the United States to help England and France, which had declared war against Germany immediately after its invasion of Poland. Mrs. Roosevelt stated, however, that the issue "is up to Congress, and I don't think my opinion is that much important."[4]

The women reporters followed her lead in playing down her statement. Black's United Press story began: "While President Roosevelt's press conferences are dominated by subjects connected with the European war, Mrs. Roosevelt's press conferences are chiefly concerned with how to make peace, and what a war situation does to White House customs." Thus she trivialized what could have been a significant news story, because Mrs. Roosevelt's comments marked an important shift in her position. Only two years earlier, under the auspices of a committee of prominent isolationists, Mrs. Roosevelt had launched a "No Foreign War" crusade in a radio address from the White House. However, after Franklin Roosevelt won his unprecedented third-term victory in 1940, she came out strongly for putting bullies in their place by answering "force with physical force."[5]

In her relations with the press women, Mrs. Roosevelt was not afraid to show occasional annoyance. She directly upbraided Winifred Mallon, a veteran reporter for the *New York Times*. Mallon had angered Mrs. Roosevelt with an article claiming that the first lady had been responsible for the appointment of an antifeminist to the Inter-American Commission of Women as well as the appointment of two men to the Interstate Commerce Commission.[6]

Three weeks before the Mallon story ran, Mrs. Roosevelt had invited Mary Winslow to appear at a press conference in what Furman called "one of her silent gestures of support." An official of the Women's Trade Union League, which Mrs. Roosevelt had supported for years, Winslow was backed for the Inter-American Commission appointment by the League of Women Voters and Secretary of Labor Perkins. She replaced the feminist Doris Stevens, a lawyer and member of the National Woman's party, who, as chairman of the commission for a decade, advocated passage of equal rights legislation, Winslow opposed it on grounds that it would interfere with protective legislation for laboring women.[7]

One male journalist, who ridiculed the furor over the Winslow appointment, called it the biggest "fight in Washington" among women since an argument between Dolly Gann, sister of Vice President Charles Curtis, and Alice Roosevelt Longworth, wife of the Speaker of the House, over which one should take precedence at Washington dinner tables. The press women, fearful of displeasing the first lady, were reluctant to bring the question up at Mrs. Roosevelt's first press conference after Mallon's story appeared. In part this was because the conference was the same one at which she was questioned about her resignation from the DAR. After unsuccessful attempts to draw out Mrs. Roosevelt on this point, the reporters proceeded with trivia. "Who is your vocal instructor?" she was asked, and "Do you take setting up exercises every day?" to which Mrs. Roosevelt replied, "Yes, every day."[8]

Then, according to Furman, "Somebody finally got up the courage to ask about the [Inter-American Commission] fight." Mallon's story had alleged that Mrs. Roosevelt interfered in "patronage matters," not only in the appointment of Winslow but in the nominations of J. Hayden Alldredge and former Representative Thomas R. Amlie to the Interstate Commerce Commission. In addressing the issue, Mrs. Roosevelt spoke to Mallon, Furman noted, in the "sweetest voice." The first lady denied that she had proposed "anybody for anything," although she said she had passed on suggestions for nominations. Looking directly at Mallon, she added, "And it is so interesting to me, Miss Mallon, that when you have an opportunity to talk to me here at these press conferences, you don't ask me, instead of printing mere rumors."[9]

Once again, Mrs. Roosevelt stated her opposition to the Equal Rights Amendment: "I happen to be connected with a group [League of Women Voters] which does not believe as the National Woman's Party does. I think they have a good argument on an ideal basis. . . . But we have to live in the world as it is." She said she asked Winslow "to this press conference as I ask anyone appointed to a new office."[10]

Although Mrs. Roosevelt's reply was not totally convincing, since the distinction between suggesting nominations and passing along suggestions may be a fine one, follow-up questions were not asked about the Stevens replacement. Black rushed in with a related query implying criticism of the Mallon story. "Now that we are clearing away the gossip," she said to Mrs. Roosevelt, "did you send cables as to what you wished done at Lima [during a meeting of the Inter-American group]?" Mrs. Roosevelt responded that she had sent no cables expressing support for protective legislation, but "I did discuss the matter in small groups." She proceeded to explain, according to Furman, "Latin American women [are] even less ready for [a] blanket equal rights treaty and loss of protective legislation than in [the] United States." The reporters then dropped the subject, moving on to questions of etiquette (shaking hands with foreign dignitaries) and White House lore (ghosts in the Lincoln bedroom).[11]

Perhaps the women's treatment of Mrs. Roosevelt stemmed in part from the excitement of being able to offer backstage guidance to a star actress in the drama of the times. The reporters knew that, to a degree, she depended on them for information. The preceding month she had not known until told at a press conference that waitresses were picketing a hotel in Alexandria, Virginia. She was scheduled to attend a ball there on her husband's birthday to raise money to fight infantile paralysis, but after being informed that the waitresses received only 50 cents a day plus tips, Mrs. Roosevelt declared that she would not cross the picket line.[12]

Moreover, the women did not probe, push, or argue in the rarefied setting of the White House because they did not think it appropriate to judge Mrs. Roosevelt's motives or to inquire too deeply into her tactics. In part, this reflected the news-gathering mores of a period when public figures were treated with more respect than today. The reporters knew Mrs. Roosevelt was a fallible human being. Increasingly deaf, she depended on Thompson to repeat questions she could not hear. If asked unwelcome questions, she silenced offending journalists with a stare, especially if the queries concerned her children. The reporters understood her sensitivity on the question of her own role because they knew she had no clearly defined path to follow.[13]

In addition, many of the reporters were not concerned with issue-oriented news like the Winslow appointment. Their expertise lay in polishing nuggets of human interest material, which Mrs. Roosevelt happily supplied. Reflecting the interests of their editors and readers, the majority were far more excited about the approaching visit of the king and queen of England in the summer of 1939 than in the direction of a Pan-American commission.

Possibly for that reason Mrs. Roosevelt's comments on her lack of political influence were not directly challenged. To most observers, the submission of names for consideration for offices would amount to substantial influence, if those suggested were at least sometimes selected. Yet Mrs. Roosevelt repeatedly denied having political influence, a fact difficult to understand except in the context of a wife disavowing that her husband paid much attention to her ideas. Perhaps in her denials Mrs. Roosevelt was voicing a sense of powerlessness. In her autobiography she wrote, "If I felt strongly about anything I told Franklin, since he had the power to do things and I did not, but he did not always feel as I felt."[14]

Certainly Mrs. Roosevelt's ability to handle sensitive subjects with diplomatic finesse was illustrated in connection with the visit of the British monarchs. Nothing could have been more serious than their intent—to seek allies in an inevitable war. But the official position of the administration required maintenance of the polite fiction that this was a pleasant tour by two attractive young sovereigns. Mrs. Roosevelt helped foster the illusion.[15]

For weeks before the visit in June 1939 questions about plans for the tour dominated the press conferences. In awe of the regal couple, the American press acted like schoolchildren suddenly transported into a storybook world of crowns and castles. A procession of royalty seeking American aid had started the previous year and would continue during World War II, but no other visitors captured the headlines like the British monarchs.

In the midst of excitement over their tour, a final report was issued on Mrs. Roosevelt's Arthurdale project in West Virginia. The report found the cost astronomically high: expenses per family unit amounted to $8,665 for each modest dwelling in an area where one could buy a substantial home with thirty-five acres of farmland for $5,000. But Mrs. Roosevelt received relatively little blame in the media. As a woman whose heart was seen to be "in the right place," she was not criticized severely when her efforts to do good had not worked out as intended. Questioned about Arthurdale at a press conference, she responded by emphasizing improvements in living conditions for the families involved.[16]

Made to order for the women reporters, the royal visit represented the zenith of society reporting. Details of itineraries, wardrobes, entertainments, ceremonial etiquette, and royal customs filled column after column, often based on press conference questions. On one occasion Mrs. Roosevelt dealt with an inquiry "asked with malice," in Furman's opinion, by a reporter not among the first lady's friends.[17]

The apparently innocuous question was whether musicians performing at a state dinner would be introduced to the king and queen. When Mrs. Roosevelt replied affirmatively, it meant that Marian Anderson would meet the monarchs. It was a symbolic gesture that the administration may have preferred to keep quiet to avoid antagonizing segregationists.[18]

Mrs. Roosevelt made sure that her reporter friends shared in the drama of the visit. The night before the state dinner for the monarchs, she invited Strayer, Herrick, Bugbee, Black, Craig, Fleeson, and Furman to dine in the White House garden. Afterward she led them inside to peek at "the most fantastic kingly cake imaginable . . . topped with a royal crown set with colored candy jewels resting upon a crimson sugar pillow," as Furman put it.[19]

The day after the dinner, Mrs. Roosevelt arranged for the women journalists to meet the king and queen following a press conference at which she lavished praise on the royal pair. When she emphasized their compassion for the unfortunate, Miller sought specific information, but Mrs. Roosevelt replied with, "My impressions are simply on general attitude." As the conference ended, the press women stood in a double line in the Blue Room leaving an open aisle for the monarchs. The queen looked at the group and said, "There are a lot of them, aren't there?" The king smiled and said nothing.[20]

The journalist who benefited the most from the visit was Mrs. Roosevelt herself. United Features guaranteed subscribers "an exclusive report from the First Lady on an important and national event." It offered to sell her column to newspapers that did not normally subscribe for the length of the eight-day visit. Fourteen daily newspapers in Europe and the British colonies took advantage of the special offer as well as six Canadian and fourteen metropolitan American papers.[21]

The women reporters eyed Mrs. Roosevelt's coverage of the visit jealously. "Are you going to scoop us in your column while the King and Queen are here?" she was asked at a press conference. Mrs. Roosevelt offered partial reassurance: "You're not in much worse position [than she herself]—you can write what you want to write. I have to be very careful."[22]

In "My Day" Mrs. Roosevelt included anecdotes for readers seeking an "insider's" story of the visit. She described the delight of little Diana Hopkins, daughter of Harry Hopkins, when she saw Queen Elizabeth in a "spangled tulle dress with her lovely jewels and her tiara in her hair." Mishaps filled another column as Mrs. Roosevelt told how the servants loaded too many dishes on a serving table so that it tipped over and "no one could think because of the noise of breaking china." Next they dropped an entire tray of glasses and bottles on the floor while "Their Majesties remained completely calm and undisturbed."[23]

Mrs. Roosevelt also used the column to defend herself. She was accused of imperiling "the dignity of our country" by serving hot dogs, among other dishes, to the royal couple at a picnic. She assured her "dear readers" that "the more important guests will be served with due formality"—even if they dined on humble hot dogs.[24]

United Features was delighted with her work, particularly when the *New York Times* reprinted the special series on the monarchs after it appeared in the rival *New York World-Telegram*, which regularly carried "My Day." The newspaper trade publication *Editor and Publisher* noted that turning out "My Day" under the pressure of acting as a state hostess represented a reportorial feat. Mrs. Roosevelt was quoted as having said that she devoted from half to three-quarters of an hour each day to the column. Although she normally dictated it, in a pinch she typed it herself as she had been forced to do when Thompson was seriously ill in 1938.[25]

"My Day" soon was to gain attention on other grounds. Three months after the royal visit, Arthur Krock of the *New York Times* labeled the column "required political reading for those seeking insight into administration policies." He speculated that Mrs. Roosevelt might be a dominant influence on her husband because she sat at the president's side during a press conference at Hyde Park and prompted him to discuss cutbacks in Works Progress Administration programs that provided jobs for the unemployed. Since Mrs. Roosevelt had raised the same issue in her column, it appeared to Krock that her husband was following her lead. Krock declared that the president and his wife seemed to be operating as "a political team," a new development in American political history.[26]

In the fall of 1939 Mrs. Roosevelt lent journalistic support to the American Youth Congress, a communist-front group that purported to represent unemployed young people, when its leaders were summoned to appear before the House Un-American Activities Committee. As Joseph P. Lash, executive secretary of the group, took the stand, Mrs. Roosevelt moved to the press table, prepared to take notes. Subsequently she reported on the hearings in her column, where she expressed her indignation over the grilling tactics of staff members.[27]

The liberal *Nation* included Mrs. Roosevelt on its 1939 honor roll for refusing to be "intimidated" by the committee. Other publications saw her committee appearance as evidence of poor judgment. The *New York World-Telegram* alleged in an editorial that the first lady had been "deceived by devious-minded followers of the party line."[28]

Indication of sympathy for fellow travelers disturbed her syndicate editors. In a tactful warning, George Carlin told Mrs. Roosevelt several months before the committee meeting that he "inwardly applauded" a comment in "My Day" attributing communism to empty stomachs, but he hoped she would never repeat it. "The word Communist is a red flag," he wrote. "It is dangerous, I think, for a column like 'My Day.'" In supporting the American Youth Congress, Mrs. Roosevelt played the role of a courageous journalist standing up for what she thought was right. When she moved to the press table, notebook in hand, she wrapped herself in the mantle of the First Amendment.[29]

By this time, Mrs. Roosevelt had mastered the techniques of utilizing the media. In December 1939 she used her press conference to deny statements attributed to her in a *Harper's Magazine* article. The author, Dorothy Dunbar Bromley, contended Mrs. Roosevelt had said in an interview that the United States should not stay out of the European war if "England and France are fighting our battles." Mrs. Roosevelt said she had been speaking only of general circumstances "in which a people had to fight or to give up principles."[30]

Bromley and other journalists raised the possibility of Franklin Roosevelt running for an unprecedented third term, or even of Mrs. Roosevelt running in his place, because of the threat of war. But Democrats wanted to mute the war issue, knowing that voters would not cast ballots to send their sons abroad to fight. When a Japanese correspondent asked Mrs. Roosevelt at a press conference on September 27, 1939, whether the start of World War II in Europe would not ensure a third term for her husband, she answered, "a little curtly," according to Strayer, "I don't see why that should have any bearing." She added, "I am just as anxious as I have ever been to see this country remain at peace, if it is possible."[31]

This statement showed how Mrs. Roosevelt had learned to give herself latitude for shifts of position when speaking for publication. In addition, the women reporters did not scrutinize her statements closely. In the story on the September 27 conference, Strayer, for instance, did not begin with Mrs. Roosevelt's comments on war, but started on a "human interest" note: "This is an important White House fashion communique — that Mrs. Roosevelt won't wear wasp-waists or bustles." The trivializing of Mrs. Roosevelt's position did not lead the public to expect consistency or intellectual vigor from the first lady.[32]

Because she was a wife, not a public official, Mrs. Roosevelt was not held to any particular standard. The public, as represented in the press, excused her failures as honorable attempts. For example, the tough-minded Dorothy Thompson, who did not hesitate to label the youth congress communist-dominated, thought Mrs. Roosevelt's support for it a reflection of her goodness: "She never suspects anyone of ulterior purposes," Thompson wrote. Mrs. Roosevelt continued to defend members of the youth congress even after a group of 4,000, assembled for a citizenship institute in Washington, jeered her husband when he admonished the delegates against attempting to subvert the Constitution.[33]

Although she mentioned the institute sympathetically in "My Day," she did not report on the president's speech or the hostile reaction to it. At a press conference, she insisted, "I still feel that, while they arrive at many of the same conclusions [as communists] because of the difficulties they face, they are not Communist controlled." She did not break with the organization until the summer of 1940 when it voted against United States defense measures and refused to condemn foreign dictatorships.[34]

In her support of the youth congress, Mrs. Roosevelt seemed determined to prove to herself, as well as to the public, that she possessed moral courage. In an article for the *Virginia Quarterly Review*, she quoted Theodore Roosevelt as saying, "When you were afraid to do a thing, that was the time to go and do it." Being afraid of communism was no excuse not to listen to youth, even "when it belongs to the Communist party," she continued.[35]

In April 1940 Mrs. Roosevelt resumed commercial broadcasting. She signed a contract with the manufacturers of Sweetheart soap for a twenty-six-week series of fifteen-minute talks over thirty-six NBC stations twice weekly in the afternoon. Sponsors soon added nine more stations for Mrs. Roosevelt's talks. The themes formed a familiar litany: White House life and history, home management, gardening, supervision of servants, air travel, the scenic beauty of the United States, political conventions and campaigns, and democratic ideals.

Time magazine reported that she received her standard fee of $3,000 for each fifteen-minute broadcast. It called her an equal mixture of celebrity based on her husband's status and achievement in her own right. A contemporary analysis of her radio performance called attention to her clear-cut articulation and cultivated Eastern accent, although it noted that her voice ranged into a falsetto, and inflections sometimes became monotonous. High marks were awarded for "the warmth, sincerity, and earnestness prevalent in her voice."[36]

Movie producers offered her a "tremendous sum" to lecture in ten short films, but she declined the offer, according to Black. In 1940, however, she donned the usual makeup worn by screen stars and made a short movie about her family's hobbies. Two months later she read a plea for religious tolerance that served to introduce an English film being distributed in the United States by her eldest son, James.[37]

But Mrs. Roosevelt emphatically turned down a proposal to play the role of first lady in a Broadway drama. Her swift rejection indicated that she would not consider outright commercialization of her ceremonial position. Similarly she vetoed numerous offers to endorse products in advertisements. She let her name be used without payment, however, in advertisements by the airline industry to promote flying among women.[38]

Carving out a few hours weekly for writing, Mrs. Roosevelt continued to work on magazine articles. In her first seven years in the White House, she sold fifty-one articles, with women's magazines her best customers. She provided their customary fare—hints to brides, advice for women in politics, and tips on good manners.[39]

Informality, if not naivete, characterized her work. "Cherry Blossom Time in Washington," which appeared in the *Reader's Digest*, typified her style. "The cherry trees are in blossom!" it began. "I think perhaps they are most beautiful by moonlight. I still catch my breath when I see them." Occasionally she dealt with current political issues. In *Liberty* in 1939 she told "Why I Am against the People's Vote on War," an attack on a proposed Constitutional amendment for a national referendum on a declaration of war.[40]

Bye insisted Mrs. Roosevelt receive at least a dollar a word. When *Better Homes & Gardens* asked her to write a series on family life, Bye rejected the payment offered. He informed the editor, "We have to protect the magazines that pay Mrs. Roosevelt's dollar-a-word rate as much as possible [although] she usually generously delivers more words than are ordered."[41]

"My Day" remained her longest-running venture, yielding from $1,000 to as much as $2,000 a month depending on subscriber interest. In 1938 she published a book of excerpts from her column. It sold poorly, yet received a favorable critical reception "by reason of its author's amazing naturalness, individuality and force of character," as one reviewer put it. Like most of Mrs. Roosevelt's writing, the column suffered from unevenness in quality. Despite the excess adjectives and clichés, examples of excellent reportorial terseness could be found, as Bromley noted. She quoted Mrs. Roosevelt's observation from a train window of "a little girl, slim and bent over, carrying two pails of water across a field to an unpainted house."[42]

Occasionally Mrs. Roosevelt offended editors by unwittingly violating newspaper taboos. During the fall of 1939, when England and France declared war against Germany, she referred to "gluing" herself to the radio for war news. Carlin passed on a complaint from a Memphis editor who objected to the inference that newspapers were secondary news sources. Mrs. Roosevelt contritely made amends. "Curious how we have settled down again after our first flurry of excitement and now turn to our newspapers for real information," she told her readers a few days later.[43]

In April 1940 United Features renewed her contract for another five years, although it was not certain that her husband would run for a third term. This was tangible recognition that she had established herself as a unique figure within the world of journalism. The renewal stimulated Mrs. Roosevelt's desire to be regarded as a legitimate journalist, although some professionals questioned her qualifications. In 1938 nine votes were cast against her election to membership in the Women's National Press Club. She was admitted only after Furman, Black, Frances Keyes, and Doris Fleeson argued on her behalf and Black denied charges that she was the first lady's "ghost."[44]

Controversy also arose over her membership in the American Newspaper Guild, a union of newspaper employees that she joined in

1936 to show support for unionization. Although she was not active in the union, she was nominated for national president in 1939. Black warned Mrs. Roosevelt radical factions were trying to use her name as a front, and Mrs. Roosevelt declined the nomination. Yet her name was mentioned in connection with charges of communist influence in guild affairs. Westbrook Pegler, the waspish columnist who earlier had called Mrs. Roosevelt "the greatest American woman," attacked the guild for being "run by Communists" and declared that it ought to "get rid of ineligibles," starting with the first lady.[45]

When Mrs. Roosevelt announced that she planned to start attending guild meetings to fight against communists, if she discovered them, Pegler was outraged. He contrasted her decision to remain in "a Soviet outpost," with her "sensational" resignation from the DAR and declared she was "not a journalist but a diarist and dilettante." Mrs. Roosevelt maintained a ladylike reserve in the face of his attacks, telling her readers she saw no reason to feud publicly. She also described her attendance at guild meetings where her ivory knitting needles clicked away, as they sometimes did at her press conferences, while she listened to long-winded talk.[46]

Pegler's venom dismayed Carlin. He wrote Mrs. Roosevelt that "My Day" had succeeded not because it was written by the president's wife, but because it was "an honest projection of one of the great personalities of our own time; a woman great in her own right, and as a newspaper columnist, possibly the best trouper of them all, never known to miss a deadline."[47]

Her stature received similar praise when she spoke at the Democratic convention that nominated Roosevelt for his unprecedented third term. When the convention balked at endorsing Roosevelt's choice for vice president, Henry A. Wallace, Mrs. Roosevelt made a spirited and high-minded appeal for party unity that led to Wallace's nomination. Among those urging her to speak was Hickok, now working for the Democratic National Committee.[48]

Republicans, who had nominated the liberal Wendell Wilkie, tried to make Mrs. Roosevelt and the Roosevelt children, whom they accused of profiting from their family position, into a campaign issue. "We don't want Eleanor either!" read the slogan on a large GOP button. But the first lady was far more an asset than a liability. During the first term Mrs. Roosevelt had aroused controversy in the media because she failed to fit the previous image of a first lady by engaging in unorthodox activities such as driving her own car and mingling easily with trade unionists and destitute miners, activities she had become accustomed to while campaigning in New York State in the 1920s. But by 1940, through her own example, Mrs. Roosevelt had transformed the image of proper conduct for a president's wife from regard for social form to a concern for social ills. It was an image well suited to an era when people needed inspiration. As Hornaday put it, "The very fact she would strike out on her own and be something, instead of just sitting in the White House and going to teas gave courage to a lot of people, especially during the Depression."[49]

Mrs. Roosevelt's trips throughout the nation also served to enhance her status in the media. Not only by giving lectures, but through meeting local reporters while on tours, she endeared herself to millions. According to Hornaday, "It was her travels that produced the news; they became local stories." On the trips, she talked to countless local journalists, ranging from high-school students to distinguished publishers.[50]

A picture in the *Decatur* (Illinois) *Herald and Review* illustrated a typical scene from Mrs. Roosevelt's travels in 1940. Captioned "The first lady seemed as eager to answer questions at the press conference as her hearers were to ask them," it showed an animated Mrs. Roosevelt discussing rural school consolidation with an attentive group of Illinois editors. Mrs. Roosevelt's secretary, Thompson, sat in a corner, looking, as the accompanying story put it, "a little bored with what to her was just one more press conference."[51]

During the presidential campaign of 1940 Mrs. Roosevelt hedged on the issue of America's possible involvement in war. Before the third term nomination was certain, "My Day" implied the inevitability of American participation. In the heat of the campaign, when Roosevelt made an ill-advised promise to keep American boys out of foreign wars, Mrs. Roosevelt tried to reinterpret his statement at a press conference on May 13, 1941. "[In] most of the things I have read and remembered hearing him say, he has always said 'unless we are attacked.' I don't see how anyone understood it any other way," she said. At the same time in her column she emphasized that the

United States had not entered the conflict: "The fact is before you that in a world of war we are still at peace." After the election, she returned to her earlier theme of the need to meet force with force.[52]

Mrs. Roosevelt also gained favorable publicity from the publication of Black's laudatory biography, which Black wrote in four and a half months in an effort to rejuvenate her career. It was not an official campaign biography but it came close to being one. To gain material, Black submitted questions to Mrs. Roosevelt and Thompson and incorporated their answers in the manuscript. In some cases, Mrs. Roosevelt told Black what she could and could not print. Problems with her mother-in-law were "not too intimate to mention," the first lady said, but she refused permission to include a vignette on her encounters with the "horsy" set of Virginia hunt country. When Mrs. Roosevelt objected to being called "Mother of the NYA," Black changed a chapter title to "Inspiration of the NYA."[53]

Titled simply *Eleanor Roosevelt*, the book was the first biography of Mrs. Roosevelt. Published on October 11, 1940, Mrs. Roosevelt's fifty-sixth birthday, it received mixed reviews, failing to fulfill Black's hopes for a financial and critical success. Even well-disposed reviewers complained of the sentimental tone. Hornaday recalled Mrs. Roosevelt as being "cold" about it and speculated that she found it shallow. Comparing it with his own firsthand knowledge of life at Val-Kill, Joseph Lash, by now the first lady's close friend, recognized that Black had not understood the tangled relationships of the Roosevelt family. Black was thrilled when Mrs. Roosevelt mentioned the book in "My Day," although she damned the volume with faint praise: "I began to feel I was being introduced to someone I really did not know."[54]

Regardless of depth, or lack of it, the book enhanced the image of Mrs. Roosevelt as a political partner with her husband. Franklin Roosevelt liked it. To a lesser degree, so did another well-informed reader, Hickok. She wrote Mrs. Roosevelt that the book gave a clear picture of her development into a public "personage." Although Hickok said she had carried on for years "an anguished and losing fight against the development of the person into the personage," she concluded, "I admire and respect the personage with all my heart."[55]

In Hickok's assessment of Mrs. Roosevelt's public transformation can be seen the commanding personality who towered over the lives of some of those around her. There was Hickok, dependent on Mrs. Roosevelt's recommendation for a job as executive secretary of the women's division of the Democratic National Committee. There was the self-effacing secretary, Malvina Thompson, who left her husband, Frank Scheider, when she moved with Mrs. Roosevelt from New York to Washington, and later divorced him.[56] Mrs. Roosevelt called Thompson "the person who makes life possible for me." She was supervisor of the White House staff of eighteen who answered Mrs. Roosevelt's mail, which totaled one million letters in 1940, and took care of social affairs. Thompson was the traveling companion who accompanied the first lady on journeys that averaged 40,000 miles a year during the first two terms. "Everything I do is conditioned by her needs," Thompson told Emma Bugbee. "So I am never worried by a conflict between my affairs and hers."[57]

As for Black, being an intimate of Mrs. Roosevelt provided dubious professional advantages, she informed a columnist. "I sometimes think her alleged 'favorites' get scooped oftener than those who are not invited to visit her, at the White House or at Val-Kill, because we often learn things in confidence which get gossiped around by non-journalists, and finally make their ways into columns," Black said.[58]

Although Mrs. Roosevelt assured Hickok that "I only like the part of life in which I am a person," she played the part of the personage superbly. Perhaps it was because of the kind of womanly self-discipline she described in a 1940 article titled "Men Have To Be Humored" in *Woman's Day*. Women, she wrote, were the stronger of the two sexes emotionally "because they have to please the gentlemen." She quoted a passage from Stephen Vincent Benét's poem "John Brown's Body," which depicted a Southern lady:

> May Lou Wingate, as slightly made
> And as hard to break as a rapier-blade.[59]

As a role model for women, Mrs. Roosevelt, who was 5 feet, 11 inches tall and weighed 160 pounds, bore little resemblance to a rapier blade. Yet she had the same kind of indestructibility. She had been forced into a position she did not want and turned it to her own advantage. As first lady, her status remained that of a wife whose accomplishments reflected favorably on her husband. In 1940 the

Divorce Reform League selected President Roosevelt as one of the five "best husbands" in the country and Mrs. Roosevelt as one of the five "most fortunate wives" because he did not restrict her activities to the home. As a celebrity, she did not stand apart from her marital partnership.[60]

Nevertheless, instead of being blinded by the spotlight of publicity, Mrs. Roosevelt had learned to use it to illuminate herself. She fit the mold of what Daniel Boorstin identified as "a new kind of eminence," that attained by celebrity status rather than pure achievement. She was known for what she did, but she was also known for who she was, which in turn influenced what she did.[61]

10

The Press as Adversary
1941–42

I don't question for a moment that any President of this country would do anything he could to keep his country out of war. But nobody can state what circumstances may exist.

—Eleanor Roosevelt, White House press conference,
May 13, 1941

People can gradually be brought to understand that an individual, even if she is a President's wife, may have independent views and must be allowed the expression of an opinion. But actual participation in the work of the government, we are not yet able to accept.

—Eleanor Roosevelt, "My Day,"
February 23, 1942

After Roosevelt's third-term inauguration in 1941, Mrs. Roosevelt began to prepare the nation's women for war. Hornaday recalled that she told the press conference group off-the-record that she "couldn't believe her husband could switch so fast" on the issue of war, after promising to keep the nation out of it. On the record, Mrs. Roosevelt warned of the likelihood of rationing. She reported that army officers in training camps were telling draftees to stop joking and start marching because they were headed for combat. As a supporter of organized labor, she tried to persuade the public, including mothers of draftees, that it was understandable why workers were striking even in defense plants.[1]

In the midst of serious discussion, a chatty, sorority house atmosphere often prevailed. "It used to be as much as a girl's reputation was worth to be seen with a soldier in uniform," one newswoman declared after hearing Mrs. Roosevelt report on an inspection trip to Fort Bragg, North Carolina. "I don't see how that can hold, when many of us have children in uniform," Mrs. Roosevelt earnestly replied.[2]

The first lady favored conscripting young women, as well as young men, for a year of compulsory service. She proposed the plan when she inaugurated a question-and-answer page, "If You Ask Me," in the *Ladies' Home Journal* in May 1941 patterned after a similar page, "Dear Mrs. Roosevelt," which ran in the *Democratic Digest* from December 1937 until January 1941.

Her proposal on conscription came in response to a question from a 19-year-old woman who wrote, "My young man has just gone to camp, and it doesn't seem right for me to sit at home and go around doing the same things I have always done." The *Journal* co-editor, Beatrice Gould, thought Mrs. Roosevelt's idea "a fine thing," but *Time* magazine commented, "No one in the government, from the President down, supported her." The plan was viewed as too radical, because it would remove women from their protected, subordinate status, although under it women could have lived at home while being trained in traditional fields like nursing, food preparation, and, as *Time* put it, "such mechanical skills as they wanted to learn."[3]

Mrs. Roosevelt was not initially a supporter of a bill introduced in May 1941 by Representative Edith N. Rogers, a Republican from Massachusetts, to create a women's army auxiliary corps. "I don't know that we will consider it a necessity here [to have women in the military]," Mrs. Roosevelt told a press conference. The legislation did not pass until six months after the United States entered World War II, following the Japanese attack on Pearl Harbor on December 7, 1941. Women were not given full army status until 1943, when the auxiliary was converted to the Women's Army Corps (WAC).[4]

Prior to United States entry into the conflict, Mrs. Roosevelt had stressed that women should be mobilized not simply for military purposes, but to carry out the New Deal vision of an improved society. Impressed by the efforts of Lady Stella Reading, director of the women's civil defense organization in England, Mrs. Roosevelt wanted to involve women in building a new social order. She interpreted civil defense as a means of improving society, not just selecting air raid wardens. At a press conference in August 1941 she criticized the national Office of Civilian Defense, headed by Mayor Fiorello H. LaGuardia of New York, because it ignored women. She saw her

own proposal to conscript young women for post–high-school training as an alternative to drafting them for defense work. Mrs. Roosevelt opposed a draft on the grounds that the nation had a surplus of
unemployed workers.[5]

In reaction, LaGuardia insisted that Mrs. Roosevelt be designated assistant director of the office. Although she was unpaid, her
appointment had to be approved by President Roosevelt. It marked
the first time a first lady had held a government office.[6]

LaGuardia called Mrs. Roosevelt "America's Number 1 volunteer." In her new post, she took charge of what the Office of Civil
Defense press releases referred to as "fortification in recreation,
health, welfare, family security, education and other types of public
and private community services." The press, however, focused not on
her task but on the unusual spectacle of a president's wife holding an
official appointment even if an unpaid one.[7]

She began her duties on September 29, 1941, under difficult
circumstances, three weeks after the death of her mother-in-law and
four days after the death of her brother, Hall Roosevelt. As she did on
other occasions, Mrs. Roosevelt used "My Day" to ventilate her personal feelings in public, while still staying within the boundaries of
good taste. She described her mother-in-law frankly in her column as
a "grande dame," concluding, "She was not just sweetness and light,
for there was a streak of jealousy and possessiveness in her where her
own were concerned."[8]

When she walked nearly a mile from the White House to her
Dupont Circle office for her first day on the job, journalists checked
her arrival time. Black's United Press story said that Mrs. Roosevelt
was on time, but other reporters said that she was ten minutes late.
"First Lady is Late for New Job," blared the headlines in the *Washington Times-Herald*. Even favorable reports pictured her as a dabbling
do-gooder. Black, in her United Press stories, quoted Mrs. Roosevelt
as saying that she would "really work" but would not observe regular
hours because of other commitments.[9]

One of Mrs. Roosevelt's first acts was to decide on admission
policies for press conferences. She announced that she would retain
women-only press conferences at the White House but would admit
men to conferences at her civil defense office. Obviously Mrs. Roosevelt wanted to retain the women's conference as a separate entity,

although a major scrutiny of accreditation standards was under way before she took the civil defense post.[10]

On May 31, 1941, Florence Shreve, formerly a government publicity writer, had been called out of a conference and "dramatically ejected from the White House by ushers," according to a newspaper column. The White House press office declared that Shreve, described in the column as a "red-haired and aggressive matron," had misrepresented herself as a reporter for the *Hemet* (California) *News*, but actually was a lobbyist for West Coast shipping and mining interests. In a confidential memo, Black informed United Press editors that Shreve had used her accreditation to the conference to "jimmy good pay out of contract-seekers and lobbyists by telling them . . . she has 'White House contacts.'"[11]

At the time of the Shreve incident it was easy for almost any woman with the slightest claim to being a correspondent for a daily newspaper to gain admission. A roster of accredited correspondents compiled in June 1941 showed 115 names of newswomen along with the names of sixteen other journalists who represented federal publicity offices. Many of the eligible women wrote only occasional feature stories for small papers such as the *Southwest Times* of Pulaski, Virginia, and the *News Telegraph* of Atlanta, Iowa.[12]

Admission to the conferences was controlled by Stephen T. Early, the president's press secretary, although he frequently delegated the task to Malvina Thompson. In February 1941 he informed Mrs. Roosevelt that he had rejected the application of Mrs. Bedford Lawson, who "represents colored weekly newspapers printed in Pittsburgh." If correspondents for weekly newspapers were admitted, he continued, the "regular attendance at these conferences probably will be increased by several hundred persons." In addition, Early saw the Lawson request as a subterfuge by "certain colored leaders" who were trying to "force their admission to the President's conferences with the press," where they were also banned on the grounds that they represented weekly, not daily, newspapers.[13]

Nine months later Thompson asked Early's opinion about admitting a black reporter from the *Washington Afro-American*, another weekly. Early reiterated his opposition. Since some of the women admitted sold free-lance articles to weekly newspapers, although they were not actually employed by them, it appeared that Early's intent was to exclude black journalists on a technicality.[14]

Following the Shreve incident, the women journalists, with Mrs. Roosevelt's approval, discussed the possibility of forming their own organization to direct the press conferences. After the United States entered World War II, the women set up such a body. At a meeting on December 22, 1941, May Craig called attention to the need "to prevent exploitation of the conference, which is more to be feared with war on; also to avoid the danger of subversive activity."[15]

The group chose the title Mrs. Roosevelt's Press Conference Association, proposed by Martha Strayer, temporary secretary. It rejected the use of "First Lady" in the name after Craig said that Mrs. Roosevelt "had made fun of the term." It also considered "Women's White House Press Conference Association," but abandoned it when Craig argued against a sex distinction.[16]

The previous week a male reporter had attended what was supposed to be a women-only conference. On that occasion Mrs. Roosevelt, to save time, had told the women journalists to meet at her civil defense office rather than at the White House. Dewey Fleming, a reporter for the *Baltimore Sun*, appeared and refused to leave, asserting his right to attend a press briefing by a public official.[17]

The issue of admitting men was not discussed immediately by the new group, however, as it debated accreditation requirements. A key question was whether to continue to admit part-time correspondents and government press officers. Speaking against the latter, Miriam Ottenberg of the *Washington Star* argued, "Is this supposed to be a propaganda bureau for Mrs. Roosevelt?" Her chief opponent was Black, who was now supplementing her United Press earnings with a part-time job, obtained through Mrs. Roosevelt's influence, at the Office of the Coordinator of Inter-American Affairs headed by Nelson A. Rockefeller. In the end the group compromised by deciding to admit government representatives but without giving them voting privileges in the organization.[18]

In the early months of 1942, Mrs. Roosevelt held a series of press conferences at the Office of Civil Defense with male reporters present. By this time she was under journalistic fire, first for alleged administrative inefficiency, and later for putting personal friends, especially Mayris Chaney, a professional ballroom dancer, on the civil defense payroll. Chaney, who originated the "Eleanor glide" in Mrs. Roosevelt's honor, was hired to set up a program to teach dancing to children in bomb shelters. The press overwhelmingly disapproved.

The revelation that Mrs. Roosevelt had favored Chaney's employment was reported in February 1942 by Christine Sadler of the *Washington Post.* According to Mary Hornaday, who had been elected the first chairman of the press conference association, this demonstrated that women reporters did not always "cover up" for Mrs. Roosevelt. Notes taken at Mrs. Roosevelt's press conferences at the Office of Civil Defense in January and February 1942 show that she was asked much harder-hitting questions than at the women-only conferences at the White House, although there is no record of whether men or women asked them.[19]

On January 5 a reporter asked, "Will you confirm or deny the accuracy of a newspaper prediction that you and Mayor LaGuardia will resign from the civilian defense?" According to Strayer's notes, "Almost for the first time in her press conferences, Mrs. Roosevelt was on the defensive." She replied, "Do they need to make predictions that absolutely are not based on fact and that put me on the spot? As far as I know, there is no truth in that whatsoever."[20]

As the questions kept on, Mrs. Roosevelt became increasingly flustered, as this exchange indicated:

Question: "Did LaGuardia fire two of your assistants, including the assistant connected with the physical fitness program?"
Mrs. Roosevelt: "If there were two assistants, there were two that I never have seen."
Question: "Did you promptly rehire them?"
Mrs. Roosevelt: "I haven't seen any. I had a staff meeting this morning and everyone on the staff was still there. I don't know."
Question: "They might have been there, because according to the report you rehired them."
Mrs. Roosevelt: "I haven't been conscious of anything."[21]

Further questions followed, implying that Mrs. Roosevelt was inefficient as an executive. In actuality the job represented an administrative nightmare that would have taxed the most experienced manager. Efforts to create a program ran afoul of bureaucratic jealousy between cabinet departments and fledgling defense agencies as well as friction with the military. Voluntary organizations sought to outdo each other to gain publicity for themselves. Volunteers lacked clearly defined tasks, and local and regional councils issued conflicting sets of instructions. The press, however, pictured the problems in simplistic terms centered around criticism of Mrs. Roosevelt herself.[22]

A chance comment in "My Day" became a target for attacks that Strayer called "the most embarrassing of all." In her column for December 24, 1941, Mrs. Roosevelt wrote that she had been late arriving at the Office of Civilian Defense because the president "finally decided to tell me that British Prime Minister, Mr. Winston Churchill, and his party were arriving sometime in the late afternoon or evening." To the Republican *New York Herald-Tribune* and other critics, this showed that Mrs. Roosevelt had "an improper attitude about getting to work on time," in an era when punctuality was taken seriously.[23]

Even before this incident, columnists had called for her resignation. The sober Walter Lippmann saw her as "sugar-coating" serious business with "all manner of fads, fancies, homilies, and programs which would have been appropriate to the activities of an excited village improvement society." He contended that the wife of the president should not confuse everybody by being "a subordinate official in a subordinate department of the government which her husband administers." The anti–New Deal columnist Frank R. Kent alleged that the talents for publicity displayed by both LaGuardia and Mrs. Roosevelt obscured administrative chaos. Presidential aides reacted to the criticism by bringing in new officials. To improve civil defense administration, James M. Landis, dean of the Harvard Law School, was appointed executive officer and Jonathan Daniels, later editor of the *Raleigh News and Observer*, was named executive aide.[24]

Mrs. Roosevelt was subjected to more sharp questioning at another press conference, and again became defensive. On January 12, 1942, a reporter asked, "Did you happen to read in the *Congressional Record* what was being said on the floor. . . . particularly the reference to your being too busy to handle the job?" Mrs. Roosevelt replied, "How specific was it? Who was it who made that? What is the definite question? What do people consider too busy?" After the reporter responded, "The point in both houses was that this is a full-time job," Mrs. Roosevelt continued, "What is a full-time job? How many hours does that mean?" She estimated that she spent twelve hours a day on civil defense but that not all were spent in her office. Knowing of her high energy level, her journalist friends did not dispute her assertion.[25]

Mrs. Roosevelt also became embroiled in policy arguments. She opposed a bill to turn civil defense over to the army, arguing it was more than a military issue. To the disappointment of feminists, she was lukewarm about using women as army volunteers. She told a press conference, "If you need them, I think it should be possible to use them; but I don't believe in obliging women to do things when it isn't necessary for them to do them."[26]

Mrs. Roosevelt also aroused hostility from segregationists who disliked her efforts to allow blacks to participate in civil defense programs. Racial integration was in line with her dream of a better world for all, a theme highlighted in Mrs. Roosevelt's speeches and writings after the United States entered World War II. In "My Day" she stressed, "If we cannot meet the challenge of fairness to our citizens of every nationality . . . if we cannot keep in check anti-semitism, anti-racial feelings as well as anti-religious feelings, then we shall have removed from the world, the one real hope for the future."[27]

The uproar over the Chaney appointment occupied reporters at a press conference on February 9, 1942. Mrs. Roosevelt admitted having suggested the dancer as director of children's civil defense activities at $4,600 annually, a salary higher than that paid to an army colonel. Questioning turned into a sparring match. "What is Miss Chaney doing? Because, of course, she must be doing something," a reporter insisted. "You're bringing up a question on the whole question of the physical fitness program," Mrs. Roosevelt countered. "I think that's not for me to discuss."[28]

Congressional Republicans seized upon the incident gleefully with the House voting to ban funds for promoting "physical fitness through dancing." A growing number of newspapers demanded Mrs. Roosevelt's resignation. Raymond Clapper, considered a nonpartisan columnist, complained, "How can you have any kind of morale with a subordinate employee, who happens to be the wife of the President of the United States, flitting in and out between lecture engagements to toss a few more pets into nice jobs."[29]

In addition the Chaney appointment provided lethal ammunition for critics already incensed because of fears that the civil defense organization harbored communist sympathizers brought in by Mrs. Roosevelt. Lash, appointed as an unpaid member of an advisory committee, came under fire. Melvyn Douglas, an actor who headed an arts division, was berated for being a radical. These efforts to attack her through her friendships proved upsetting, Mrs. Roosevelt noted in her autobiography.[30]

The February 9 press conference marked the last of Mrs. Roosevelt's attempts to combine a session for women reporters with a conference open to men. Before admitting the male journalists, she met with the women alone. She instructed them to return to the White House for subsequent conferences, commenting, "Miss Thompson tells me that you really find it better at the White House, and there is this difficulty here that other people [men] want to come."[31]

By this time the women's association had agreed on a procedure for conference accreditation. Each applicant was directed to submit a letter from her employer, clippings of recently published work, and a statement of her plans for attendance. This was a concern because only about half of the accredited group usually showed up for the conferences, perhaps because many of the women were feature writers whose work appeared only intermittently in their newspapers.[32]

In mid-February 1942 Mrs. Roosevelt informed the chairman, Mary Hornaday, that the Secret Service "because of the war, has asked me to place a limit on the size of the groups which are admitted to the White House." Mrs. Roosevelt then specified that attendance should be restricted to employees of daily newspapers, press associations, broadcasting companies and weekly news magazines. By excluding part-time journalists, the new requirements sharply cut the number of women eligible to attend. From the total of 115 accredited in June 1941 the number dropped to thirty-three.[33]

The actual accreditation was left to a five-member committee. It included Hornaday, Strayer, Craig, Gertrude Chesnut of Transradio

Press Service, and Esther Van Wagoner Tufty, who represented a group of Michigan newspapers. Admission of government publicity women was left to Mrs. Roosevelt.[34]

According to Strayer, "many 'fringe' or 'free lance' writers were eliminated, much to the regret of everybody, including Mrs. Roosevelt, [because] the eliminated writers had done well by her." These women had written features presenting "usually kind pictures of the depression model First Lady," Strayer noted. Most of these articles were published in small-town newspapers otherwise lacking in White House coverage.[35]

As the waves of criticism over the Chaney appointment mounted, even Mrs. Roosevelt's staunchest friends among the women reporters questioned her action. Strayer wrote years later that Mrs. Roosevelt's "friends and admirers regretted that she had accepted this federal post. It undoubtedly was a mistake."[36]

Mrs. Roosevelt resigned her civil defense post on February 20, 1942. The press immediately softened its condemnation by portraying Mrs. Roosevelt as a woman of honorable intentions, if poor judgment. *Time* pictured her as "a kind lady" giving the nation "a lesson in good manners" by resigning in the best interests of civil defense. Calling her failure "inevitable," because of the vagueness of her responsibilities, the *New York Times* said that her resignation did not reflect upon "her ability, her goodwill and her unselfish devotion to the general welfare."[37]

In her own defense Mrs. Roosevelt sidestepped criticism of specific actions by casting the issue in broader terms. In "My Day" she made a feminist claim, ignoring the question of her civil defense performance itself. Portraying herself as the victim of her position, she wrote it was impossible for anyone who was first lady to be "looked upon as an individual."[38]

After Mrs. Roosevelt's resignation, questions at press conferences reverted to the details of White House life during wartime, particularly sugar rationing and the prospects for a victory garden, which was not planted after the soil was found to be unsuitable. Questioned about the role of women, she gave conservative replies. She foresaw no possibility of a woman admiral, although women were being accepted into the navy WAVES, because "there is no question of women running ships in any capacity."[39] Defending the administration in the spring of 1942, Mrs. Roosevelt supported the internment of citizens of Japanese descent. She insisted that many Japanese-Americans she had met realized their removal from their homes was for their own good and for the good of the country. She added that many would suffer unjustly but said the war required extreme measures.[40]

As head of the conference association, Hornaday asked Mrs. Roosevelt in November 1942 to relax her rule forbidding direct quotations except by special permission. "Since the size of the conference has been drastically reduced and its caliber increased accordingly (we hope), we do not believe you would have much trouble with being misquoted," Hornaday argued on behalf of the group. Privately, she had doubts. "It was hard to take Mrs. Roosevelt's statements down," recalled Hornaday years later. "Her language was vague. You couldn't get it down fast. She kind of wandered. Covering her was the only time I wished I knew shorthand."[41]

Responding to Hornaday's request to relax the "no quote" rule, Mrs Roosevelt at first held out for advance approval. She said, "I'm quite willing if you just simply say, 'Is this all right to quote, to have you quoted.' If I say anything that I want to have off the record, I'll say, 'This is off the record.' " Six months later Hornaday again sought blanket permission for direct quotes except when Mrs. Roosevelt stated otherwise. By 1944, the association's rules provided that any statement made by Mrs. Roosevelt at a press conference could be used in direct quotes unless she specified that it was for indirect quotation only or entirely off the record.[42]

After the civil defense debacle, Mrs. Roosevelt insisted that her press conference be barred to men. When Gordon Cole, a reporter for the liberal New York newspaper *PM*, requested admission, the conference association itself divided. "Some members seemed to feel it is up to us to end the discrimination against men; others felt that women have so many strikes against them in this business that it is wise to keep this one advantage," Hornaday informed Mrs. Roosevelt. When the first lady warned the group she might end the conferences if men were admitted, the association rejected Cole's application. Esther Van Wagoner Tufty, a member of the standing committee, stressed to her colleagues that the women-only conferences were "precious" to Mrs. Roosevelt.[43]

A month after she left the civil defense office, Mrs. Roosevelt cast herself in the role of a dutiful, traditional wife. "I guess I'd list myself as a housewife—with some experience in writing a column and in speaking—and that's all," Mrs. Roosevelt told her press conference in March 1942. Other comments reinforced various government campaigns to persuade housewives to work in defense plants and service industries but only until the war emergency was over. In an era of serious debate over the propriety of women wearing slacks, Mrs. Roosevelt remarked she would not want a secretary working for her to wear them.[44]

Her retreat into the role of a self-sacrificing wife was illustrated by her stand on a proposal that would require married couples to file a joint income tax return. She said that she agreed with the object of raising money for the war by combining two incomes to force a couple into a higher tax bracket. Women's groups argued that it would penalize working women, and some columnists, including Arthur Krock of the *New York Times*, objected on grounds that it would turn back the clock on social progress. He pointed out that Mrs. Roosevelt was speaking as the president's wife in upholding the plan and not as the well-paid career woman that she also was.[45]

Before the attack on Pearl Harbor, Mrs. Roosevelt had signed a contract with the Pan-American Coffee Bureau, which represented eight coffee-exporting nations, for a series of twenty-eight Sunday evening broadcasts. (By today's standards, it would be almost inconceivable for a president's wife to receive similar payments from foreign governments. At the time there was little concern, probably because the public was used to Mrs. Roosevelt's broadcasts.) From October 1941 through April 1942 the broadcasts praised homemakers as "the first line of defense in the war." They urged women to accept food rationing and described Mrs. Roosevelt's visits to defense installations. *Time* magazine said that the programs were carried by more NBC outlets than the popular "Fibber McGee and Molly" comedy show.[46]

The programs, for which Mrs. Roosevelt reportedly received a total of $28,000, also afforded her an opportunity to defend her civil defense activities. Mrs. Roosevelt told her listeners that a professional dancer like Chaney was needed for a physical fitness program, and labeled her critics enemies of the New Deal. In a broadcast on February 22, 1942, she called them "the same group which has felt that everything which was done to make life pleasanter and easier for the people as a whole, was in some way useless, and therefore, should be branded as boondoggling." On the one side, she said, were the "virtuous Westbrook Peglers," and on the other, "the boondogglers, so-called. . . . It is a question of privilege or equality."[47]

This marked one of the few times that Mrs. Roosevelt directly attacked Pegler, whom she usually ignored, following her husband's advice not to get into a "bad smells" contest. Pegler mocked the dilettantish quality of Mrs. Roosevelt's column in a devastating parody written a few months later. Written shortly after he had won a Pulitzer prize for an exposé of scandals in organized labor, the parody drew appreciative responses even from Mrs. Roosevelt's friends. Few could dispute the element of haziness in Mrs. Roosevelt's enthusiasms that Pegler encapsulated. He began: "Yesterday morning I took a train to New York and sat beside a gentleman who was reading the 1937 report of the international recording secretary of the World Home Economics and Children's Aptitude and Recreation Foundation of which my very good friend, Dr. Mary McTwaddle, formerly of Vassar, is the American delegate. This aroused my interest and I ventured to remark that I had once had the pleasure of entertaining a group of young people who were deeply concerned with the neglected problem of the unmarried father. It turned out that gentleman himself was an unmarried father so we had a very interesting chat until he got off at Metuchen."[48]

Yet even as Pegler ridiculed Mrs. Roosevelt, he unintentionally presented her in a quasi-favorable light as a well-meaning lady whose heart outran her head. A less vitriolic columnist, Raymond Clapper, raised the same point after Mrs. Roosevelt invited Secretary of Agriculture Claude R. Wickard to appear on her radio program to advise housewives of an impending sugar shortage. The warning led to a rash of hoarding, which prompted Clapper to ask why the shortage was announced before rationing measures were put into effect. "Sometimes Mrs. Roosevelt seems so naive that you wonder whether it isn't something just a little more subtle," Clapper wrote. He suggested that the naivete masked a strong character whose will to do good overpowered her judgment.[49]

In the wake of the civil defense fiasco, Mrs. Roosevelt found herself without any definite responsibility in the war effort. Wartime restrictions halted her lecture tours and precluded any new contracts for radio commentaries, although she continued to keep individual speaking engagements as well as to write. Her duties as a hostess multiplied, with royalty and prime ministers parading through the White House. Yet in the midst of hectic days, Mrs. Roosevelt lamented, "I do not seem to be doing anything useful." Soon, however, she would begin a round of travel that would make her a figure known worldwide.[50]

During World War II Eleanor Roosevelt traveled all over the world visiting American troops. This cartoon was drawn by Herblock for NEA shortly after the British commando raid on Dieppe in August 1942. © 1942 Newspaper Enterprise Association, Inc.

Eleanor Roosevelt holding a press conference at the Royal Hawaiian Hotel, Oahu, on September 21, 1943, during a trip to the Pacific. Franklin D. Roosevelt Library.

Eleanor Roosevelt and Clementine Churchill addressed the Canadian people over the radio from the Chateau Frontenac during the second Quebec conference of President Roosevelt and Prime Minister Winston Churchill, September 11–16, 1944. Franklin D. Roosevelt Library.

Called the "First Lady of Radio" for her frequent broadcasts, most often on the NBC radio network, Eleanor Roosevelt became one of the best-known radio performers in the United States during her White House years. Here she is shown broadcasting a message to Americans on Victory-in-Europe Day, May 8, 1945, less than a month after the death of President Roosevelt. UPI.

Reporters questioned Eleanor Roosevelt at a press conference at the United Nations in Paris on December 9, 1948, after the adoption of the Declaration of Human Rights. Franklin D. Roosevelt Library.

Eleanor Roosevelt on the "Meet the Press" broadcast in New York, April 8, 1949. Left to right: Martha Roundtree, Lawrence Spivak, Mrs. Roosevelt, Murray Davis, May Craig, Henry La Cossitt, and Warren Moscow. Franklin D. Roosevelt Library.

The first telecast of "Eleanor Roosevelt's Weekly Forum" on February 11, 1950, featured a discussion of "What to Do with the Hydrogen Bomb." Participants were (left to right): Senator Brian McMahon, Hans A. Bethe, Mrs. Roosevelt, David E. Lilienthal, and J. Robert Oppenheimer. Leonard McCombe, *Life* Magazine, © Time Inc.

The twentieth anniversary reunion of Eleanor Roosevelt's first White House press conference took place at a luncheon in 1953 at the Algonquin Hotel in New York City. Attending (clockwise from left) were: Lorena A. Hickok, Edith Asbury, Corinne Frazier, Mrs. Roosevelt, Emma Bugbee, Mary Hornaday, Margaret Parton, Dorothy Ducas, Kathleen McLaughlin, and Malvina Thompson. Cosmo-Sileo photo furnished by the Western History Research Center, University of Wyoming.

Eleanor Roosevelt presided at a press conference in January 1962 to announce plans for the President's Commission on the Status of Women. Franklin D. Roosevelt Library.

11

Promoting the War Effort
1942–45

Women are often attacked because no radical changes have occurred since they obtained their rights as full citizens of this democracy, and now is the time to show they recognize their responsibilities.
— Eleanor Roosevelt, "My Day,"
January 14, 1944

Because I was the wife of the President certain restrictions were imposed upon me. Now I am on my own and I hope to write as a newspaper woman.
— Eleanor Roosevelt, "My Day,"
April 18, 1945

In October 1942 Mrs. Roosevelt flew to England as the guest of Queen Elizabeth to examine the contribution of British women to the war. Mrs. Roosevelt attributed the invitation to her career activities, ignoring the obvious, her position as wife of the president. "The queen, knowing I wrote a column and made speeches fairly frequently, felt, I think that I had access to the people here," Mrs. Roosevelt wrote in her autobiography. She said that she welcomed the trip after her "recent experience" in the Office of Civilian Defense because it "seemed to offer me a chance to do something that might be useful."[1]

Staying in Buckingham Palace, inspecting the destruction wrought by the German bombings of London, touring American military installations, and visiting servicemen, Mrs. Roosevelt spent twenty-one exhausting days in England. She also continued to send back her column, with the assistance of her secretary, Thompson, who accompanied her. As she contributed to morale, she projected the image, according to a London newspaper, "of a personality as symbolically American as the Statue of Liberty itself."[2]

Upon her return, Mrs. Roosevelt called upon American women to draw inspiration from the example of their British sisters and to contribute more to the war effort. "If women are willing to do more work than seems necessary, I think there would be released more manpower to do the essential things," she said at a press conference. Again she pictured women as auxiliaries to men.[3]

By this time the leadership of her press conferences was passing to a new generation of reporters. Two of her closest friends, Furman and Black, were no longer permitted to ask questions, since both were now government employees. Furman had become assistant chief of the magazine division of the Office of War Information, where she worked under another reporter friend of Mrs. Roosevelt, Dorothy Ducas Herzog. Black had resigned from the United Press in the spring of 1942, after new accreditation rules allowed only full-time reporters to attend. Although the wire service had offered her a full-time job, she became angry when it refused to pay her more than the minimum set in its contract with the Newspaper Guild. After her resignation, Black became a full-time publicist for the Office of the Coordinator of Inter-American Affairs. The United Press then depended on Strayer of the *Washington Daily News* to cover the conferences for it as well as for her own paper.[4]

The rule against questions by government employees was based on the theory press officers would be likely to ask questions worked out in advance with Mrs. Roosevelt while reporters would not. Black fought the ban with Mrs. Roosevelt's encouragement. Mrs. Roosevelt told Black her questions were "usually the most intelligent," Black confided to Rosamond Cole, who had worked for Black's news bureau. Perhaps Mrs. Roosevelt thought so because she herself occasionally suggested to Black the topics that she raise.[5]

When Black met with the standing committee of the press conference association to fight the ban on questions by government employees, Furman withdrew her initial support. She stated that the Office of War Information had decided its employees were to ask "no more planted questions." After May Craig said that she opposed any "hint of government propaganda" at Mrs. Roosevelt's conferences, the group refused to support Black.[6]

Among younger reporters at the press conferences was Ann Cottrell, who succeeded Hornaday as chairman of the association in

1943. An English major at Columbia University, she had worked on the *Richmond Times-Dispatch* before beginning her Washington career in 1940 as the first woman in *Newsweek's* bureau. From there she moved to the *Chicago Sun.* In 1943 she became the first woman in the *New York Herald-Tribune's* Washington bureau, an example of the women being hired to replace male journalists who had gone to war.

A former editor of a fashion magazine, Cottrell was struck by the appearances of her older colleagues, who amazed her with "surprising agility and ferocious front-row-seat grabbing." Years later she recalled them as extraordinary individualists: Marie Manning Gasch, of International News Service, a commanding, kindly woman who originated an advice to the lovelorn column under the name "Beatrice Fairfax," and who, like Strayer, dressed in mannish suits and flat-heeled shoes; Esther Van Wagoner Tufty, so tall and imposing she was called "Duchess," a nickname that stuck after she was mistaken for royalty in Europe; and May Craig, who usually wore blue and was known for her spunk along with her perky hats. Among the oldest were white-haired Maud McDougall, whose career dated back to the days of McKinley, and feisty Winifred Mallon, of the *New York Times*, who peered at the others over spectacles that were always slipping down her nose.[7]

Cottrell looked back on her employment by the *Herald-Tribune* as a way for the newspaper to get fresh coverage of Mrs. Roosevelt's press conferences. "I remember my boss, Bert Anderson, saying 'Nobody writes this right. Go in there 'n' picture it. Just put in everything.' I wrote long detailed stories. They wanted them, they really did," she said.[8]

No exposés of Mrs. Roosevelt resulted. The headlines on Cottrell's stories called attention to Mrs. Roosevelt's use of the conferences to advance war aims along traditional lines. "Mrs. Roosevelt Praises Spirit of War-Wounded" was typical. The most provocative headline, "Mrs. Roosevelt Assails Stories about Waacs [Women's Auxiliary Army Corps, later the Women's Army Corps]," reported Mrs. Roosevelt's denial of stories about widespread immorality among servicewomen. She branded these tales as originating in a Nazi-inspired whispering campaign.[9]

Partly by her manner, which approached the regal, Mrs. Roosevelt kept the conferences from deteriorating into a mere device for personal publicity. In 1984 Cottrell recalled how the women stood as Mrs. Roosevelt swept into the room and shook hands with each reporter after exclaiming, "Good morning, ladies." In the first lady's "brisk, yet gracious manner," Cottrell sensed Mrs. Roosevelt's determination to make the conferences an instrument of social change.[10]

According to Tufty, Mrs. Roosevelt refused to wallow in sentiment. On one occasion, Tufty remembered, a reporter asked Mrs. Roosevelt, "Why don't you have a flag in the window, with your stars for each one of your sons that's in the service?" She replied, according to Tufty, "I'm not going to take any glory for having given sons to war," and asked the newswomen not to write about the exchange. Tufty saw it as an example of Mrs. Roosevelt, whose four sons were in the armed forces, passing up a chance to "pull out the throbs." Her idea of news "was to get done the things she wanted."[11]

To help the war effort, however, Mrs. Roosevelt often turned into a publicist for the government. In numerous columns she ignored the diary format and turned instead to patriotic messages from the Office of War Information, along with descriptions of her travels to far-flung theaters of war and letters from servicemen. Sending Mrs. Roosevelt a copy of her "brain child," a booklet titled "War Jobs for Women," Furman prevailed upon Mrs. Roosevelt to give it "a little mention in your column." Another "My Day" column urged Congress to continue food subsidies to combat wartime inflation. This prompted a gentle rebuke from Carlin, who enclosed a letter from the editor of the *New York World-Telegram* objecting to the "political speech."[12]

Mrs. Roosevelt muted her concern for women's rights during the war. Asked whether women should give up jobs to returning servicemen, she declared, "It seems to me to be clear that every serviceman has been promised he will be restored to his former job." In a 1945 "My Day" column, she commented, "The need for being a feminist is gradually disappearing in this country," although, she added, "we haven't quite reached the millenium." As one example of the "little ways in which women are discriminated against," she cited the policy of specifying "men only" for "higher positions" in the civil service.[13]

To some extent she spoke out more boldly for racial justice, although she emphasized a gradualist approach. While she worked behind the scenes to aid blacks, her public pronouncements counseled restraint. In an article called "If I Were Colored," written for the *Negro Digest* in 1943, she said, "I would take every chance to prove my quality and my ability, and if recognition was slow, I would continue to prove myself, knowing that in the end, good performance has to be acknowledged." Her willingness to speak up for blacks in even moderate terms, however, made her a heroine to the black press.[14]

When a letter was circulated from Mrs. Roosevelt to a Southern white woman denying Mrs. Roosevelt's advocacy of "social equality," the black press tried to minimize it. The *Baltimore Afro-American*, for example, excused her by saying, "Mrs. Roosevelt receives so many letters that this reply is evidently composed by a secretary." The letter ended with a statement that could be interpreted as having racial overtones: "We made a grievous mistake in bringing the Negroes here and we cannot undo that." The *Afro-American* called this an obvious bid for Southern white votes in the approaching 1944 election.[15]

Racial issues were raised at Mrs. Roosevelt's press conferences when she was forced to discount "Eleanor Club" stories. The "clubs" were alleged to be groups organized to remove black women from domestic service and put white women in their places. In 1942 Mrs. Roosevelt announced that the Federal Bureau of Investigation had failed to find evidence of any such "clubs" in Southern states. At another conference she denied a rumor that she had appeared at leading Washington hotels, which were segregated, bringing "colored persons" as her guests. She branded the story "of value to the Nazis."[16]

Mrs. Roosevelt saw the racial situation in the United States in relation to world changes as World War II brought an end to colonialism. She saw the need for Americans to overcome prejudice toward different racial groups. This attitude prevailed in her hospitality to Madame Chiang Kai-Shek, wife of the generalissimo of China, who visited the White House in 1943. When she appeared at Mrs. Roosevelt's press conference, Madame Chiang was asked to comment on the proposed Equal Rights Amendment pending in Congress. "I have never known brains to have any sex," she said. This last sentence was the only one reporters were allowed to quote directly.[17]

Mrs. Roosevelt, however, had reservations about the conduct of this aristocratic visitor, some of which she shared with the women reporters. Tufty remembered years later, "When Madame Chiang Kai-Shek came, she [Mrs. Roosevelt] said how often she had to have the sheets changed in Madame Chiang's bed, seven times a day or something." It was, Tufty recalled, the kind of thing Mrs. Roosevelt would say "always with a smile [meaning] isn't this amusing, and unimportant, but amusing." Tufty compared it to the way Mrs. Roosevelt had joked with the women about her mother-in-law, saying, "Mama called Franklin and wants to do this." The women reporters considered these hints of displeasure unsuitable for publication. "We were not writing opinion, we were covering her—what she was doing," Tufty said.[18]

In support of the war effort, Mrs. Roosevelt favored all programs for increased racial and religious harmony at home and abroad. In "My Day" she advocated efforts to "save the Jews in Europe and to find them homes," although she said that she did not know what could be done. Her description of Jews in her column, while offensive today, at that time was intended to counter prejudice. She noted, "There are able people among them. . . . people of extraordinary intellectual ability along many lines." On the other hand, she said, "Largely because of environment and economic conditions, there are people among them who cringe, who are dishonest, who try to take advantage of their neighbors, who are aggressive and unattractive." She concluded, "They are a cross-section of the human race."[19]

Mrs. Roosevelt's worldwide travels brought her extensive attention from the media during World War II. Admirers praised her willingness to visit American forces all over the world, but detractors charged that she violated wartime travel restrictions. In August 1943 Mrs. Roosevelt, as a special Red Cross representative, undertook a 25,000-mile trip to the Pacific, which included stops at seventeen islands, as well as Australia and New Zealand.

When she returned home, she held her first White House press conference at which men were allowed, after male reporters pleaded that the trip was "of such unusual significance that it justifies an exception to your rule of restricting your press coverage to women." Some stories about this conference highlighted the presence of men, with the result that war-between-the-sexes features overshadowed more substantive news. "12 Gentlemen and 40 Ladies of the Press showed up, the Ladies grabbing all the best positions, leaving the Gentlemen on the fringe to gasp at the brazen questions put by their feminine colleagues," reported *PM* in a story headlined "Males Squirm at First Lady's Parley." An example was given of a "brazen" question: "Mrs. Roosevelt, aren't you a lot thinner?" One male reporter was quoted as saying, "I felt like I had blundered into the powder room of an art gallery."[20]

Women reporters avoided ridiculing the conferences, even though they attacked Mrs. Roosevelt herself. Helen Essary of the *Washington Times-Herald*, which sniped continuously at the Roosevelt administration during World War II, wrote that Mrs. Roosevelt "talked, not as a woman who had gone traipsing off on her own to see the sights, but as the other half of a working team." This, of course, was the team of Franklin and Eleanor, which, Essary added, in a gibe at the probability of a fourth term, meant to keep on working "maybe for five or six terms."[21]

Still, it was a kinder portrait of the first lady than Essary had painted in her column six months earlier. Then she professed dismay over a "My Day" column in which Mrs. Roosevelt had told of cutting a birthday cake at a San Francisco shipyard before visiting disabled veterans in a naval hospital, after which she had eaten an extremely good lunch. She said that she had worked up her appetite by walking through hospital wards. The column concluded with Mrs. Roosevelt mentioning tours through more wards before taking tea with a vice admiral and visiting her newest grandchild. Essary stated that she felt ill when the first lady "spoke of cake and legless men and tea and concussions of the brains and of seeing the new grandchild and miles of suffering human beings and too much lunch, all in the same jolly breath."[22]

In the spring of 1944 Mrs. Roosevelt took a 10,000-mile trip through the Caribbean to inspect army and navy bases. As on the tour of the Pacific, she packed her typewriter so she could write "My Day," doing the typing herself since her secretary did not accompany her. According to a Gallup poll in May 1944 Americans were split in their opinions on the propriety of her trips, with 45 percent opposed on the grounds that she had claimed travel privileges denied to most Americans, 36 percent in favor, 6 percent without opinion and 13 percent claiming that it was none of their business. Reacting to the attacks, Mrs. Roosevelt made them the basis for an article titled "How to Take Criticism" in the *Ladies' Home Journal*. "If you run counter to others now and then, you have enemies," she philosophized, "but life would become unbearable if you thought about it all the time, so you have to ignore the critics."[23]

In general, the journalistic criticism of Mrs. Roosevelt was influenced by two factors—politics and sex-stereotyping. Representatives of newspapers like the *Washington Times-Herald* that had split with the Roosevelt administration searched for whatever could be construed as flaws in Mrs. Roosevelt's performance. Their attacks often took the form of criticism of her judgment, as in the Chaney incident. Apart from partisan considerations, some journalists tended to discount Mrs. Roosevelt's activities as legitimate news because they did not fit male-oriented definitions. The world of journalism thrives on coverage of wins and losses, successes and defeats, conflict and controversy. Because she was not an elected official, Mrs. Roosevelt's endeavors could not be placed within this context. Therefore her detractors saw her as a woman simply seeking personal publicity in part because the conventional news formula was inadequate to provide for a president's wife who sought to speak out but still had to be careful what she said. An unflattering poem, titled "The Lady Eleanor," expressed the critics' view:

> And despite her global milling,
> Of the voice there is no stilling
> With its platitudes galore, . . .
> Advertising Eleanor."[24]

A fixture of the *Ladies' Home Journal* during the World War II period, Mrs. Roosevelt wrote articles about her travels in addition to her advice column. She continued to picture women as subordinates in the war effort. In a *Reader's Digest* article in 1944, she stated that women were content only if they "feel they are contributing something toward the speedier ending of the war and a better chance for their particular men in the world of the future." She offered a faint hope of postwar equality, noting in a subsequent *Reader's Digest* piece, "Men are now giving up, though rather reluctantly, their ancient prerogatives of deciding, without feminine assistance, the great questions of public policy."[25]

As the war years went by, Mrs. Roosevelt's activities possessed what one reporter termed a "diminishing novelty." An element of monotony crept into articles about her travels and endeavors to aid the war effort. Nevertheless the press conferences still produced news, often with political overtones. For example, with the election of 1944 on the horizon, Mrs. Roosevelt assured the conference group that her husband's health would not prevent his continued performance in office. To get stories like this, the reporters still pressed for accreditation, and the number admitted increased from thirty-three in 1942 to fifty-six in 1945.[26]

Women who attended the conferences were divided between her loyal friends and those who viewed Mrs. Roosevelt less warmly. In the first category remained Furman, who had been hired in 1943 by the Washington bureau of the *New York Times*. Her stories focused on Mrs. Roosevelt's concern for social improvements in the postwar world and similar topics that painted Mrs. Roosevelt as a humanitarian.[27]

In the second category was Ruth Montgomery of the anti-Roosevelt *New York Daily News*. In her memoirs she described Mrs. Roosevelt as conducting the conferences "with the giddy informality of an Aunt Nellie." According to Montgomery, some of Mrs. Roosevelt's answers to questions "evoked squirming discomfort" from Stephen Early. She cited this example: "Did Mrs. Roosevelt think it was right for her to accept an $11,000 mink coat during wartime, a gift from the Canadian mink ranchers? Mrs. Roosevelt assured us that she did, since there were no legal restrictions against a President's wife receiving presents."[28]

During the 1944 campaign, Mrs. Roosevelt assured the women reporters that she was not a factor in the election. But Republicans tried to make her one. They introduced Frances Hutt Dewey, the wife of the Republican presidential candidate, Thomas E. Dewey, as a homebody who thought a first lady "should pretty largely stay put in the White House."[29]

After Roosevelt's victory, Mrs. Roosevelt asked members of the conference association how the sessions could be made more "productive of useful news relating to wartime and post-war issues." Eighteen months earlier in a speech before the Women's National Press Club, she had said that she was not satisfied "that I get all that I should out of my conferences." She wanted the reporters to give more space to her causes and opinions. "I am sorry that the reporters could not make me a better conveyor of ideas and of information and of thoughts that they could make use of," she stated.[30]

Certainly Mrs. Roosevelt did not want the conferences to bog down into fishing expeditions for scandalous tidbits about the Roosevelt family. When reporters asked about a *Washington Post* story that alleged her daughter, Anna Boettiger, had ordered priority travel on a military plane for a dog owned by her brother Elliott, Mrs. Roosevelt snapped, "I wouldn't know, and I wouldn't comment if I did know."[31]

The reporters' dissatisfaction with Mrs. Roosevelt's rambling statements and guest appearances by minor figures surfaced at an association meeting on February 13, 1945. Members objected to Mrs. Roosevelt's desire to make her press conferences "into sessions resembling a forum." The reporters insisted that the conferences were "for the sake of getting news from the person being interviewed and not for the sake of crusading ideas, however worthwhile the ideas may seem to be."[32]

The press women were also unhappy with guests whose appearances did not lead to sparkling copy. Their report stated that the group wished to "discourage the inclusion of visitors who are persons to whom the reporters can go any time to ask questions." At this point, guests were not royal dignitaries or important government officials, but were individuals like Helen Ferris, director of the Junior Literary Guild, who spoke on the inadequate salaries of children's librarians.[33]

Some of the reporters still shielded Mrs. Roosevelt from touchy situations, the report stated, whereas a majority of the members believed "reporters should back each other up in such a situation instead of killing off such a story by 'rescuing' Mrs. Roosevelt." Most of them wanted more human interest stories from Mrs. Roosevelt based on her activities. They also requested permission to accompany her on trips outside of the United States, even though wartime restrictions made it unlikely that this would be granted.[34]

When Montgomery, now chairman of the group, gave the report to Mrs. Roosevelt, the first lady was "most co-operative," Montgomery told association members. She agreed not to invite low-level government officials to appear at the conferences but added that she couldn't refuse those who specifically asked to come.[35]

Outside the association, the press conferences continued to draw fire. In a "Washington Merry-Go-Round" column for April 8, 1945, Drew Pearson referred repeatedly to the "press girls." He charged that there was a "cooling in relationship between Mrs. Roosevelt and the ladies of the press" after Jonathan Daniels, then a White House press aide, alleged a reporter had misquoted Mrs. Roosevelt. At issue was her comment on whether the United States would be able to raise enough food for Europe after the war. The reporter claimed that Mrs. Roosevelt had said this nation would not feed Europe. As refutation, Mrs. Roosevelt referred to the shorthand notes made by her secretary, Thompson. Pearson alleged that Thompson had "doctored" the transcript, an accusation denied by Montgomery on behalf of the conference association.[36]

The issue dominated the discussion at Mrs. Roosevelt's press conference on April 12, 1945. A *Washington Star* reporter asked Mrs. Roosevelt if she agreed with Pearson's assertions. As Mrs. Roosevelt started to answer, Bess Furman suggested that the question be addressed to the conference association. After a debate on whether a vote to refer the issue should be taken, Mrs. Roosevelt gave an off-the-record answer. She said that Pearson's charge did not merit a reply.[37]

Aside from this controversy, the April 12 news conference seemed an ordinary event. Most of the reporters focused their stories on Mrs. Roosevelt's comments about Germany. She asked the public to withhold judgment on postwar treatment of Germany until the United States government provided more information.[38]

No one had an inkling that this was to be the last gathering. That afternoon Franklin D. Roosevelt died of a massive stroke at Warm Springs, Georgia. It was the end of the association, since Bess Truman, who succeeded Eleanor Roosevelt as first lady, declined to hold press conferences.

On April 19, 1945, Mrs. Roosevelt gave a farewell tea at the White House for the newspaperwomen, but she did not hold a news conference. Fifty-seven newswomen attended, the total membership of the association at the time. Some had notebooks in hand, but Mrs. Roosevelt declined to permit direct quotes. At the end she wished them well and then repeated the announcement she had made in "My Day" a few days earlier. She said she now intended to join their ranks as another newspaperwoman. Indeed she had resumed her "My Day" column on April 16 just four days after Franklin Roosevelt's death. It was an obvious statement of determination to continue her professional career.[39]

12

International Fame
1945–62

My devotion to my country and to democracy is quite as great as that
of Senator McCarthy. I do not like his methods or the results of his methods
and I would like to say to my correspondent that I think those of us who
worked with young people in the thirties did more to save many of them
from becoming Communists than Senator McCarthy has done for his fellow
citizens with all his slurs and accusations.

I know the danger of communism. I know it perhaps better than many
other American citizens because for nearly five months of every year for the
last six years, I have sat in meetings with the Communist representatives of
the USSR.

I despise the control they insist on holding over men's minds. And that
is why I despise what Senator McCarthy has done, for he would use the same
methods of fear to control all thought that is not according to his own pattern
—in our free country.

> —Eleanor Roosevelt, "My Day,"
> August 29, 1952

The world's most famous widow, Eleanor Roosevelt, at the age
of sixty did not foresee a career for herself in politics after the death
of her husband. Although urged to run for the Senate from New
York, she ruled out that possibility because she did not want to interfere with the political aspirations of her sons. She planned to pursue a
career as a journalist, concentrating on her column and her question-
and-answer page for the *Ladies' Home Journal.* President Truman,
however, mindful of Mrs. Roosevelt's influence with women and
black voters, sought her as a member of his administration.[1]

Instructed by Truman to find an appointment for Mrs. Roosevelt, Secretary of State James Byrnes proposed that she be named the
only woman delegate from the United States to the first United Na-

tions General Assembly meeting in London, scheduled to begin on January 10, 1946. The nomination sailed through Congress with only one dissenting vote—that of the racist Senator Theodore Bilbo of Mississippi. Aside from Pegler, influential journalists hailed the appointment as ideal, on the grounds that Mrs. Roosevelt stood for her husband's dedication to world peace. Mrs. Roosevelt viewed her appointment as an inherited responsibility, passed on to her "largely because my husband laid the foundations for the organization through which we all hope to build world peace."[2]

As she became increasingly familiar with her new duties, she publicized the United Nations in her column. She pictured it as central to "the preservation and continuance of our civilization." But her support for the United Nations did not prevent Mrs. Roosevelt from noting its flaws.[3]

She told her readers she was disappointed by the small number of women delegates. After meeting with the meager total of eighteen women who were delegates, alternates, or advisors, she reported on the group's recommendation for increased participation by women in the United Nations. "My Day" also mentioned her dismay at the bickering of male colleagues over parliamentary rules: "I find that, if anything, the men here take more words to express their thoughts than the women. The answer will doubtless be that they have more thoughts to express. . . . but if you want to get work done quickly oratory is not half as important as putting your thoughts clearly."[4]

These little barbs attacked colleagues who, without consulting her, had assigned Mrs. Roosevelt to Committee Three, which dealt with humanitarian, educational, and cultural questions. In her autobiography, she observed that she suspected the "gentlemen of the delegation" had assigned her to the relatively noncontroversial committee, thinking, "She can't do much harm there." To their surprise, they found her a worthy antagonist against Russian opposition. Although she did not mention it in "My Day," she made front-page headlines by persuading Committee Three to vote against a Russian proposal that would have denied displaced persons in refugee camps the opportunity for relocation in the noncommunist world instead of being repatriated to the Soviet sphere. Subsequently she debated the Russian delegate, Andrei Vishinski, on the same issue. In a letter to Joseph Lash, she expressed her pleasure over winning "hands down" and demonstrating a woman's competence: "You will be amused that when Mr. [John Foster] Dulles said good bye to me this morning he said, 'I feel I must tell you that when you were appointed I thought it terrible & now I think your work here has been fine.' So—against odds the women inch forward, but I'm rather old to be carrying on this fight."[5]

So Mrs. Roosevelt portrayed herself—an old woman making a lonely fight for self-fulfillment, as well as human rights, on the world stage where fate had placed her. She did not mention the debate in "My Day," no doubt because she considered it impolitic for a diplomat to comment publicly on besting a rival. Any indication of reveling in a triumph would also have undermined one of her main journalistic themes—that international debate transcended personalities and re-volved around matters of principle. She herself continued to present to the public an image of a gracious, dignified lady with a motherly concern for oppressed peoples everywhere.[6]

It was an image that she retained throughout the rest of her career as a United Nations delegate, which continued until Dwight D. Eisenhower was elected president in 1952. Chosen chairman of the Commission on Human Rights in 1947, she was the moving spirit behind the creation of the Universal Declaration of Human Rights to set forth standards for the civilized world. When the General Assembly passed the declaration on December 10, 1948, the delegates rose in a standing ovation to Mrs. Roosevelt, who had come, more than anyone else, to epitomize the human rights cause. The media saluted her as "First Lady of the United Nations."[7]

Yet there was another side to her, a hard, practical side that astute observers recognized. A *New Yorker* profile pointed out her occasional haste to answer another delegate: "Actually her haste is apt to be prompted by her familiarity with newspaper deadlines and by her extremely practical realization that a rebuttal attains widest notice if published coincidentally with the remarks that provoked it." She used other techniques, too, designed to enable a woman to manipulate in the world of men, the profile continued: " 'Now, of course, I'm a woman and I don't understand all these things,' she will remark softly, almost maternally, 'and I'm sure there's a great deal to be said for your arguments, but don't you think it would be a good idea if—.' . . . This might be called the Mother technique. A State

Department career man, after watching her artfully maneuver her way through a delicate discussion, once murmured, 'Never have I seen naivete and cunning so gracefully blended.' " [8]

During her United Nations years Mrs. Roosevelt declared that she finally considered herself free to express her own views. She told a writer for the *New York Times* that her ideas could no longer react against anyone but herself. Still, because of her desire to mobilize support for the United Nations in the face of growing anticommunist hysteria in the United States, her public statements projected more positive hopes for world peace than she actually held. In a 1946 memorandum to President Truman, Mrs. Roosevelt warned of Stalin's desire to expand into Iran and Eastern Europe as well as Russian designs on Western Europe. Nevertheless in her columns, articles, and speeches, she asked the American public to understand that the cause of Soviet belligerency lay in Russia's history of isolation. Just as she had been a voice for social reform during the depression, she now spoke on behalf of international understanding. [9]

As before, there were those who found her position unacceptable. This was reflected in the handling of her newspaper column. By the end of 1945, Lee Wood, editor of the *New York World-Telegram* and a critic of Mrs. Roosevelt, had moved her column to the back of his paper except when she was in the news.

"My Day" became the platform in 1947 for her sponsorship of the newly formed Americans for Democratic Action, intended to be a liberal alternative to Henry Wallace and his communist-linked Progressive party. Two years earlier she had used her column to announce that because she had "experienced the deception of the American Communists I will not trust them," although, she added, she believed that Americans could "co-operate with the U.S.S.R. and its people." [10]

To some, "My Day" reflected an attitude of accommodation toward communists that might menace the security of the United States. Among its readers were agents of the Federal Bureau of Investigation, who maintained a file on Mrs. Roosevelt that included many of her columns. Clippings were brought to the personal attention of J. Edgar Hoover, the bureau director, who occasionally scribbled handwritten notes in the margins. [11]

Hoover's dislike of Mrs. Roosevelt dated back to 1941, when she had complained to Hoover of "Gestapo methods" employed by bureau agents in conducting investigations of two of her most trusted assistants, Edith B. Helm, the White House social secretary, and Malvina Thompson. Hoover told her the investigation of Helm had been ordered by the Council of National Defense and that the bureau would not have become involved had it known of Helm's White House duties. He tried to make amends by denying that there was any investigation of Thompson and declaring, "I deeply regret the resentment which this incident has caused you, and particularly the impression which I fear you gained as to the position of the Bureau in this matter," but distrust between him and Mrs. Roosevelt grew. During World War II, Hoover monitored Mrs. Roosevelt's activities closely, warning Harry Hopkins in 1944 that she should not address an interracial group in Detroit lest she spark a race riot.[12]

In spite of Mrs. Roosevelt's vigorous upholding of United States policy in the United Nations, Hoover and his agents saw her as a possible communist dupe. He perused not only "My Day," but also articles about Mrs. Roosevelt for evidence of any disloyalty. When the *Washington Times-Herald* complimented her on "waking up to the true character" of communism because she had warned of Soviet aggression in a speech to the Women's National Press Club, Hoover decided that perhaps she had changed her mind, but noted on the margins of the clipping, "not before doing much harm!"[13]

When "My Day" extolled the efforts of the FBI, Hoover was not convinced of Mrs. Roosevelt's sincerity. Questioning the role of congressional committees in ferreting out alleged communists, Mrs. Roosevelt wrote a column in 1948 in which she called the FBI the "proper agency" to investigate spies. "Well, well I am amazed at her 'confidence' in the FBI!!!" Hoover scrawled on a copy of the article. "She can't help but make snide remarks about us," he penned next to a clipping of another "My Day" column in which Mrs. Roosevelt described herself as "bewildered" by a character in a play by T. S. Eliot who "acted as a kind of super FBI man."[14]

Any hint of criticism disturbed Hoover, even when his agency was not directly named. During the rise in influence of Senator Joseph McCarthy with his demagogic charges of internal communist subversion, "My Day" cautioned against "the establishment of a Gestapo in our midst, and the curtailment of the right of free speech and free association," warnings that Hoover took to be attacks on the FBI.

Beside the article he wrote: "I often wonder whether she is so naive as she professes or whether it is just a blind to lull the unsuspecting."[15]

Hoover's agents also scanned Mrs. Roosevelt's magazine advice column, "If You Ask Me," for evidence of communist sentiment. In 1953 they clipped her answer to a question from a reader who asked if a professor should be permitted to tell his classes that congressional committees on un-American activities were "ruining our reputation in the rest of the world." Her reply: "I think this professor's statement is absolutely correct."[16]

In 1949, Mrs. Roosevelt had shifted her column from the *Ladies' Home Journal* to *McCall's* after a dispute with the Goulds over the manuscript of the second volume of her autobiography, *This I Remember*, which covered her White House years. In writing the manuscript, she had enlisted the aid of Lorena Hickok, then living in retirement on Long Island because of ill health. But the *Journal* editors wanted her to work with a professional collaborator, complaining to Malvina Thompson, "She's written this as though she were typing it on a bicycle on the way to a fire." In a meeting with Elliott Roosevelt and Thompson, to whom Mrs. Roosevelt had assigned one-half of the royalties from the serial rights in return for her clerical and research help, Bruce Gould demanded three more months of work. "And then Mr. Gould only hoped that it would suit him," Mrs. Roosevelt wrote Martha Strayer.[17]

Bypassing Mrs. Roosevelt's agent, George Bye, Elliott Roosevelt contacted *McCall's*, the *Journal*'s chief competitor, which offered $150,000 sight unseen for the autobiography. After Mrs. Roosevelt accepted *McCall's* offer, which included a $15,000 commission for her son, Bruce Gould told her to "take your Question and Answer page there, too," a move that he later regretted. The incident also ruptured the relationship between Bye and Mrs. Roosevelt because he insisted that Mrs. Roosevelt and Thompson pay him a $15,000 commission, too. *McCall's* agreed to pay her $3,000 a month for the question-and-answer page, which was $500 more than she had received from the *Journal*, and to give her a five-year contract in contrast to the Goulds' month-to-month contract.[18]

Fortunately for *McCall's*, as well as for Mrs. Roosevelt, *This I Remember* proved to be a great success with readers and critics. Published as a book by Harper and Brothers, it drew rave reviews. A critic writing in the *Saturday Review of Literature* called it "the most exciting book of the year," next to a biography of Stalin. "Only a great woman could have written it," proclaimed Arthur Schlesinger, Jr. A perceptive reviewer in the *New York Times* noted that it pictured a wife who "unable to dedicate herself to her husband—why, we shall never be sure—ended by dedicating herself to his work."[19]

Mrs. Roosevelt wrote her relatives that she was concerned because Pegler, who had switched to the Hearst papers after his column was dropped by the *New York World-Telegram*, had chided her for failing to mention the fact that Lucy Mercer Rutherford was at Warm Springs when Franklin Roosevelt died. But in public she usually ignored Pegler's attacks. In a letter to her daughter, she referred to a Pegler column that insinuated incorrectly that Franklin Roosevelt had accumulated a vast fortune and commented, "It is taking much self-control to keep quiet." Victorian gentility sometimes underlaid her reticence. "There are certain things you did not entirely understand and of course, certain things that neither you nor anyone else knows anything about outside of the few people concerned," she wrote to John Gunther after reading his biography of her husband. "Whether it is essential they should ever know is something on which I have not made up my mind since they are personal and do not touch on public service."[20]

The *McCall's* contracts helped Mrs. Roosevelt to solve some of her financial problems. After the death of her husband, she estimated that her annual income would be about $80,000, including $30,000 from his estate, more than half of which was earmarked for taxes. Her income from "My Day" rose and fell with the number of newspapers subscribing. This fluctuated from ninety, immediately following the death of President Roosevelt, when readers were curious about her reaction to widowhood, to seventy-five in 1952. The United States paid her at a rate of $12,000 a year as a delegate to the United Nations, but paid only for the days she worked.[21]

Mrs. Roosevelt relinquished her rights to a $5,000-a-year pension given other widows of presidents, but she accepted franking privileges for her mail. She needed money. In addition to her personal expenses, she faced demands to contribute to charity and to aid her children, particularly Elliott and Anna. She had joined Elliott in a money-losing venture to operate a commercial farm at Val-Kill.

Anna's second marriage had foundered, leaving her with debts that Mrs. Roosevelt tried to help her repay.

Radio and television appearances to benefit her son and daughter presented logical ways to augment her income. In 1948–49, she and Anna appeared on 200 stations of the American Broadcasting Company in a fifteen-minute daytime talk show that was broadcast from three to five times a week for thirty-nine weeks. Mrs. Roosevelt recorded her portion, sometimes in Europe, while her daughter handled a live opening and closing from Hollywood. According to the producer, "Mrs. Roosevelt dealt with the more serious side of news, such as world affairs, United Nations, etc., while her daughter dealt with theatre, motion pictures, fashion and the lighter side of the news." Guests who appeared for interviews included General George Marshall, Dr. Ralph Bunche, Vincent Sheehan and Tallulah Bankhead.[22]

Although the program was dropped for lack of a commercial sponsor, it drew critical acclaim. The *Hollywood Reporter* praised the show as "the first network recognition of female intelligence in daytime programming" and said that it "should convince the nets that the ladies aren't as zany about soap operas as network and agency masterminds have figured." Of the first broadcast *Time* said, "Speaking by transcription from Paris, where she is a member of the U.S.'s Social, Humanitarian and Cultural Committee, Commentator Roosevelt let fire with some salvos that were notable for both clarity of diction and political candor."[23]

Her next radio series, "The Eleanor Roosevelt Show," a forty-five-minute program presented five days a week in the afternoon, began on her birthday, October 11, 1950, and ended on August 31, 1951. Originating on WNBC in New York, it was syndicated to about twenty other stations. Produced by Elliott Roosevelt and Martin Jones, the program featured a question-and-answer period by Mrs. Roosevelt and her son, followed by interviews with famous persons, many of them Mrs. Roosevelt's friends.

In the spring of 1950 Mrs. Roosevelt agreed to let Elliott feature her in a Sunday television talk show with a tea party format, which he sold to NBC after he had offered assurances that his mother would secure as guests world-famous figures including Winston Churchill and Andrei Vishinski. Although neither of them agreed to appear, Mrs. Roosevelt was successful in obtaining Albert Einstein, who ordinarily refused invitations from the media, as one of eight distinguished persons who appeared on her first program to discuss "The H-Bomb and Atomic Energy." A *New Yorker* reviewer thought it an embarrassment of riches, commenting, "Mrs. Roosevelt lost her bearings and felt that the mere presence of big experts was an adequate substitution for the proper study of a big problem."[24]

The show, with Mrs. Roosevelt's share of the proceeds going to Anna, ran from February 12, 1950, until July 15, 1951. Critical response was generally good: *Newsweek*, for example, referred to Mrs. Roosevelt's "gifts of charm and personality" as she chatted with notables over a tea table. The guest list, which included European heads of state, continued to be impressive. The program failed, however, to attract a sponsor because of Mrs. Roosevelt's controversial liberal views. Even though she agreed, at NBC's request, to drop Paul Robeson, a left-leaning black singer, sponsors were wary. One famous individual who declined to participate was J. Edgar Hoover, whose assistants gave as an excuse Hoover's "terrifically heavy schedule."[25]

Henry Morgenthau III, who assisted Elliott Roosevelt in producing the radio series, recalled that "Mrs. Roosevelt was anxious at that time to do things to help Elliott and to make money for him—or allow him to make money." It was not "an easy situation," Morgenthau remembered, because Elliott's partner, Jones, wanted to have "various people" on the show, including Senator Owen Brewster of Maine, an extreme right-wing partisan. "And Mrs. Roosevelt, who would generally accept almost anyone, at one point said, 'I think if I have to have Senator Brewster on our program again, I'll be ill.'"[26]

Eventually, Morgenthau noted, he resigned from the show "because I knew that she could be persuaded to do things that really were against her better judgment and her taste." Questions of taste emerged in Elliott's handling of commercials in which he informed the audience that "mother uses" the kind of soap and other products manufactured by sponsors of the show. It proved, according to *Billboard*, "that a boy's best friend is his mother."[27]

The issue of freedom of speech arose in connection with Mrs. Roosevelt's program on KFWB in Los Angeles. When a group of women calling themselves an anticommunist consumers' league exerted pressure on two sponsors to drop the program, the radio station stood up for First Amendment rights and scheduled the show twice a day instead of only once. The station manager received more than 600 letters of praise and only three that opposed his decision. Many letters came from persons who said that they did not particularly admire Mrs. Roosevelt but wanted to protect her right to be heard.[28]

One program incensed J. Edgar Hoover, who had also refused to appear on the radio show, again citing "the pressure of official duties" plus "the necessity of frequently being in travel status." The FBI obtained a transcript of the program on April 4, 1951, after an agent's wife reported hearing Mrs. Roosevelt say that she thought the FBI did not merit additional funds until it raised the caliber of its personnel. The transcript showed that Mrs. Roosevelt's remarks were unclear: "Sometimes when I have heard of the investigators, I have felt they were not always, now this does not always hold good, they were not always of the caliber to find out things."[29]

Hoover wrote her to complain, and she replied that an acquaintance had been visited by an FBI agent who told him that it was "dangerous" to read a controversial publication. Hoover sought more details so that he could identify the agent, but Mrs. Roosevelt expressed her regret that she could not furnish them. Subsequently Hoover scrawled in her file next to a newspaper clipping about a speech by Mrs. Roosevelt in which she accused Senator Joseph McCarthy of smear tactics: "She has done exactly this in her attacks on the FBI & when I called upon her to produce facts she was unable to do so."[30]

According to Elliott Roosevelt, the radio program left the air because his mother returned to Paris for the meeting of the United Nations in the fall of 1951, and "NBC felt that the shows emanating from Europe lost audience because of foreign accents." Mrs. Roosevelt continued to perform on radio and television, however, frequently appearing on "Meet the Press." She also spoke in French over the Voice of America. This proved so successful in the creation of goodwill for the United States that she subsequently did broadcasts in German, Spanish, and Italian. A writer for the *New York Times* observed that she had "assets possessed in Europe by no one else — a beloved and respected name, a reputation in her own right as a diplomat and a fighter for social justice, and a simple feminine manner which appeals to the average listener."[31]

As a journalist, Mrs. Roosevelt urged Americans to interest themselves in international affairs. In magazine articles aimed primarily at women, she wrote on the role of politics in a democracy, the United Nations, human rights, and the common interests of women around the world. After a trip to the Middle East and India in 1952, she wrote a book titled *India and the Awakening East,* in which she expressed her belief in foreign aid to encourage Third World support for democracy. Three years earlier she had been a coauthor of a book titled *Partners: The United Nations Youth,* which explained the workings of the United Nations to young people.

But it was in "My Day" that Mrs. Roosevelt appeared most controversial and perhaps most influential during the United Nations years. A year after she left the White House, the Advertising Research Foundation called her "the columnist with most reader appeal to U.S. women," read by 37 percent of women newspaper readers and ranked ahead of Dorothy Thompson. Although the column still featured a recital of her activities, the principal subject matter ranged far beyond that traditionally designed for women readers. It included her support for the state of Israel, which she pictured as a brave new nation struggling against feudal Arabs in a fight "reminiscent of all other pioneer movements where people have tried to establish themselves in new places to flee oppression and interference elsewhere."[32]

Often speaking out on pending legislation in "My Day," she drew bitter criticism from the Roman Catholic church after she supported the Barden bill, which provided for federal aid to education but excluded private and parochial schools. In an open letter, Francis Joseph Cardinal Spellman, archbishop of New York, violently accused her of conducting an anti-Catholic campaign. He ended his letter on a furious note: "Your record of anti-Catholicism stands for all to see —a record which you yourself wrote in the pages of history which cannot be recalled—documents of discrimination unworthy of an American mother." Spellman also deplored her failure to support Cardinal Mindszenty, an anticommunist Hungarian imprisoned in Budapest, whom Mrs. Roosevelt had attacked for opposing agrarian reform. Responding in "My Day," Mrs. Roosevelt informed the cardinal she would send him a letter of reply and restated her belief in freedom of religion.[33]

For years Catholic leaders had been unhappy with Mrs. Roosevelt. In the 1930s they had disliked her stand against the Franco regime in Spain, her quiet support of birth control, and her closeness to the Red-dominated American Youth Congress. In 1948 she protested when New York City's public schools bowed to the Catholic hierarchy and removed the *Nation* magazine from their libraries because it contained an article on Catholic power in the United States. In addition, she had opposed in the United Nations the return of ambassadors to Franco's Spain until that government had agreed to reforms. The United Nations issue, Mrs. Roosevelt believed, was the "real count" against her, not simply her position on federal aid to education.[34]

In her letter to the cardinal, published in the *New York Times*, she gave her views on the separation of church and state. She wrote that she had protested the imprisonment of Mindszenty, and ended with a devastating retort: "I assure you that I had no sense of being 'an unworthy American mother.' The final judgment, my dear Cardinal Spellman, of the worthiness of all human beings is in the hands of God." Although *Catholic World* backed the prelate, the Jesuit publication *America* "did not dare take up the cudgels for the Cardinal," noted newspaperwoman Doris Fleeson, who had been raised as a Catholic, in a letter to Mrs. Roosevelt. Another friend from Mrs. Roosevelt's press conference days, May Craig, commented, "It has stirred up a lot of anti-Catholic feeling that was lying just under the surface and had, I hoped, melted into tolerance." Mrs. Roosevelt's mail, normally about 1,000 letters a week, jumped to 4,000, with about 90 percent favorable to her, according to Malvina Thompson.[35]

Eventually a compromise was reached, apparently after Pope Pius XII, acting at the behest of Ed Flynn, boss of the New York Democratic party, secretly ordered the cardinal to make peace with Mrs. Roosevelt. Both Mrs. Roosevelt and the cardinal worked out statements clarifying their views. Mrs. Roosevelt then quoted the cardinal in "My Day" as urging funds for parochial schools only to cover "auxiliary services" and not advocating "general public support of religious schools."[36]

Not long afterward, Spellman dropped in for tea at Hyde Park.

Mrs. Roosevelt, at the request of a church representative, mentioned the visit in "My Day." She commented only, "The Cardinal had dropped in on his way to dedicating a chapel in Peekskill. We had a pleasant chat and I hope the country proved as much as a tonic for him as it always is for me."[37]

The innocuous phraseology of "My Day" provided a shield for Mrs. Roosevelt's true feelings. She confided to a friend that the cardinal impressed her "with a horrible feeling of insincerity," adding, "I think the Barden bill was something through which they hoped to hurt my influence which has been exerted on the UN delegation against returning ambassadors to Spain." But she soon changed her stand on diplomatic relations with Spain, explaining that it was inconsistent to have ambassadors in other nations with repressive governments and not have them in Spain.[38]

It was in "My Day," too, that Mrs. Roosevelt battled Senator Joseph McCarthy's communist-hunting tactics in the early 1950s. She expressed her dislike of both McCarthy and Stalin. Russia, she thought, should be contained through NATO and through involvement of the United States in the Korean war.

Most of the mainstream media delighted in praising her, often implying that she was able to retain her womanly attributes while matching wits with men. In 1948, *Time* called her "perhaps the best known woman in the world." It added a quotation from the *London News Chronicle*, "Immersed in politics, she has never acquired the hard professionalism of the politician." In 1951, the *Saturday Review of Literature* poll on the greatest living persons named her both the "greatest living American woman" and the "greatest woman in the world." A survey of journalists, parents, and educators by editors of the *Book of Knowledge* placed Mrs. Roosevelt at the top of the list of the "world's twelve smartest women" for four straight years.[39]

Still she was censured for stepping out of a woman's subordinate role. "She has been severely criticized for failing to comply with the notion that woman's place is in the home," observed *Newsweek*. Mrs. Roosevelt was also blamed for the "long record of divorce among her children," the magazine stated.[40]

Her old friends among the press corps noted her regal manner. "There was something about Mrs. Roosevelt that was almost like a monarch," recalled Mary Hornaday. "I remember once interviewing her at the United Nations. My pencil broke —but do you think she would get up to get me another one? No, she just sat there to let me struggle along as well as I could." [41]

In 1952, Mrs. Roosevelt addressed the Democratic national convention that nominated Adlai Stevenson for president. She spoke first of her husband's memory and then in support of the United Nations. Her speech set off a resounding spontaneous demonstration, which prompted Agnes E. Meyer, a journalist, women's rights advocate, and wife of the owner of the *Washington Post*, to write, "It certainly must have been a relief for the women of the country to realize that one could be a woman and a lady and yet be thoroughly political." Calling other "political women . . . vulgar in their speeches and in their appearances," Meyer complimented Mrs. Roosevelt: "You were the only one who was suitably garbed." [42]

When Dwight D. Eisenhower was elected president by a landslide vote, Mrs. Roosevelt turned in the letter of resignation traditionally submitted by diplomats when new administrations take office. To the surprise of her supporters, Eisenhower accepted it, perhaps in response to conservative pressure or perhaps because of pique after he was told that Mrs. Roosevelt had once inquired if Mrs. Eisenhower had a drinking problem. In her last speech at the United Nations, Mrs. Roosevelt raised the question of the international political rights of women. She contended that men dominated decision-making so completely that "whatever of special value women have to offer is shunted aside without expression." [43]

Although she was being shunted aside by a Republican administration, Mrs. Roosevelt was determined not to retire from public life. She was sixty-eight years old but she was not yet ready to withdraw from the political fray. Volunteering her services to the American Association for the Advancement of the United Nations, she worked diligently for that organization from an austerely furnished office. Critics accused her of "an insatiable craving for attention," but if her psyche demanded that she vindicate her life through publicizing worthy causes, she succeeded in the eyes of millions throughout the world. [44]

After leaving the United Nations, Mrs. Roosevelt embarked in 1953 on a world tour of Japan, Greece, Turkey, and Yugoslavia, accompanied during part of the journey by Minnewa Bell, Elliott

Roosevelt's fourth wife. Bell was struck by her mother-in-law's zest for travel. "She was invited to go and see [Marshal Josip Broz] Tito," Bell recalled. "When she was invited to go somewhere in the world by a person of political importance, she had to [go]." Bell attributed this, in part, to Mrs. Roosevelt's desire to find fresh journalistic material. "I think her work was as important to her as, say, a business is to a man," Bell said. After interviewing Tito, for example, Mrs. Roosevelt compared his fears of Russian aggression to those of the United States in an article for *Look* magazine.[45]

As a role model for American women during the 1950s, Mrs. Roosevelt provided an example of a woman who combined feminine qualities with the influence usually reserved for men. It was a time when American women were engulfed by social change that few understood. Married women working outside the home had become an accustomed part of the American social scene by 1950. Women, particularly those over thirty-five years of age, had not disappeared from the labor force, as expected, after World War II, but had been joined by an increasing proportion of those who were married. In 1952, some 10.4 million wives held jobs—two million more than during the war and about three times the number in 1940. At the same time, the press, particularly the women's magazines, featured innumerable articles asserting that women had ventured too far from their accustomed roles. Mrs. Roosevelt, it appeared, was one of the few individuals who had solved what *Life* magazine called the "woman's dilemma"—the conflict between traditional notions of a woman's role and the new reality of her activity outside the home.[46]

In 1954, when Mrs. Roosevelt celebrated her seventieth birthday, her earned income proved that she certainly had not retired. She paid taxes on a total of about $90,000 that year derived from writing and speaking; it included $36,000 from *McCall's*, $28,000 from "My Day," and $25,000 from lecture tours. When the press asked her on her birthday to name her greatest achievements, she responded, "I just did what I had to do as things came along. I got the most satisfaction from my work in the UN." It was a modest answer, surely, but also one that inadvertently pictured the world's most admired woman as something of a dilettante, reacting to events instead of trying to take charge of her life. It failed to acknowledge Mrs. Roosevelt's efforts to establish herself as a person in her own right, but it fit well with society's view of women as reactive, dependent beings in comparison with men.[47]

Although Mrs. Roosevelt remained the quintessence of a maternal figure, in her final years her intimate associates were not members of her family. As she had once lavished attention and friendship on friends like Earl Miller, Lorena Hickok and Joseph Lash, from 1947 until her death Dr. David Gurewitsch, her physician, shared her confidences and accompanied her on her travels. In her last years, she shared a house in New York with Gurewitsch and his wife, Edna. To Gurewitsch, as she once had to Hickok, she distinguished between her public and private self: "The people I love mean more to me than all the public things even if you do think that public affairs should be my chief vocations." Another beloved friend was the humorous, intellectual Adlai Stevenson, in whom she saw the leadership potential of Franklin Roosevelt. In his 1956 Democratic campaign for president, Mrs. Roosevelt worked in his behalf day and night. She even modified her usually strong stand on civil rights to accord with Stevenson's moderate position.[48]

When she discussed the Republican candidates, President Eisenhower and Vice President Richard M. Nixon, on "Meet the Press," she showed herself capable of dealing a man-sized political blow concealed in grandmotherly prose. She deftly put down Nixon, using one of her favorite devices, that of deriding her opponents as immature: "I am told that Mr. Nixon is a very fine young man by many Republican people whom I know, particularly young people, and that he has matured and grown in many ways." After referring to the senatorial campaign in which Nixon had branded his opponent, Helen Gahagan Douglas, as a communist, although "he knew quite well" that she was not, Mrs. Roosevelt observed that he lacked "the character that I really admired in public life." As for Eisenhower, she sweetly noted that "he has a great admiration for the achievement of the successful business man because he has never been a successful business man and you always admire what you really don't understand."[49]

"My Day" promoted Stevenson's campaign after Israel attacked in the Sinai following Egypt's seizure of the Suez Canal. Mrs. Roosevelt blamed the Republican leadership when Britain and France entered the conflict on the side of Israel while the United Nations sided against Israel's allies and with Russia in calling for a withdrawal of troops. In "My Day" she exclaimed, "I think if we elect Adlai Stevenson and Estes Kefauver next Tuesday we will not find ourselves in situations of this kind."[50]

Her partisanship almost brought an end to "My Day." The number of subscribing newspapers declined to about forty, after the Scripps-Howard chain canceled the column. This drastically cut her "My Day" income from $28,000 in 1956 to $9,630 in 1957. She suggested that she give up the column, but United Features Syndicate urged her to continue, in hopes of regaining clients. The syndicate, however, asked her to curb her advocacy of political candidates, and for this reason she declined membership on an advisory committee of the Democratic National Committee. The loss of the Scripps-Howard papers had at least one happy outcome. In New York City, "My Day" was picked up by the liberal *New York Post*, which featured it far more prominently than the *World-Telegram*.[51]

In 1957 and 1958, Mrs. Roosevelt made two trips to the Soviet Union. She traveled with Dr. Gurewitsch and Maureen Corr, who had replaced Malvina Thompson as Mrs. Roosevelt's secretary following Thompson's sudden death in 1953. In 1957, she was granted an interview with Khrushchev, who subsequently visited Mrs. Roosevelt in the United States in 1959 and 1960. While she insisted she was traveling as a reporter, Khrushchev treated her as an honored guest, engaging her in his first frank exchange with a Westerner on cold-war issues.[52]

The text of the Khrushchev interview became one of the highlights of the third volume of her autobiography, *On My Own*, published in 1958, after it had been excerpted in the *Saturday Evening Post*. In the autobiography she spoke of the need for "Americans and the rest of the free world . . . [to] understand the nature of the struggle against Communism as exemplified by the Soviet Union." By this she meant it was essential for Americans to comprehend Russian culture and experiences, which were so different from their own.[53]

Her philosophy was expounded in "My Day," which FBI agents continued to read diligently. A memorandum in Mrs. Roosevelt's FBI file, dated September 16, 1957, began, "Communist propaganda appears in many guises. It is transmitted throughout the world in many ways. Perhaps the most insidious method used for its transmittal involves the use of dupes." It went on to state that "Eleanor Roosevelt, in her syndicated newspaper column which is read by millions, has been telling her readers of her travels in the Soviet Union," including her visit to Zagorsk, where she saw a shrine and monastery. "Mrs. Roosevelt apparently would have her readers believe that Communist leaders have changed their views on religion," the memo noted, quoting passages from Marx and Lenin to show the atheistic nature of communism.[54]

The following year, J. Edgar Hoover's personal attention was directed to a "My Day" column that criticized officials of the American Legion for alleging that there was communist activity within the Methodist church. After receiving a copy of the Legion's response to the charge, Hoover wrote: "A devastating reply but I doubt it will have any effect on the old hoot owl and her clique."[55]

Although viewed suspiciously by the right wing, Mrs. Roosevelt remained a power in political circles, even after her dream of seeing Stevenson as the Democratic presidential candidate in 1960 was not realized. Initially hostile to John F. Kennedy, whom she accused of failing to stand up to McCarthy, she agreed to support the Massachusetts senator after he called on her at Val-Kill following his nomination. Two days after his visit, she told "My Day" readers of her new impression of Kennedy: "I left my conversation with him with the feeling that here is a man who wants to leave a record of not only having helped his countrymen, but having helped humanity as a whole."[56]

Although her health had begun to fail, she kept up the pace of a much younger woman. At seventy-five, she accepted an appointment as a visiting lecturer at Brandeis University, declining to be called "professor" because she claimed that she did not merit the title. A book, *You Learn by Living*, written with a collaborator, appeared in 1960. It set forth her philosophy of life. "Women," she wrote, "have one advantage over men." Forced throughout history to make adjustments to husbands and children, "it is less difficult for a woman to adjust to new situations than it is for a man." Later she wrote, "Nothing ever happens to us except what happens in our minds. Unhappiness is an inward, not an outward, thing."[57]

She continued her efforts to conquer the infirmities of old age by keeping busy and remaining in the public eye. She moderated a program, "The Prospects of Mankind," for Brandeis University, on educational television, the forerunner of public broadcasting. The program featured interviews with well-known figures, and was produced by Henry Morgenthau III, who found Mrs. Roosevelt's offhand manner somewhat disconcerting. He recalled years later: "Sometimes I felt that she would spend no more time thinking about or preparing herself for something of this kind than she would, say, if an old school friend had asked her to talk to a group of girls. . . . Everybody, just as a human being, deserved equal treatment, equal concern. I think in a way that she also did that in her writing: that she would perhaps spend no more time writing her column than she would dashing off a letter to a friend. And I think sometimes she didn't even read those columns." [58]

Morgenthau questioned her "sense of the value of human beings and the equality of human beings," which made a television program no more important than a speech to a group of Girl Scouts. He saw it both as "the key to her whole philosophy" and also as a weakness, a lack of discrimination between the significant and the trivial. But it was in keeping with Mrs. Roosevelt's image of herself as a woman adjusting to the needs of those around her. [59]

Still she sought the income that provided tangible evidence of professional achievement. She agreed to do a television commercial for margarine, hoping to prove that she was not too controversial to have a regular sponsored show. For the appearance she received $35,000, which she spent on CARE packages for the relief of hunger. Some critics, like Jack Gould of the *New York Times*, were horrified by Mrs. Roosevelt "linking her concern for the world's needy with the sale of a food product at a retail counter." But Mrs. Roosevelt maintained that she wanted a television platform to talk about hunger. No sponsored program, however, materialized. Nevertheless, in 1961, the same year that the Gallup poll found her America's "most admired woman," Mrs. Roosevelt's professional income came to more than $100,000, of which lectures accounted for $33,500 and payments for her writing close to $60,000. She also received $6,500 from Brandeis and $7,794 from "My Day," which had tapered off into a three-day-a-week feature. [60]

President Kennedy, grateful for her campaign help in his narrow victory, found roles for her to play in his administration. He named her to the United States delegation at a special General Assembly session. When he appointed a Commission on the Status of Women at the end of 1961, she was chosen its head. According to Esther Peterson, vice chairman of the commission, Mrs. Roosevelt emphasized the need for the commission to publicize its activities. "She thought the media was very important," Peterson said.[61]

By this time Mrs. Roosevelt had dropped her opposition to the Equal Rights Amendment, on grounds that unionization had made protective legislation unnecessary, but she refused to work for the amendment. Asked by a commission member whether the commission was set up to promote the amendment, she replied, "It is odd, because for many years I opposed the equal rights of women," and did not clearly state that she no longer objected. The final commission report, issued after Mrs. Roosevelt's death, concluded that an equal rights amendment "need not now be sought."[62]

To publicize the work of the commission, Mrs. Roosevelt appeared on the ABC public affairs program "Issues and Answers" on August 26, 1962. The moderator, Peggy Whedon, knowing that Mrs. Roosevelt had been ill, lined up a makeup man, a hairdresser, and a medical student to assist Mrs. Roosevelt and instructed a dozen pages to watch for the former first lady to enter the ABC studios in New York. Yet they failed to identify her, telling Whedon only that "an old lady in a funny white hat" wanted to see her. Mrs. Roosevelt refused to avail herself of the makeup artist and the hairdresser and insisted on wearing the hat on the air, even though Whedon was sure it would shade her face and detract from her presentation.[63]

But her fears proved unfounded. "The minute that little red light flashed on, and she realized that she was on camera, the old pro took over," Whedon wrote in her memoirs. "Under that ghastly white hat, her face was so luminous, her mind was so facile, and her ideas were so far ahead of her time that we listened, and learned, avidly." On the program Mrs. Roosevelt expressed support for the Kennedy administration's "equal pay for equal work" bill to benefit working women and said she thought a career woman could be a successful wife and mother if she had a cooperative family.[64]

As Mrs. Roosevelt's health failed, she worked on her last book, *Tomorrow Is Now*, written with Elinore Dennison. She called it a record of "one woman's attempt" to analyze the problems of democracy. Relatively little was specifically addressed to women, although she stated, as she had many times before, "The average housewife can be a real force in her community. She can join the organizations that represent her ideas, and those that are working for peace, and those that provide a better understanding in the world." That the majority of women might cease to be housewives and pursue the goals of women's liberation lay in a future which Mrs. Roosevelt did not see.[65]

Eleanor Roosevelt died of a rare form of tuberculosis at the age of seventy-eight on November 7, 1962, in New York City. The spring before her death, she had invited old friends from her press conference group to lunch with her in New York. One was Bess Furman, who had been named head of the press information section of the Department of Health, Education and Welfare in 1962, as a consequence of Mrs. Roosevelt's efforts to persuade Kennedy to appoint qualified women to top governmental posts. Dorothy Ducas, former director of public relations for the March of Dimes, Emma Bugbee, still with the *New York Herald-Tribune*, Mary Hornaday, still with the *Christian Science Monitor*, and Kathleen McLaughlin, former women's page editor of the *New York Times*, also were there. Ruby Black, however, was missing. She had died in a fire in 1959, a victim of alcoholism in her later years. After Mrs. Roosevelt's funeral, her secretary, Maureen Corr, told the press women, "She knew at the time that she was going to die. She was saying good-bye." Thus at the end, Mrs. Roosevelt remembered the women who had done so much to make her the public figure she had become.[66]

Conclusion

Eleanor Roosevelt was exceptional because of her combination of accomplishments and position. In some ways she did not break new ground. Other women before her had used the media to publicize social causes, particularly the suffragist movement. Yet as the wife of the only man ever to be elected president of the United States for four terms, Mrs. Roosevelt held an unparalleled position. Whatever she did was invested with dignity and significance in the eyes of millions of admirers. When she chose to draw attention to herself and her causes through the use of mass communications, she also focused attention on the communications process itself and legitimized its use by other women.

Esther Van Wagoner Tufty, a Washington correspondent for half a century, assessed the impact of Mrs. Roosevelt on the press during her centennial in 1984. Tufty summed it up in a few words: "Eleanor Roosevelt caused more to be written by, for and about women than any other woman." A study of Mrs. Roosevelt's career supports this generalization. Mrs. Roosevelt strived to communicate as one woman to another. In her efforts to reach a mass audience, she sensed the isolation that marked the lives of many American women in the 1930s. During this period the overwhelming majority of women labored within their family units, cut off from positions of authority within the social structure. Due to rigid sex-typing of occupations, many of the 25 percent who held jobs in the 1930s were confined to low-status clerical, trade, and service occupations. Through the medium of mass communications, Mrs. Roosevelt encouraged them to take a more active role in public affairs. Although her message was framed in traditional terms, which called on women to put their family responsibilities foremost, nevertheless it carried revolutionary overtones.[1]

Her press conferences provided Mrs. Roosevelt with an opportunity to put both women journalists and women's issues on the nation's communications agenda. As she encouraged women to carry on public discussion of their own interests, separate from the concerns of men, she acted to enhance the status of women in society. The conferences emphasized the multifaceted nature of her position as first lady, which encompassed ceremonial obligations along with her personal humanitarian, political, and career interests. By publicizing her own activities, Mrs. Roosevelt enlarged the boundaries of proper conduct for women, making it acceptable for them to seek a greater role in the media.

In addition, by insisting on only women reporters at the press conferences, Eleanor Roosevelt forced the press to make at least token changes in its treatment of women. At the beginning of the conferences, she forced the hiring of a few individual reporters, like Ruby Black, although Mrs. Roosevelt by no means brought about an influx of women reporters in Washington in the 1930s. The Washington bureau of the Associated Press, for example, had only one woman out of an eighty-member staff until World War II. Only then, when men went into the armed forces, were women hired in significant numbers by major news organizations.[2]

Therefore Mrs. Roosevelt and the women who covered her may be viewed as a group of pioneers, engaged in a symbiotic process of negotiating a new type of news agenda for women. Unlike President Roosevelt, whose press conferences dealt with obvious questions of affairs of state, the first lady had no definite rationale for meeting the press. Since Mrs. Roosevelt occupied no policy-making post, both she and the reporters needed to justify the conferences by making sure they produced suitable news stories. In their exchanges the first lady had to present material the reporters could write about and the reporters had to ask questions that would produce newsworthy items. The fact that the conferences lasted throughout Mrs. Roosevelt's entire twelve years in the White House testified to the ability of both Eleanor Roosevelt and the women reporters to carry out obligations of mutual benefit. Without doubt the conferences did generate news that had not appeared before —news written by women about a different kind of president's wife who actively sought to be a role model for other women.

On both sides the conferences proved learning experiences, although the first lady emerged as the chief gainer in the transaction. Through the conferences, Eleanor Roosevelt grew expert in dealing with the press, mastering skills that she demonstrated during her later career at the United Nations. Some of the reporters gained experience they would have been denied if men had been allowed to cover the conferences. (If this had occurred, however, the conferences might have ended, because male reporters, having access to varied news sources, probably would have had less of a vested interest than women in seeing them continue.) For many of the women, the first lady was the most newsworthy individual with whom they came in contact.

The conferences had negative as well as positive aspects. The careers of a few of the women closely associated with them, particularly those of Black and Herrick, eventually faltered, like that of Hickok, perhaps because of too much dependence on Mrs. Roosevelt. Initially the conferences were open to almost all women, as long as they were white, no matter how marginal their journalistic achievements. This created a quasi-social atmosphere that lent itself to ridicule and was disliked by the members who represented significant news operations. As the years went by, the reporters themselves tried to upgrade the standards for admission to the conferences, attempting to eliminate those with tenuous claims to professional status. When the group organized as Mrs. Roosevelt's Press Conference Association, it carefully scrutinized applications to keep out women who were not employed full-time as journalists.[3]

The women also became increasingly critical of the newsworthiness of the conferences. Some of the reporters expressed resentment at Mrs. Roosevelt "scooping" them by running news items in her column rather than publicizing them through the conferences. In addition, during the World War II period, evidence of an adversarial relationship between Mrs. Roosevelt and some of the reporters began to appear. Interestingly, this occurred at a time when the women as a group were obtaining jobs previously held by men. Since male reporters had a tradition of adversarial relationships with political sources in Washington, this can be viewed as an example of women adopting male values as they moved from the periphery toward the center of a male-dominated occupation.

The fact that the conferences succeeded as well as they did testified to the impact of Eleanor Roosevelt's extraordinary personality. Therein lay both their success and their defect. As an individual with a unique capacity for both personal development and involvement in the world around her, Eleanor Roosevelt made the conferences into a vehicle of commentary on her times. Yet she was not able to institutionalize them into a permanent feature of American political life. Although Eleanor Roosevelt hoped her successor as first lady, Bess Truman, would carry on the conferences, Mrs. Truman declined to do so. While subsequent first ladies have met the press from time to time, none has done so with the regularity or the zeal to communicate shown by Mrs. Roosevelt. While a cynic might conclude that Eleanor Roosevelt manipulated the press, a more sophisticated observation would be that she demonstrated, through the force of her personality combined with the status of her position, how the press can be influenced to respond to an individual.

Certainly Mrs. Roosevelt's personality also emerged as the most salient feature of her newspaper column, her magazine articles, her broadcasts, and her books. For a woman of her day Eleanor Roosevelt earned an astonishing amount of money while she was first lady: $75,000 as an advance on her autobiography, for example, and an estimated $156,000 from her radio broadcasts in 1940 alone. Obviously she needed psychologically to demonstrate her self-worth by earning money, the tangible symbol of accomplishment in a capitalistic society. Her interest in monetary rewards went far beyond a desire to purchase Christmas presents, to help individual members of her family, and to contribute to charity. Still, her money-making activities, like her press conferences, generally were linked to political ends—the promotion of her husband as president. Yet they spoke to women in symbolic terms broader than the purely political.

Apart from actresses and movie stars, American women in the New Deal era had almost no role models in the mass media, except for Eleanor Roosevelt. She served as a more realistic mentor than a Hollywood beauty queen, even though women as a whole may have been more attracted to the silver screen than to Mrs. Roosevelt's example of social concern. Surrounding Eleanor Roosevelt, however, was an aura of respectability that no star could ever match. She made it respectable for respectable women to participate in the man's world of public controversy. In this connection the amateurish qualities of Mrs. Roosevelt's activities proved an asset rather than a liability.

It fit the public conception of a woman's limitations for her to write columns and articles that lacked the polish of a professional writer and to give speeches that did not display the vocal qualities of the trained orator. "My Day," for example, touched the heart of a young woman from Austria who arrived in the United States in 1939 unsure of the English language. "Her writing was so simple, even I could understand it," Stella K. Hershan wrote in a letter to the *New York Times* in 1986 during the centennial celebration of the Statue of Liberty. "From her I learned about America." To Hershan, as to others before her, Eleanor Roosevelt embodied the spirit of the statue.[4]

The stereotypical woman of the day often was pictured as somewhat inept but highly moral and Mrs. Roosevelt fit this image perfectly during her years in the White House. If Mrs. Roosevelt had been more intellectually precise, it is likely she would have been less effective as a public communicator. Certainly she used the media as a vehicle for self-assertion in her life, much of which was a struggle between the Victorian idea of womanly subordination and the modern concept of self-actualization. But no matter how much she portrayed herself as an individual, she also pictured herself in the context of a wife helping her husband. Perhaps for this reason the public did not display greater resentment over the money she made, although it was generated largely by her husband's position. She was seen simply as a well-meaning wife earning extra income for good works. As first lady, Mrs. Roosevelt never surrendered the image of conventional femininity. Had she been more radical, it is doubtful she would have achieved the acclaim she gained. By emphasizing that she upheld old-fashioned, family-centered values, Mrs. Roosevelt shielded herself with the Victorian ideal of womanhood while she pushed forward to claim a place in the modern world. It was a place she claimed on behalf of other women as well as herself.

As a celebrity known, in Boorstin's words, "for who she was, which in turn influenced what she did," Mrs. Roosevelt triumphed in the media in part because of a combination of social and economic factors. She got her media start in the 1920s when print—in the form of both newspapers and magazines—reigned supreme. No longer made up simply of units owned by individual editors and publishers, the print medium had become part of a vast industry characterized by chain ownership and carrying not only information but entertainment, both of which served to sell the wares of national advertisers. Although Mrs. Roosevelt's activities did not always fit within the conventional definitions of news, their range and emotional appeal made her an ideal subject for the print medium's fascination with national personalities.[5]

During the depression when print lost ground to radio, the economics of survival caused publishers to turn increasingly to syndicated columns, since these cost less to obtain than news written locally. Newspapers needed to attract women readers to keep important local advertisers like department stores. Publishers' willingness to purchase "My Day," advertised as a personal visit by the first lady to millions of American homes, can be seen partly as a response to economic needs. Similarly, economic pressures played a role in the attendance at Mrs. Roosevelt's press conferences. Dozens of women found the conferences a useful way to gain subject matter for Washington columns that could be sold for small sums to their hometown newspapers. In addition, wire service stories about Mrs. Roosevelt may have filled newspapers across the country in part because newspapers received them as part of their normal complement of national feature news at no extra cost.[6]

In terms of broadcasting, Mrs. Roosevelt benefited from the fact that she entered radio when it was a new field. True, some of the criticism of her voice stemmed from general complaints about women's voices on the air in the 1920s and 1930s. Both critics and listeners contended that the low-pitched voices of men transmitted better than the higher-pitched voices of women over the microphones of the era. But aside from this, it was an advantage for Mrs. Roosevelt to be a pioneer in radio because no clear-cut guidelines existed as to what was or was not appropriate for a president's wife to do on the air. The public seemed willing to accept her sponsored broadcasts because it considered her simply a "lady" earning money for charity and helping her husband. That opponents were not able to stir up much of an outcry against her sponsored broadcasts stands in marked contrast to what might be expected today if a president's wife received a personal financial reward for being featured in the media.[7]

In addition, the appeal of Mrs. Roosevelt—the warmth and sincerity she conveyed—might not have been valued to the same extent if she had appeared on the television of today instead of being heard on early-day radio. Network television time is both so costly and limited that it is unlikely Mrs. Roosevelt would have had an opportunity for the kind of lengthy exposure she received as a pioneer radio commentator. Moreover, most of the women who succeed on contemporary television are judged largely on the basis of youthful appearance, an area in which Mrs. Roosevelt could not have competed. Although Mrs. Roosevelt was an effective performer on television in the 1950s and early 1960s, it should be noted that she was unable to obtain the sponsorship she sought.

It was fortunate for Mrs. Roosevelt's personal development that she was first lady before the impact of television created a complex political communication system involving the manipulation of political figures and their wives by sophisticated political consultants. Although Mrs. Roosevelt was advised by a brilliant political master, Louis Howe, in the 1930s image making was not the high-powered science of today. Mrs. Roosevelt was not dominated by advisors who orchestrated her every move. As first lady she was able to lead an independent life, developing a public personality for herself instead of being forced to rely on paid image merchants.

A possible measure of Eleanor Roosevelt's influence, or at least of the way she foreshadowed the future, can be gained by noting what has occurred in American society since she passed from the scene. Today it is customary for a woman to combine marriage and a family with work outside the home. Like Eleanor Roosevelt, the typical woman continues to cling to the traditional at the same time she broadens her role. Since this pattern often is blamed for a fragmentation of activity and a social ethic requiring the performance of a superwoman, it is appropriate to recall the random nature of Mrs. Roosevelt's pursuits and the hectic pace of her life. Nevertheless there is no doubt she projected an image of women as competent and active individuals.

In her own career, in her expression of popular attitudes, and in her sense of women's priorities, Eleanor Roosevelt displayed an intuitive grasp of what actually would occur in the evolution of American women. The extent to which she consciously contributed to this development—or whether her own attempt to combine marriage with a career merely predated what was certain to take place—is unknown. Nevertheless, when the most prominent woman of the day presents herself through the mass media as a model for women and in succeeding years it becomes the norm for women to follow this model—the role of the media in affecting social change arises as an intriguing question.

In recent years historians have disagreed over the extent of Eleanor Roosevelt's commitment to feminism, but arguments over this issue obscure a significant point. Mrs. Roosevelt's social and cultural ideas were those of the social feminists and advocated by many educated women of her period. She publicized and popularized ideas important to her, usually by taking the raw material of her own life and transforming it through the media into a message for the masses, particularly other women. Perhaps her greatest single contribution to feminism was to insist on the right of every woman, regardless of her husband's status, to earn money for herself.

There were numerous inconsistencies and contradictions in Eleanor Roosevelt's life, as there are in the lives of most individuals. Yet she remained remarkably consistent, in what she both said and did, regarding one major point: the need for women to create their own identities to enhance, not to relinquish, their traditional roles. Thus she took a conservative position and transmitted it to the public through modern technology. For good or ill, Eleanor Roosevelt prefigured the pattern for American women and she did it through the media. She was the first important American woman in public life to demonstrate the power of the media.

Notes

Introduction

1. Eleanor Roosevelt, *This Is My Story* (New York: Harper and Brothers, 1937), p. 5.

2. Merriman Smith, UPI dispatch headlined "She Found Truth; It Made Her Free," *Boston Sunday Globe*, Nov. 11, 1962; "Mrs. Roosevelt," editorial, *New York Journal-American*, Nov. 8, 1962; "FDR's Illness Turned Shy Wife into Dynamic Leader," *New York Journal-American*, Nov. 8, 1962; "Mrs. Roosevelt, First Lady 12 Years, Often Voted 'World's Most Admired Woman,'" *New York Times*, Nov. 8, 1962; "Eleanor Roosevelt Chose a Life of Usefulness," *Washington Star*, Nov. 8, 1962, clippings contained in "The Death of Eleanor Roosevelt," a scrapbook compiled by John F. McHugh, Allentown, Pa.

3. Alice C. Desmond, *Martha Washington: Our First Lady* (New York: Dodd, Mead and Co., 1951), p. 223. See also Mary W. Ashworth, "Martha D. Washington," *Notable American Women* 3 (Cambridge, Mass.: Belknap Press of Harvard University Press, 1980), pp. 549–50, and "The World of Nancy Reagan," *Newsweek*, Dec. 21, 1981, pp. 22–27.

4. Speculation on Eleanor Roosevelt's sexual relationships is assessed by William H. Chafe in a "Biographical Sketch" in Joan Hoff-Wilson and Marjorie Lightman, eds., *Without Precedent: The Life and Career of Eleanor Roosevelt* (Bloomington: Indiana University Press, 1984), p. 17. Chafe concludes that it was unlikely an individual of Mrs. Roosevelt's upbringing was able to fulfill her sexual drives outside of marriage. It must be noted, however, that Mrs. Roosevelt stepped far beyond her upbringing in other areas of her life, so the question remains one of conjecture. Franklin Roosevelt's affair with Lucy Page Mercer, Mrs. Roosevelt's social secretary, is detailed in Joseph P. Lash, *Eleanor and Franklin* (New York: Signet, 1973), pp. 302–11. The impact of the Mercer affair is discussed in James Roosevelt, *My Parents: A Differing View* (Chicago: Playbook Press, 1976), p. 98, and in Elliott

Roosevelt and James Brough, *Mother R: Eleanor Roosevelt's Untold Story* (New York: Putnam, 1977), pp. 29–30. A suggestion of a homosexual relationship between Eleanor Roosevelt and Lorena A. Hickok emerged in Doris Faber, *The Life of Lorena Hickok* (New York: Morrow, 1980), a biography based on some 3,000 letters that the two women exchanged over a thirty-year period. This allegation is denied by members of the Roosevelt family. See Henry Mitchell, Megan Rosenfeld, and Arthur Schlesinger, Jr., "Eleanor Roosevelt and the Styles of Friendship," *Washington Post*, Oct. 23, 1979, pp. C1–2, 4.

Chapter 1, "First Exposure"

1. Frank Freidel, *Franklin D. Roosevelt: The Apprenticeship* (Boston: Little, Brown, 1952), p. 78; "President in Town," *New York Times*, Mar. 18, 1905, p. 2; Roosevelt, *This Is My Story*, p. 126; Lash, *Eleanor and Franklin*, p. 205.

2. Roosevelt, *This Is My Story*, p. 22.

3. Ibid., p. 111; Elliott Roosevelt and James Brough, *The Roosevelts of Hyde Park: An Untold Story* (New York: Putnam, 1973), p. 33.

4. Roosevelt, *This Is My Story*, p. 181; James Brough, *Princess Alice* (Boston: Little, Brown, 1975), p. 130; Lash, *Eleanor and Franklin*, p. 309.

5. Sylvia Jukes Morris, *Edith Kermit Roosevelt: Portrait of a First Lady* (New York: Coward, McCann and Geoghegan, 1980), p. 3.

6. *New York Times*, Aug. 11, 1932, as quoted in Morris, *Edith Kermit Roosevelt*, p. 477; David McCullough, *Mornings On Horseback* (New York: Simon and Schuster, 1981), p. 353.

7. Roosevelt, *This Is My Story*, p. 192.

8. *New York Times*, July 17, 1917; Lash, *Eleanor and Franklin*, p. 290; Kenneth S. Davis, *FDR: The Beckoning of Destiny 1882–1928* (New York: Putnam, 1971), p. 491.

9. Davis, *FDR: The Beckoning of Destiny*, p. 490; Elliott Roosevelt and James Brough, *The Roosevelts*, p. 25.

10. Lash, *Eleanor and Franklin*, p. 290.

11. Elliott Roosevelt and James Brough, *The Roosevelts*, p. 123; Lash, *Eleanor and Franklin*, pp. 308–11.

12. Elliott Roosevelt and James Brough, *The Roosevelts*, pp. 122–23.

13. Roosevelt, *This Is My Story*, p. 314.

14. Ibid., p. 315.

15. Hilda R. Watrous, *In League with Eleanor: Eleanor Roosevelt and the League of Women Voters, 1921–1962* (New York: Foundation for Citizen Education, 1984), p. 3; Roosevelt, *This Is My Story*, pp. 323–24.

16. Rita H. Kleeman, *Gracious Lady: The Life of Sara Delano Roosevelt* (New York: Appleton-Century, 1935), p. 214; Eleanor Roosevelt, *The Autobiography of Eleanor Roosevelt* (New York: Harper, 1961), p. 113.

17. J. William T. Youngs, *Eleanor Roosevelt: A Personal and Public Life* (Boston: Little, Brown, 1985), p. 129.

18. Watrous, *In League with Eleanor*, pp. 3, 6; Lash, *Eleanor and Franklin*, p. 357.

19. *Poughkeepsie* (N.Y.) *Eagle News*, and Eleanor Roosevelt's diary, May 24, 1921, as quoted in Lash, *Eleanor and Franklin*, p. 358.

20. Kenneth S. Davis, *Invincible Summer: An Intimate Portrait of the Roosevelts Based on the Recollections of Marion Dickerman* (New York: Atheneum, 1974), pp. 12–15; Susan Ware, "ER and Democratic Politics: Women in the Postsuffrage Era," in Hoff-Wilson and Lightman, eds., *Without Precedent*, p. 47.

21. Ware, "ER and Democratic Politics," p. 49.

22. Eleanor Roosevelt, "The American Peace Award," *Ladies' Home Journal* 40 (Oct. 1923): 54.

23. Charles de Benedetti, "The $100,000 American Peace Award of 1924," *Pennsylvania Magazine of History and Biography* 98 (1974): 239, 245–47. Among those preparing plans was Franklin D. Roosevelt, during his recuperation from the infantile paralysis that had struck him in 1921. See Frank Freidel, *Franklin D. Roosevelt: The Ordeal* (Boston: Little, Brown, 1954), pp. 127–29. Freidel notes that Roosevelt apparently did not submit the plan to the contest because of his wife's involvement. In her autobiography, Mrs. Roosevelt does not clarify this point. See Eleanor Roosevelt, *This I Remember* (New York: Harper, 1949), pp. 23–24. Mrs. Roosevelt included the plan, which her husband reviewed in connection with the establishment of the United Nations, as Appendix I, pp. 353–66.

24. As quoted in Lash, *Eleanor and Franklin*, p. 383.

25. Ibid., p. 377.

Chapter 2, "Finding a Voice"

1. Eleanor Roosevelt, "Why Democrats Favor Smith," *North American Review* 224 (Nov. 1927): 472–75; "Jeffersonian Principles the Issue in 1928," *Current History* 28 (June 1928): 354–57, and "Governor Smith and Our Foreign Policy," *Woman's Journal* 12 (Oct. 1928): 21.

2. Davis, *Invincible Summer*, pp. 27–28; Alfred B. Rollins, Jr., *Roosevelt and Howe* (New York: Knopf, 1962), p. 208.

3. Eleanor Roosevelt to Marion Dickerman, Aug. 14, 1925, box 4,

Marion Dickerman Papers, Franklin D. Roosevelt Library, Hyde Park, N.Y. (hereafter referred to as FDRL).

4. Ann Davis, "The Character of Social Feminism in the 30's: Eleanor Roosevelt and Her Associates in the New Deal," unpublished paper presented at the centennial conference on Franklin D. Roosevelt: The Man, the Myth, the Era, Hofstra University, Hempstead, N.Y., Mar. 6, 1982, p. 2.

5. See Eleanor Roosevelt, "What I Want Most out of Life," *Success Magazine* 11 (May 1927): 16–17, 70; "Women Must Learn to Play the Game as Men Do," *Redbook Magazine* 50 (Apr. 1928): 78–79, 141–42; "Education for Girls," *Independent Education* 3 (Dec. 1929): 7–8; "Servants," *Forum* 83 (Jan. 1930): 24–28; "Mrs. Franklin D. Roosevelt Looks at this Modern Housekeeping," *Modern Priscilla* 44 (Apr. 1930): 13, 64; "What Is a Wife's Job Today? An Interview with M. K. Wisehart," *Good Housekeeping* 91 (Aug. 1930): 34–35, 166, 169–73; "Ten Rules for Success in Marriage," *Pictorial Review* 33 (Dec. 1931): 4; "Grandmothers Can Still Be Young," *Liberty* 9 (Feb. 20, 1932): 38–40; "What Do Ten Million Women Want?" *Home Magazine* 5 (Mar. 1932): 19–21, 86; "Today's Girl and Tomorrow's Job," *Woman's Home Companion* 59 (June 1932): 11–12; "Wives of Great Men," *Liberty* 9 (Oct. 1, 1932): 12–16; "What Are the Movies Doing to Us," *Modern Screen* 4 (Nov. 1932): 27, 102.

6. Eleanor Roosevelt, manuscript for article, "Ten Rules for Success in Marriage," box 3023, speech and article file, Eleanor Roosevelt Papers (hereafter referred to as ERP), FDRL, p. 2; Roosevelt, *This I Remember*, p. 349.

7. Eleanor Roosevelt, unpublished manuscript, "The Ethics of Parents," box 3022, speech and article file, ERP, FDRL, p. 9.

8. Ibid.

9. Ibid., p. 2.

10. Eleanor Roosevelt, untitled manuscript for *Vogue*, 1929, box 3022, speech and article file, ERP, FDRL, p. 1.

11. Interview with Frances A. Perkins, vol. 3, part 3, oral history collection, Columbia University, New York, N.Y., pp. 532, 540; Charles H. Trout, "Frances Perkins," *Notable American Women* 4:538.

12. Roosevelt, "What Is a Wife's Job Today?" pp. 166, 169.

13. Ibid., p. 170.

14. Ibid., p. 171.

15. James Roosevelt, *My Parents: A Differing View*, p. 122.

16. Roosevelt, "What Is a Wife's Job Today?" pp. 172–73.

17. Perkins interview, vol. 3, part 1, p. 22.

18. Rollins, *Roosevelt and Howe*, pp. 271–72.

19. James Roosevelt, *My Parents: A Differing View*, p. 127; Lash, *Eleanor and Franklin*, p. 437; Eleanor Roosevelt, typescript of editorial dated Jan. 22, 1929, for the *Women's Democratic News*, box 3025, ERP, FDRL. Other contributions, most of which are undated, are in the same box. See also Mrs. Franklin D. Roosevelt, "A Summer Trip Abroad," *Women's Democratic News* 5 (Apr. 1930): 2, and 6 (June 1930): 16.

20. Eleanor Roosevelt, manuscript for article, "What Do Ten Million Women Want?," box 3023, ERP, FDRL, pp. 1–3.

21. Ibid., p. 4.

22. William H. Chafe, *The American Woman: Her Changing Social, Economic, and Political Roles, 1920–1970* (London: Oxford University Press, 1972), p. 31.

23. Ibid., p. 57; Susan Ware, *American Women in the 1930s: Holding Their Own* (Boston: Twayne, 1982), p. 69.

24. Bernard Asbell, ed., *Mother and Daughter: The Letters of Eleanor and Anna Roosevelt* (New York: Coward, McCann and Geoghegan, 1982), p. 33.

25. Elliott Roosevelt and James Brough, *The Roosevelts*, p. 281; Eleanor Roosevelt to Franklin Roosevelt, Apr. 14, 1928, as quoted in Lash, *Eleanor and Franklin*, p. 417.

26. Lash, *Eleanor and Franklin*, p. 436.

27. Ibid., p. 460.

28. Roosevelt, *This I Remember*, p. 74.

29. Lorena A. Hickok, *Reluctant First Lady* (New York: Dodd, Mead, 1962), foreword.

Chapter 3, *"Lorena A. Hickok, Unlikely Mentor"*

1. Ishbel Ross, *Ladies of the Press* (New York: Harper, 1936), pp. 12–13.

2. Hickok, *Reluctant First Lady*, pp. 10, 16–17.

3. Hickok, chapter 1, "The Making of an Introvert," unfinished autobiography, box 14, Lorena A. Hickok Papers (hereafter referred to as LHP), FDRL, p. 6.

4. Hickok, outline, unfinished autobiography, p. 1. See also Faber, *The Life of Lorena Hickok*, p. 45.

5. Hickok, foreword, unfinished autobiography, p. 2.

6. Ibid.

7. Ibid.

8. John P. Broderick, "An Interviewer Interviewed," unpublished article, n.d., box 14, LHP, FDRL, pp. 3–4.

9. Lorena A. Hickok to Bess Furman [1930], box 44, Bess Furman

Papers (hereafter referred to as BFP), Library of Congress (hereafter LC), Washington, D.C.

10. Ibid.

11. Hickok, chapter 7, "The Lindbergh Kidnaping Story," unfinished autobiography, pp. 8–9, 1, 10.

12. Ross, *Ladies of the Press*, p. 204.

13. Hickok, *Reluctant First Lady*, pp. 35, 46.

14. Faber, *The Life of Lorena Hickok*, pp. 92–93; Hickok, *Reluctant First Lady*, p. 44.

15. Perkins interview, vol. 3, part 2, p. 266; see chapter on "Eleanor and the Corporal" in Joseph P. Lash, *Love, Eleanor: Eleanor Roosevelt and Her Friends* (Garden City, N.Y.: Doubleday, 1982), pp. 111–23.

16. Joseph Alsop, *FDR: A Centenary Remembrance* (New York: Viking, 1982), pp. 109–10.

17. Dorothy Strachey-Bussy, *Olivia* (London: Hogarth, 1948), p. 22; Blanche W. Cook, "Exploitative Book Distorts Relationship," *New Directions for Women*, Mar./Apr. 1980, p. 13; Lash, *Love, Eleanor*, pp. 18–19.

18. See account of Hickok's relationship with Judge Marion Harron in Faber, *The Life of Lorena Hickok*, pp. 290–98; Carroll Smith-Rosenberg, "The Female World of Love and Ritual: Relations between Women in Nineteenth-Century America," *Signs* 1 (Autumn 1975): 1–2.

19. Lorena A. Hickok to Eleanor Roosevelt, [1932], box 1, LHP.

20. Lash, *Eleanor and Franklin*, p. 469; Hickok, *Reluctant First Lady*, p. 43; Associated Press news copy initialed KB and marked "hold," Sept. 1932, box 14, LHP.

21. Lorena A. Hickok byline, Associated Press news copy, Potsdam, N.Y., Oct. 30, 1932, box 14, LHP.

22. Memo to WWC [W. W. Chapin] from LAH, [1932], box 14, LHP.

23. Hickok, *Reluctant First Lady*, p. 57; Bess Furman, *Washington By-Line* (New York: Knopf, 1949), p. 133.

24. Memo to WWC [W. W. Chapin] from LAH, Nov. 1932, box 14, LHP; Associated Press news copy, New York, Nov. 8, 1932, box 14, LHP.

25. Associated Press news copy, New York, Nov. 9, 1932, box 14, LHP; Hickok, *Reluctant First Lady*, pp. 57, 86.

26. Hickok, *Reluctant First Lady*, p. 84; Associated Press news copy, New York, Nov. 9, 1932, box 14, LHP.

27. Associated Press news copy, New York, Nov. 10, 1932, box 14, LHP.

28. Ibid.

29. Associated Press news copy, New York, Nov. 11, 1932, box 14, LHP.

30. Lorena A. Hickok to Malvina Thompson, July 23, 1949, box 17, LHP.

31. Hickok, *Reluctant First Lady*, p. 86; Lash, *Eleanor and Franklin*, p. 454.

32. Hickok, *Reluctant First Lady*, pp. 78–84; Lash, *Eleanor and Franklin*, p. 473.

33. "On Girls Learning to Drink," *Literary Digest* (Jan. 7, 1933): 20; Lorena A. Hickok to Malvina Thompson, July 23, 1949, box 17, LHP.

34. Lash, *Eleanor and Franklin*, pp. 473–74. See also Lorena A. Hickok, Associated Press news copy, New York, Feb. 4, 1933, box 51, BFP.

35. Hickok, *Reluctant First Lady*, pp. 53, 61, 64–65.

36. Ibid., pp. 103–7; Roosevelt, *This I Remember*, p. 78; Furman, *Washington By-Line*, p. 150.

37. Lorena A. Hickok byline, "Nation's 'First Lady' Outlines Plans As She Begins White House Residence," clipping, *La Crosse* (Wisc.) *Tribune*, Mar. 5, 1933, Ruby A. Black papers (hereafter referred to as RBP), in the possession of her daughter, Cornelia J. Motheral, Arlington, Va.; Furman, *Washington By-Line*, pp. 150–51.

38. Hickok, *Reluctant First Lady*, p. 151; Furman, *Washington By-Line*, p. 151.

39. Lash, *Eleanor and Franklin*, p. 476; Hickok, *Reluctant First Lady*, p. 96.

40. Eleanor Roosevelt to Lorena A. Hickok, Mar. 5, 1933, box 1, LHP. The correspondence between Eleanor Roosevelt and Lorena Hickok constitutes the bulk of the 16,000-page collection of Hickok papers at the Franklin D. Roosevelt Library.

41. Lorena A. Hickok byline, AP news story, "Mrs. Roosevelt Adds 'Anna Blue' Wrap and Hat to Ensemble as She Tries on Inaugural Gown," unidentified clipping, Mar. 1933, RBP; Hickok, *Reluctant First Lady*, p. 86; Roosevelt, *This I Remember*, p. 102; Faber, *The Life of Lorena Hickok*, p. 106.

42. Faber, *The Life of Lorena Hickok*, p. 106.

Chapter 4, "The 'Newspaper Girls'"

1. Jane Grey Swisshelm, *Half a Century* (Chicago: Jansen, McClurg and Co., 1880), p. 130: Marion Marzolf, *Up From the Footnote: A History of Women Journalists* (New York: Hastings House, 1977), p. 51.

2. Roosevelt, *This I Remember*, p. 102.

3. Typed notes from Furman diary, entry for Jan. 25, 1933, box 51, BFP; Furman, *Washington By-Line*, pp. 59–61.

4. Marguerite Young to Ruby Black, Jan. 9, 1933, RBP.

5. Lorena A. Hickok to Bess Furman, [Jan. 1933], box 26, BFP; Ruby A. Black to Nelson A. Crawford, May 26, 1929, and Crawford to Black, June 8, 1929, RBP.

6. Ruby A. Black, biographical sketch prepared for A. M. Brayton, June 29, 1942; chronology of employment, [1941]; Fred S. Ferguson to Ruby A. Black, Apr. 21, 1923; Black to Ferguson, May 2, 1923; all from RBP.

7. Ruby A. Black to Eleanor Roosevelt, Jan. 12, 1933, RBP.

8. Martha Strayer, typescript, unpublished book on Mrs. Roosevelt's press conferences, box 2, Martha Strayer papers (hereafter referred to as MSP), University of Wyoming, p. 5; Ishbel Ross, *Grace Coolidge and Her Era* (New York: Dodd, Mead, 1962), p. 108.

9. Eleanor Roosevelt to Ruby Black, Jan. 24, 1933, and Black to Roosevelt, Jan. 30, 1933, RBP.

10. Memo from Ruth E. Jones to Stephen T. Early, Feb. 24, 1932, president's personal file, Franklin D. Roosevelt papers, FDRL, as cited in Betty H. Winfield, "Mrs. Roosevelt's Press Conference Association: The First Lady Shines a Light," *Journalism History* 8 (Summer 1981): 54; list of newspaper representatives certified to attend Mrs. Roosevelt's press conferences by Stephen T. Early on Mar. 9, 1933, box 2997, ERP, FDRL.

11. Richard L. Rubin, *Press, Party and Presidency* (New York: Norton, 1981), p. 86; catalogue of "FDR: The Intimate Presidency—Franklin D. Roosevelt, Communication and the Mass Media in the 1930s," Smithsonian Institution exhibition, Washington, D.C., 1982; Graham J. White, *FDR and the Press* (Chicago: University of Chicago Press, 1979), p. xi; Edwin Emery and Michael Emery, *The Press and America: An Interpretative History of the Mass Media*, 5th ed. (Englewood Cliffs, N.J.: Prentice-Hall, 1984), p. 426.

12. Lash, *Eleanor and Franklin*, pp. 475–76.

13. Dorothy Roe Lewis, "A First Lady as an Inside Source," *New York Times*, Mar. 13, 1981, p. A31.

14. Interview with Dorothy Ducas Herzog by Maurine Beasley, Sept. 11, 1982, South Salem, N.Y.

15. Hickok, *Reluctant First Lady*, p. 63.

16. "New Mistress of White House Plans Conferences with Press," clipping from *Christian Science Monitor*, Mar. 4, 1933, box 1, Mary Hornaday papers (hereafter referred to as MHP), University of Wyoming.

17. Ross, *Ladies of the Press*, p. 335; autobiographical sketch provided by Mary Hornaday during a personal interview with Maurine Beasley, Red Bank, N.J., May 21, 1979.

18. Lash, *Eleanor and Franklin*, p. 480; Roosevelt, *This I Remember*, p. 102.

19. Autobiographical sketch given by Hornaday to Beasley; Roosevelt, *This I Remember,* p. 102.

20. Roosevelt, *This I Remember,* p. 102.

21. Daniel J. Boorstin, "From News Gathering to News Making: A Flood of Pseudo-Events," in his *The Image: A Guide to Pseudo-Events in America* (New York: Atheneum, 1978), pp. 7–44, 57.

22. Everette E. Dennis and Arnold H. Ismach, *Reporting Processes and Practices: Newswriting for Today's Readers* (Belmont, Calif.: Wadsworth, 1981), pp. 87–88.

23. Furman typescript of notes on Mrs. Roosevelt's press conference, Mar. 6, 1933; Roosevelt, *This I Remember,* p. 103. Unfortunately the Thompson notes are not preserved with the rest of the Mrs. Roosevelt's papers at the Franklin D. Roosevelt Library and are believed to be lost. Also Edith B. Helm, *The Captains and the Kings* (New York: Putnam, 1954), p. 171.

24. Furman typescript of notes on Mrs. Roosevelt's press conference, Mar. 6, 1933; Roosevelt, *This I Remember,* p. 102; Lela Stiles, *The Man Behind Roosevelt: The Story of Louis McHenry Howe* (Cleveland: World, 1954), p. 211.

25. Roosevelt, *This I Remember,* p. 102; Furman typescript of notes on Mrs. Roosevelt's press conference, Mar. 6, 1933.

26. Ross, *Ladies of the Press,* p. 344; Winifred Mallon, "The Whole Truth, as Far as It Goes, about Ourselves," unpublished manuscript, archives, Women's National Press Club, National Press Club Library, Washington, D.C.

27. Lorena A. Hickok to Malvina Thompson, July 23, 1949, box 17, LHP. In the letter Hickok exploded, "God damn it, professionally I ranked so far above the rest of that mob, except Geno." Hickok wrote Thompson in 1949 after being sent a draft of Mrs. Roosevelt's autobiography, which mentioned the exclusive inauguration day interview. Hickok was offended by Mrs. Roosevelt's statement that after granting the interview she realized that "in the White House one must not play favorites." Denying "I got that story just because I was a nice, tame, pet reporter," Hickok contended, "I got the story because I earned it. . . . I had . . . the kind of assignments for the AP that even Geno never got"; also Ross, *Ladies of the Press,* pp. 539–42.

28. Ibid., pp. 335–36; Jennifer L. Tebbe, "Elisabeth May Adams Craig," in *Notable American Women* 4, pp. 171–72.

29. Roosevelt, *This I Remember,* p. 104.

30. The shorthand notes taken by Strayer are contained in Maurine H. Beasley, ed., *The White House Press Conferences of Eleanor Roosevelt* (New York: Garland, 1983). A biographical sketch of Strayer appears on p. 3. See also Ross, *Ladies of the Press,* p. 510.

31. Ross, *Ladies of the Press*, p. 122.

32. Ibid., p. 316; Jean E. Collins, *She Was There: Stories of Pioneering Women Journalists* (New York: Messner, 1980), p. 40.

33. Typed notes from Bess Furman's letter to her family, [Mar. 1933], box 51, BFP.

34. Ross, *Ladies of the Press*, p. 309; Furman, *Washington By-Line*, p. 153; Mary Hornaday, untitled manuscript on Mrs. Roosevelt's press conferences given to Beasley, Red Bank, N.J., May 21, 1979, p. 2.

35. Ross, *Ladies of the Press*, p. 309.

36. Ruby A. Black, "Covering Mrs. Roosevelt," *Matrix* 18 (Apr. 1933): 1.

37. Lewis, "A First Lady as an Inside Source," p. A31.

38. Typed notes from letter by Bess Furman to her family, Apr. 1933, box 51, BFP.

39. Personal interview with Rosamond Cole by Maurine Beasley, Washington, D.C., Apr. 20, 1979.

40. Typed notes from Bess Furman's diary, Mar. 15, 1933, box 51, BFP; Black, "Covering Mrs. Roosevelt," p. 4.

41. Anne Hard to Eleanor Roosevelt, Mar. 27, 1933, box 2997, topical file, ERP; Ross, *Ladies of the Press*, p. 317.

42. Hard to Roosevelt, Mar. 27, 1933; Black, "Covering Mrs. Roosevelt," p. 1; Ross, *Ladies of the Press*, p. 317.

Chapter 5, *"Headlines and Friendships"*

1. Lash, *Eleanor and Franklin*, p. 481.

2. Martha Strayer to Eleanor Roosevelt, [Mar. 30, 1933], box 2997, topical file, ERP; Roosevelt to Lorena Hickok, Apr. 3, 1933, box 1, LHP; "Beer To Be Served at White House," clipping, *New York Times*, Apr. 4, 1933, Roosevelt scrapbooks, box T-121, FDRL.

3. Strayer to Roosevelt, [Mar. 30, 1933].

4. Ruby A. Black to Eleanor Roosevelt, Apr. 8, 1933, RBP; "Curb on Women Hit by Mrs. Roosevelt," *New York Times*, Apr. 11, 1933, p. 21; Lois Scharf, *To Work and to Wed* (Westport, Conn.; Greenwood, 1980), pp. 49–50.

5. Emma Bugbee, "Horse Throws Mrs. Roosevelt into Mud Hole," clipping, *New York Herald-Tribune*, Apr. 13, 1933, Roosevelt scrapbooks, box T-121, FDRL.

6. Faber, *The Life of Lorena Hickok*, p. 123; Roosevelt to Hickok, Mar. 8, 1933, box 1, LHP; Roosevelt to Furman, Apr. 15, 1933, and Apr. 26, 1933, box 32, BFP.

7. Furman diary, entry for Apr. 20, 1933, box 1, BFP; Roosevelt to Furman, Apr. 15, 1933.

8. Roosevelt to Hickok, Apr. 20, 1933, box 1, LHP; enclosure from Furman to Roosevelt, Roosevelt to Hickok, June 15, 1933, box 1, LHP.

9. Enclosure, Furman to Roosevelt, Roosevelt to Hickok, June 15, 1933; Furman typescript of Mrs. Roosevelt's press conference, June 15, 1933, box 76, BFP.

10. Katharine M. Brooks, "Some Recollections of the American Newspaper Women's Club," Sept. 1970, files of the American News Women's Club, Washington, D.C., p. 2.

11. Ducas interview with Beasley, Sept. 11, 1982; Cole interview with Beasley, Apr. 20, 1979.

12. Ducas interview with Beasley, Sept. 11, 1982.

13. Collins, *She Was There*, pp. 36–37.

14. Personal interview by Maurine Beasley with Anne W. Arnall, Laurel, Md., Apr. 27, 1984; personal interview by Beasley with Sally L. Smith, daughter of Isaac Liberman, president of Arnold Constable department store, Washington, D.C., May 22, 1984.

15. William D. Mohr transcription of Strayer shorthand notes, Jan. 30, 1936, box 10, MSP; typescript of unpublished book on Eleanor Roosevelt's press conferences, box 2, MSP, p. 80.

16. Frances Parkinson Keyes, *Capital Kaleidoscope: The Story of a Washington Hostess* (New York: Harper, 1937), p. 295; Ducas interview with Beasley, Sept. 11, 1982.

17. Personal interview by Maurine Beasley with Hope Ridings Miller, Washington, D.C., May 3, 1979.

18. Strayer typescript, box 2, MSP, p. 11.

19. "Women's Forest Work Camps May Be Set Up," clipping, *New York Times*, May 24, 1933, Winifred Mallon scrapbook (of articles written for the *New York Times*), box 154, BFP; Furman, *Washington By-Line*, p. 174.

20. "Mrs. Roosevelt and Party Visit Lee Shrine," clipping, *New York Times*, May 18, 1933, and "First Lady Visits Jefferson's Home," clipping, May 31, 1933, *Washington Star*, White House social secretary's 1933 scrapbook of newspaper articles, box T-121, FDRL; Furman diary, entry for May 31, 1933, box 1, BFP; Lash, *Eleanor and Franklin*, p. 481; Furman diary, entry for Mar. 30, 1933, box 1, BFP.

21. Roosevelt to Hickok, May 31, 1933, box 1, LHP.

22. Furman typescript, notes of Eleanor Roosevelt's press conference, June 25, 1933, box 76, BFP.

23. Emma Bugbee, "Eleanor Roosevelt Denies Slight to Mrs. Fergu-

son," *New York Herald-Tribune*, June 14, 1933, Roosevelt scrapbook, box T-121, FDRL.

24. Furman, *Washington By-Line*, p. 158; Roosevelt to Hickok, Apr. 3, 1933, box 1, LHP.

25. Eleanor Roosevelt appointment books, 1933 to 1945, ERP, FDRL. The appointment books for 1933 to 1944 are in box 3000 and for 1945 in box 3001. A breakdown of the number of press conferences by year, according to the appointment books: 1933, 29; 1934, 38; 1935, 30; 1936, 24; 1937, 24; 1938, 21; 1939, 27; 1940, 25; 1941, 30; 1942, 33; 1943, 36; 1944, 28; 1945, 13. Press engagements crossed out in the books have been omitted in making the tabulations.

26. "Mrs. Roosevelt Hits Low Pay for Women Enrolled as Skilled Relief Workers," *New York Times*, Dec. 5, 1933, Mallon scrapbooks, box 154, BFP.

27. Strayer to Roosevelt, Oct. 12, 1933, series 100, box 1279, ERP.

28. Roosevelt to Hickok, Oct. 7, 1933, box 1, LHP; Furman to Roosevelt [Sept. 1933], enclosure in Roosevelt to Hickok, Sept. 21, 1933.

29. Keyes, *Capital Kaleidoscope*, pp. 289–90; Strayer to Roosevelt [Oct. 8, 1933] and [Oct. 15, 1933], series 100, box 1279, ERP.

30. Strayer to Roosevelt [Oct. 15, 1933].

31. Keyes, *Capital Kaleidoscope*, p. 290.

32. Roosevelt to Hickok, Aug. 10, 1933, box 1, LHP; telephone interview with India Edwards, a close personal friend of Geno Herrick, by Maurine Beasley, Washington, D.C., Apr. 27, 1983.

33. Ruby A. Black, "'New Deal' for News Women in Capital," *Editor and Publisher* (Feb. 10, 1934): 11.

34. Black to Roosevelt, Nov. 2, 1933, RBP.

35. Ruby A. Black byline, copy for United Press copyrighted story, Nov. 22, 1933, RBP.

36. Black, "'New Deal' for News Women in Capital," p. 11.

37. Eleanor Roosevelt, statement to the press, Jan. 29, 1934, box 76, BFP; Black, "'New Deal' for News Women in Capital," p. 11.

38. Furman diary, entry for Dec. 27, 1933, box 1, BFP; Furman, *Washington By-Line*, p. 189.

39. Furman typescript, notes of Mrs. Roosevelt's press conference, Apr. 11, 1934, box 76, BFP; Malvina Thompson, transcription of Mrs. Roosevelt's press conference, Apr. 23, 1934, box 3026, speech and article file, ERP.

40. Furman diary, entries for Apr. 2, Feb. 5, and Apr. 23, 1934, box 1, BFP.

41. Roosevelt to Strayer, Aug. 27, 1934, series 100, box 1321, ERP.

42. Hickok, *Reluctant First Lady*, pp. 136–41. See also report from Hickok to Harry L. Hopkins, Aug. 16–26, 1933, in Richard Lowitt and Maurine Beasley, eds., *One Third of a Nation: Lorena Hickok Reports on the Great Depression* (Urbana: University of Illinois Press, 1981), pp. 14–24; "News and Comment from the National Capital," *Literary Digest*, Nov. 28, 1933, p. 12. See also Searle F. Charles, *Minister of Relief: Harry Hopkins and the Depression* (Syracuse, N.Y.: Syracuse University Press, 1963), p. 140; Roosevelt to Hickok, Nov. 12, 1933, box 1, LHP.

43. Collins, *She Was There*, p. 43; Furman, *Washington By-Line*, pp. 195–96; Ruby A. Black, news article copy on Mrs. Roosevelt's tour for *La Democracia*, Feb. 14, 1934, RBP; news article, *Time*, Feb. 19, 1934, as quoted in Faber, *The Life of Lorena Hickok*, pp. 158–59.

44. Furman diary, entry for Mar. 20, 1934, box 1, BFP; Furman, *Washington By-Line*, p. 200; Beasley interview with Ducas, Sept. 11, 1982.

45. Roosevelt, *This I Remember*, pp. 138–40; Eleanor Roosevelt to Lorena Hickok, Dec. 7, 1933, box 1, LHP.

46. Black, "'New Deal' for News Women in Capital," p. 11; Mary Hornaday, "Mrs. Roosevelt's Role," in column headlined, "The Wide Horizon," *Christian Science Monitor*, Jan. 14, 1934, box 1, MHP.

47. Black to Roosevelt, Aug. 9, 1934, RBP; Geno Herrick to Roosevelt, Sept. 9, 1934, series 100, box 1301, ERP; Roosevelt to Furman, Aug. 29, 1934, box 32, BFP; Strayer to Roosevelt, Aug. 20, 1934, and Roosevelt to Strayer, Aug. 27, 1934, series 100, box 1321, ERP; Roosevelt to Hickok, Jan. 15, 1934, box 1, LHP.

48. Furman diary, entries for Oct. 7, Oct. 15, Nov. 6, Nov. 23, Nov. 29, Dec. 4, Dec. 9, Dec. 12, and Dec. 24, 1933.

49. Kathleen McLaughlin to Maurine Beasley, July 7, 1979.

50. Furman diary, entry for Dec. 26, 1933, Jan. 23 and Jan 26, 1934, box 1, BFP.

51. Roosevelt to Hickok, Jan. 15, 1934; Roosevelt, *This I Remember*, pp. 141–42; Hickok, *Reluctant First Lady*, pp. 158–61.

52. Ducas interview with Beasley, Sept. 11, 1982.

53. Associated Press news copy, as quoted in Furman, *Washington By-Line*, p. 194.

Chapter 6, "Building a Career"

1. Elliott Roosevelt and James Brough, *The Roosevelts*, p. 299; Interview with James A. Halsted by Emily Williams, May 17, 1979, Hyde Park, N.Y., p. 7, and transcript of interview with John R. Boettiger by Emily

Williams, Aug. 1, 1979, Northampton, Mass., p. 58, Eleanor Roosevelt oral history archives, FDRL.

2. "Passing Thoughts of Mrs. Franklin D. Roosevelt," *Women's Democratic News* 8 (Feb. 1933): 6; Eleanor Roosevelt, "What I Hope to Leave Behind!" typescript for *Pictorial Review* article, Apr. 1933, box 3028, speech and article file, ERP, p. 3.

3. Memo, "Suggested Topics for Articles for Baby Magazine," box 3025, speech and article file, ERP; Lash, *Eleanor and Franklin*, p. 494.

4. Roosevelt to Hickok, Apr. 11, 1933, box 1, LHP.

5. Lash, *Eleanor and Franklin*, p. 494; Gertrude B. Lane to Eleanor Roosevelt, May 10, 1933, box 3026, speech and article file, ERP.

6. Lane to Roosevelt, May 17 and May 22, 1933, box 3026, speech and article file, ERP; "Mrs. Franklin D. Roosevelt's Page: Ratify the Child Labor Amendment," *Woman's Home Companion* 60 (Sept. 1933): 4.

7. Roosevelt to Aron Mathieu, May 9, 1933, as quoted in Lash, *Eleanor and Franklin*, p. 495; Lane to Roosevelt, May 22, 1933.

8. "Mrs. Franklin D. Roosevelt's Page," *Woman's Home Companion* 60 (Aug. 1933), (Dec. 1933), and (Nov. 1933): 4.

9. Lash, *Eleanor and Franklin*, p. 494; North American Newspaper Alliance copyrighted article, "White House Home to Mrs. Roosevelt," clipping, *New York Times*, [Apr. 2, 1933], box 51, BFP; typescript, marked for "Northern Newspaper Alliance," Apr. 25 [1933], box 3026, speech and article file, ERP.

10. Merritt Bond to Eleanor Roosevelt, May 8, 1933; typescript for North American Newspaper Alliance article, July 1933; both in box 3026, speech and article file, ERP.

11. "White House Home to Mrs. Roosevelt."

12. Typescript for North American Newspaper Alliance article for Aug. 1933, box 3026, speech and article file, ERP, p. 2.

13. Bond to Roosevelt, Aug. 18, 1933, box 3026, speech and article file, ERP.

14. Charles B. Driscoll to Malvina Thompson Scheider, Nov. 20, 1933, box 3027, speech and article file, ERP.

15. Eleanor Roosevelt to McNaught Syndicate, Feb. 2, 1934, box 3027, speech and article file, ERP; File of clippings of McNaught Syndicate articles headlined "President's Wife Gives Views about Women Holding Jobs," Jan. 13, 1934; "First Lady Declares Crime Now Largest Item in Budget," Jan. 20, 1934; "Conditions in Prisons Discussed," Mar. 19, 1934; and "Parks Afford Ideal Spots for Recreation," Feb. 2, 1934, from *Muscatine* (Iowa) *Journal*, RBP; Memo from George Allen to Eleanor Roosevelt, Nov. 8, 1934, box 3028, speech and article file, ERP.

16. Driscoll to Malvina Thompson Scheider, May 8, 1934, box 3027, speech and article file, ERP; Eleanor Roosevelt, *It's Up to the Women* (New York: Stokes, 1933), p. 206.

17. Furman diary, entry for May 14, 1934, box 1, BFP; Lash, *Eleanor and Franklin*, p. 551.

18. Eleanor Roosevelt to Edward G. Skdahl, May 21, 1934, as quoted in "Mrs. Roosevelt Feels Overpaid," clipping, *New York Times*, box 51, BFP; script for Simmons broadcast, Sept. 18, 1934, box 3027, speech and article file, ERP, p. 9.

19. Script for Simmons broadcast, July 9, 1934, box 3027, speech and article file, ERP, p. 9.

20. Script for Simmons broadcast, Sept. 25, 1934, box 3027, speech and article file, ERP, p. 5.

21. Script for Selby Shoe Co. broadcast, Mar. 22, 1935, RBP, pp. 1–2.

22. Ibid., p. 3.

23. Lash, *Eleanor and Franklin*, p. 551; Ruby A. Black, United Press dispatches from Washington, Jan. 16, 1935, and Jan. 11, 1936, RBP.

24. James R. Kearney, *Anna Eleanor Roosevelt* (Boston: Houghton Mifflin, 1968), pp. 224–25.

25. Black, UP dispatch from Washington, Jan. 11, 1936; Dorothy Dunbar Bromley, "The Future of Eleanor Roosevelt," *Harper's Magazine* 58 (Jan. 1940): 137; Lash, *Eleanor and Franklin*, pp. 551–52.

26. Lash, *Eleanor and Franklin*, p. 552; Kearney, *Anna Eleanor Roosevelt*, pp. 224–25, 227.

27. Beasley interview with Ducas, Sept. 11, 1982; Kearney, *Anna Eleanor Roosevelt*, pp. 116–17; Heywood Broun, "It Seems to Me," *Washington Daily News*, clipping, Oct. 27, 1934, RBP.

28. Charles Hurd, *When the New Deal Was Young and Gay* (New York: Hawthorn, 1965), p. 213; Mildred Gilman Wohlforth to Maurine Beasley, Mar. 23, 1983.

29. Beasley interview with Hornaday, May 21, 1979.

30. Ruby A. Black, typescript of article titled "Is Mrs. Roosevelt a Feminist?" [1935], RBP; Black, United Press dispatch from Washington, Mar. 3, 1935, RBP.

31. Eugene A. Kelly, "Distorting the News," *American Mercury* (Mar. 1935): 308–13; Ruby A. Black to Edward J. Ziegler, Dec. 12, 1935, RBP.

32. Bess Furman, proof of article titled "Life and Manners," distributed by AP feature service, May 1, 1935, enclosed with memo from Furman to "E.R.," series 100, box 1338, ERP.

33. Ware, *Holding Their Own*, pp. 23–24; William H. Chafe, *The American Woman*, p. 108.

34. Martha Strayer, "Mrs. Roosevelt Says 'Ladies' Are Plentiful in U.S. Today," *Washington Daily News*, Mar. 14, 1935, p. 16.

35. Roosevelt to Hickok, Oct. 3, 1934, and Oct. 10, 1934, box 2, LHP.

36. Roosevelt to Hickok, May 18, 1935, box 2, LHP.

37. Roosevelt to Hickok, Aug. 1, 1935, and Hickok to Roosevelt, Aug. 7, 1935, box 2, LHP.

38. As quoted in Lash, *Eleanor and Franklin*, p. 559.

39. Eleanor Roosevelt to George T. Bye, May 23, 1935, and June 30, 1935, folder of personal letters from Roosevelt to Bye, James Oliver Brown papers (hereafter referred to as JOBP), special manuscripts collections, Columbia University.

40. Roosevelt to Bye, July 16, 1935, JOBP.

41. Roosevelt to Hickok, Sept. 7, 1935, and Sept. 8, 1935, box 2, LHP.

42. Roosevelt to Hickok, Sept. 5, 1935, box 2, LHP; Roosevelt to Hickok, June 24, 1935, box 2, LHP.

43. Malvina Thompson Scheider to Jasper Spock, Aug. 9, 1935, folder of personal letters from Eleanor Roosevelt to George T. Bye; Roosevelt to Bye, Aug. 29, 1935, JOBP.

44. Roosevelt to Hickok, Apr. 6, 1935, box 2, LHP.

45. Typescript of "Can a Woman Be Elected President of the United States?" attached to letter from Roosevelt to Hickok, July 30, 1935, box 2, LHP, pp. 13–14.

46. Roosevelt to Hickok, May 2, 1935, box 2, LHP.

47. Roosevelt to Bye, Sept. 25, 1935, JOBP.

48. "Ban on War Asked by Mrs. Roosevelt," clipping, *New York Times*, Sept. 25, 1935, Mallon scrapbooks, box 155, BFP; Roosevelt to Bye, Sept. 25, 1935, JOBP.

49. Thompson to Bye, Dec. 11, 1935, box 313, JOBP.

50. Bye to Marjorie Knight, Nov. 25, 1935, and Nov. 29, 1935, box 313, JOBP.

51. Ware, *Holding Their Own*, pp. 16–17.

Chapter 7, "My Day"

1. Roosevelt, *This I Remember*, p. 177; Roosevelt to Bye, June 14, 1935, JOBP.

2. Kearney, *Anna Eleanor Roosevelt*, p. 132; Roosevelt to Hickok, Dec. 17, 1935, box 2, LHP.

3. Roosevelt, *This I Remember*, p. 177; Roosevelt to Hickok, Dec. 17, 1935, box 2, LHP; "My Day," sample column no. 1, box 3170, ERP.

4. Monte F. Bourjaily to Eleanor Roosevelt, Dec. 14, 1935, box 4873, ERP.

5. Ibid.

6. Bourjaily to Malvina Thompson Scheider, Dec. 14, 1935, box 4873, ERP.

7. Bourjaily to Roosevelt, Dec. 14, 1935, ERP.

8. Roosevelt to Hickok, Mar. 5, 1933, and typescript by Hickok of letter to her from Roosevelt, Nov. 14, 1933, box 1, LHP; Roosevelt to Hickok, July 31, 1935, box 2, LHP. (Hickok typed some of Roosevelt's letters preparing to edit them for publication, but the project did not materialize.)

9. Bourjaily to Roosevelt, Dec. 27, 1935, box 4873, ERP.

10. Susan Ware, *Beyond Suffrage: Women in the New Deal* (Cambridge: Harvard University Press, 1981), p. 74.

11. Caroline Bird, *The Invisible Scar* (New York: McKay, 1966), pp. 287–88.

12. "My Day," Dec. 30, 1935, box 3170, ERP.

13. Bourjaily to Roosevelt, Jan. 24, 1936, box 4873, ERP; "My Day," Jan. 15, 1936, box 3170, ERP.

14. Bourjaily to Roosevelt, June 3, 1936, and Dec. 27, 1935, box 4873, ERP.

15. Bourjaily to Roosevelt, June 3, 1936, ERP.

16. Bourjaily to Roosevelt, June 3, 1936, ERP; Mohr transcription of Strayer shorthand notes, Mrs. Roosevelt's press conference, Jan. 16, 1936, box 10, MSP.

17. Beasley interview with Miller, May 3, 1979; Ross, *Ladies of the Press*, p. 318.

18. Mohr transcription of Strayer shorthand notes, Jan. 16, 1936, MSP.

19. Memo for Mrs. [Malvina Thompson] Scheider from Stephen T. Early, Jan. 31, 1936, box 2997, ERP.

20. Ruby A. Black byline, "Dinner Table Talk in Washington," undated clipping, RBP.

21. Ibid.

22. Roosevelt to Hickok, Nov. 27, 1933, box 1, LHP.

23. Lash, *Eleanor and Franklin*, pp. 560–61; "My Day," Dec. 31, 1935, Jan. 8, 1936, and Jan. 1, 1936, box 3170, ERP.

24. Mildred Gilman Wohlforth to Maurine Beasley, Mar. 23, 1983.

25. Elliott Roosevelt and James Brough, *The Roosevelts*, p. 268; "My Day," Feb. 1, 1936, box 3170, ERP.

26. "My Day," Dec. 4, 1937, and Mar. 6, 1937, box 3171, ERP.

27. Mary J. Moffat and Charlotte Painter, eds., *Revelations: Diaries of Women* (New York: Random House, 1975), p. 5.

28. "My Day," Jan. 7, 1936, and Roosevelt to Hickok, Jan. 16, 1936, box 3, LHP.

29. Bourjaily to Roosevelt, Feb. 12, 1936, box 4873, ERP.

30. "My Day," Aug. 20, 1936, box 3170, ERP.

31. Edwin Emery and Michael Emery, *The Press and America* (Englewood Cliffs, N.J.: Prentice-Hall, 1978), p. 436.

32. Margaret Marshall, "Columnists on Parade," *Nation* 137 (Feb. 26, 1938): 14–15.

33. George Carlin to Eleanor Roosevelt, Apr. 10, 1937, memo to Carlin from JC (unidentified editor), Apr. 8, 1937, and Roosevelt to Carlin, Apr. 16, 1937, box 4873, ERP.

34. Roosevelt, *This I Remember*, p. 178; Lash, *Eleanor and Franklin*, p. 561; "My Day," Mar. 11, 1937, Sept. 3, 1937, and Dec. 30, 1937, box 3171, ERP.

35. Malvina Thompson Scheider to George T. Bye, Dec. 17, 1935, box 313, JOBP; Bourjaily to Scheider, Mar. 7, 1936, box 4873, ERP.

36. Roosevelt to Hickok, Jan. 24, 1936, and Mar. 13, 1936, box 3, LHP.

37. Lash, *Eleanor and Franklin*, p. 555; Furman typescript, notes of Mrs. Roosevelt's press conference, Feb. 27, 1939, box 78, BFP.

38. Roosevelt, *This I Remember*, p. 178; James MacGregor Burns, *Roosevelt: The Lion and the Fox* (New York: Harcourt, Brace and World, 1956), p. 317: White, *FDR and the Press*, p. 70.

39. Lash, *Eleanor and Franklin*, p. 588; Eleanor Roosevelt, *My Days* (New York: Dodge, 1938), pp. 79–80.

40. Ruby A. Black, *Eleanor Roosevelt* (New York: Duell, Sloan and Pearce, 1940), p. 115; "My Day," Aug. 8, 1936, box 3170, ERP; Kearney, *Anna Eleanor Roosevelt*, p. 133.

41. Faber, *The Life of Lorena Hickok*, pp. 207–8; "My Day," May 11, 1936, box 3170, ERP; Roosevelt to Hickok, May 7, 1936, box 3, LHP.

42. Roosevelt to Hickok, June 12, 1936, box 3, LHP.

43. Mohr transcription of Strayer shorthand notes, Sept. 27, 1939, box 10, MSP.

44. Bourjaily to Roosevelt, July 17, 1936, box 4873, ERP; "My Day," July 17, 1936, box 3170, ERP.

45. "My Day," Oct. 28, 1936, and Oct. 30, 1936, box 3170, ERP; Kearney, *Anna Eleanor Roosevelt*, pp. 133–34.

46. "My Day," July 17, 1936.

47. William Stott, *Documentary Expression and Thirties America* (New

York: Oxford, 1973), p. 4; "My Day," Jan. 30, 1937, and Feb. 6, 1937, box 3171, ERP; Kearney, *Anna Eleanor Roosevelt*, p. 134.

48. "My Day," Jan. 26, 1937, and Feb. 1, 1937, box 3171, ERP.

49. Dr. Edward Safford Jones, "U. of B. Psychologist Analyzes Mrs. Roosevelt from Her 'My Day' Series," clipping, *Buffalo* (N.Y.) *Times*, Mar. 29, 1936, RBP; Roosevelt to Hickok, July 27, 1936, and Hickok to Roosevelt, July 31, 1936, box 3, LHP.

50. Hickok to Roosevelt, July 31, 1936, Roosevelt to Hickok, Aug. 3, 1936, and Oct. 16, 1936, box 3, LHP.

51. "My Day," Sept. 23, 1936, box 3170, ERP.

52. Mohr transcription of Strayer shorthand notes, Sept. 27, 1939, box 10, MSP; Roosevelt, *This I Remember*, p. 178.

53. Lash, *Eleanor and Franklin*, p. 587.

54. Beasley interview with Ducas, Sept. 11, 1982; Beasley interview with Hornaday, May 21, 1979.

55. George Carlin to Malvina Thompson Scheider, Dec. 21, 1936, box 4873, ERP; "My Day," Feb. 27, 1937, box 3171, ERP; Asbell, ed., *Mother and Daughter*, p. 79.

56. Asbell, ed., *Mother and Daughter*, p. 79; Kearney, *Anna Eleanor Roosevelt*, p. 137; "My Day," Feb. 13, 1937, box 3171, ERP.

57. "My Day," Feb. 8, 1937, box 3171, ERP; Kearney, *Anna Eleanor Roosevelt*, p. 237.

58. "My Day," Feb. 8, 1937, ERP.

59. "My Day," Mar. 30, 1937, box 3171, and June 25, 1938, box 3172, ERP.

60. "My Day," Dec. 14, 1936, box 3170, ERP.

Chapter 8, "Successful Image Making"

1. "Mrs. Landon Will Be Seen, Not Heard, She Declares," clipping, *Washington Evening Star*, July 24, 1936; Laurence L. Winship to Ruby A. Black, July 3, 1936, and Black to Winship, July 6, 1936, RBP.

2. Eleanor Roosevelt appointment books, 1933 to 1945, boxes 3000–3001, ERP.

3. Lash, *Eleanor and Franklin*, p. 587.

4. Elaine M. Smith, "Mary McLeod Bethune and the National Youth Administration," in Mabel E. Deutrich and Virginia C. Purdy, eds., *Clio Was a Woman: Studies in the History of American Women* (Washington, D.C.: Howard University, 1980), pp. 152, 156.

5. Strayer typescript, report of Mrs. Roosevelt's press conference, May 15, 1936, box 2, MSP, p. 33.

6. Ibid., pp. 36–37; interview with Frances M. Lide by Maurine Beasley, Nov. 1, 1984, Alexandria, Va.

7. Roosevelt, *This I Remember*, p. 164; Kearney, *Anna Eleanor Roosevelt*, pp. 72–73.

8. Lash, *Eleanor and Franklin*, p. 585.

9. Black to Roosevelt, Oct. 27, 1936, and Roosevelt to Black [Oct. 1936], RBP.

10. George Wolfskill and John Hudson, *All But the People: Franklin D. Roosevelt and His Critics* (New York: Macmillan, 1969), p. 38.

11. Mary Hornaday, "Mrs. Roosevelt—A Campaign Issue" clipping, *Christian Science Monitor*, June 24, 1936, box 1, MHP; Perkins interview, vol. 2, part 2, p. 170.

12. Kathleen McLaughlin, "Mrs. Roosevelt Goes Her Way," *New York Times Magazine*, July 5, 1936, p. 7; Ruby A. Black, United Press dispatch from Washington, May 26, 1937, RBP; Roosevelt to Black, Feb. 12, 1937, Feb. 16, 1937, and May 3, 1937, RBP.

13. Lash, *Eleanor and Franklin*, p. 598.

14. Black to Roosevelt, Dec. 19, 1937, RBP.

15. McLaughlin, "Mrs. Roosevelt Goes Her Way," p. 7; Frances Perkins, *The Roosevelt I Knew* (New York: Viking, 1947), p. 70; Beasley interview with Miller, May 3, 1979; Mildred Gilman Wohlforth to Maurine Beasley, Mar. 23, 1983.

16. Beasley interview with Miller, May 3, 1979.

17. Furman diaries, entries for Mar. 25, 1935, May 27, 1935, and Feb. 10, 1936, box 1, BFP; McLaughlin, "Mrs. Roosevelt Goes Her Way," p. 15.

18. Furman diary, entries for Mar. 4, 1935 and Nov. 16, 1935, box 1, BFP.

19. Black, " 'New Deal' for News Women in Capital," p. 11; "First Lady: Press Conferences Help Pet Projects and F.D.R.," *Newsweek*, Apr. 17, 1937, p. 24; Black, "Dinner Table Talk in Washington."

20. Furman diaries, entries for Apr. 30, 1935, and Jan. 5, 1936, box 1, BFP.

21. Furman, *Washington By-Line*, p. 253; Black to Roosevelt, Oct. 27, 1935, RBP.

22. Lash, *Eleanor and Franklin*, p. 588.

23. Roosevelt to Hickok, Nov. 11, 1936, box 3, LHP; Lash, *Love, Eleanor*, p. 245.

24. "My Day," Jan. 23, 1937, and Jan. 18, 1937, box 3171, ERP; Roosevelt to Hickok, Jan. 21, 1937, box 4, LHP.

25. Roosevelt to Hickok, Aug. 9, 1936, box 3, LHP.

26. Faber, *The Life of Lorena Hickok*, p. 215; Roosevelt to Hickok, Sept. 10, 1936, box 3, LHP.

27. Hickok to Roosevelt, Nov. 13, 1936, and Dec. 7, 1936, box 3, LHP. Hickok's reports finally appeared in Lowitt and Beasley, eds., *One Third of a Nation*.

28. Hickok to Roosevelt, Jan. 2, 1937, and Jan. 18, 1937, box 4, LHP.

29. Radio script attached to letter from Emma Bugbee to Eleanor Roosevelt [Jan. 1937], series 100, box 1417, ERP.

30. "First Lady: Press Conferences Help Pet Projects and F.D.R.," p. 24; Jean Eliot, "Romeos, Juliets Steal Show at Gridiron Widows' Festival," clipping, *Washington Post*, Dec. 22, 1936, scrapbook, MHP; Furman diary, entry for Dec. 14, 1936, box 1, BFP.

31. Furman diary, entry for Mar. 5, 1935, box 1, BFP; Emma Bugbee, "'Mrs. Roosevelt' of Press Skit Stages White House Sit-Down," clipping, *New York Herald-Tribune*, Mar. 2, 1937, scrapbook, MHP.

32. Furman, *Washington By-Line*, pp. 260–62; Beasley interview with Ducas, Sept. 11, 1982.

33. "First Lady: Press Conferences Help Pet Projects and F.D.R.," p. 24.

34. Beasley interview with Hornaday, May 21, 1979; Rebecca West, "Finds Mrs. Roosevelt 'Timid,'" clipping, *Philadelphia Bulletin*, Feb. 2, 1937, box 1025, ERP.

35. West, "Finds Mrs. Roosevelt 'Timid'"; Mildred Gilman Wohlforth to Beasley, Mar. 23, 1983.

36. Roosevelt to Hickok, Oct. 16, 1936, box 3, LHP.

37. Transcript of interview with Bruce and Beatrice Gould, Oct. 7, 1975, vol. 3, oral history collection, Columbia University, p. 306.

38. Interview with Bruce and Beatrice Gould, p. 304.

39. Interview with Bruce and Beatrice Gould, p. 305; Faber, *The Life of Lorena Hickok*, p. 222; Katherine Woods, "Mrs. Roosevelt's Own Story," *New York Times Book Review*, Nov. 21, 1937, p. 1.

40. Mary Ross, "The Girl Who Married Franklin Roosevelt," *New York Herald-Tribune Books*, Nov. 21, 1937, p. 1; Woods, "Mrs. Roosevelt's Own Story," p. 30.

41. Kearney, *Anna Eleanor Roosevelt*, pp. 6, 11.

42. Roosevelt, *This Is My Story*, p. 264; Lash, *Eleanor and Franklin*, p. 568.

43. Eugene F. Saxton to George T. Bye, Jan. 6, 1938, box 313, JOBP.

44. Wolfskill and Hudson, *All But the People*, p. 40.

45. Drew Pearson and Robert S. Allen, "Washington Merry-Go-

Round," May 14, 1938, clipping, unidentified newspaper, box 27, May Craig papers (hereafter referred to as MCP), LC; Beasley interview with Hornaday, May 21, 1979.

46. Interview with Beth Campbell Short by Maurine Beasley, Nov. 1, 1984, Alexandria, Va.

47. "My Day," Mar. 5, 1937, ERP; Lash, *Eleanor and Franklin*, p. 552; script for Pond's program, Apr. 21, 1937, RBP.

48. Memo, Stephen Early to Eleanor Roosevelt, June 23, 1937, box 15, Stephen T. Early papers (hereafter referred to as SEP), FDRL.

49. "My Day," Jan. 15, 1937, box 3017, ERP; Ruby A. Black, United Press dispatch, Washington, Jan. 14, 1937, RBP; "My Day," Feb. 5, 1937, box 3017, ERP.

50. "My Day," Feb. 11, 1938, box 3072, ERP; Mohr transcription of Strayer shorthand notes, Mrs. Roosevelt's press conference, Feb. 14, 1938, box 10, MSP.

51. Mohr transcription of Strayer shorthand notes, Mrs. Roosevelt's press conference, Jan. 17, 1939, box 10, MSP.

52. Bess Furman and Lucile Furman, "Discover Your Home Town," *Democratic Digest* (Mar. 1940), pp. 18–19, 37; Furman diary, entries for July 16 and Oct. 8, 1937, and Jan. 13, 1938, box 1, BFP.

53. Furman and Furman, "Discover Your Home Town," p. 19; Furman diary, entry for Nov. 29, 1937, box 1, BFP.

54. Furman and Furman, "Discover Your Home Town," p. 19; Mohr transcription of Strayer shorthand notes, Mrs. Roosevelt's press conference, Jan. 29, 1940, box 10, MSP.

55. Mohr transcription of Strayer shorthand notes, Jan. 29, 1940, box 10, MSP.

56. Black, *Eleanor Roosevelt*, p. 302.

57. Frank C. Waldrop, "Are the Roosevelts for Suffrage or Not?" clipping, *Washington Times-Herald*, Feb. 10, 1940, RBP.

58. "First Lady Drops Own Rule, Gives Congress Advice," United Press dispatch from Washington, clipping, *New York Post*, May 26, 1937, RBP; " 'Woman-for-President' Boom Punctured by Mrs. Roosevelt," Associated Press dispatch from Washington, Nov. 13, 1937, clipping from unidentified newspapers, RBP.

59. "Women Up Chins at President's Job," Associated Press dispatch from New York, Nov. 26, 1937, clipping from unidentified newspaper, RBP; "More Women in Public Office Urged by First Lady," *Washington Herald*, Dec. 17, 1937, p. 6.

60. United Press dispatch from Washington, Feb. 24, 1938, RBP; Mohr

transcription of Strayer shorthand notes, Mrs. Roosevelt's press conference, Feb. 14, 1938, box 10, MSP.

61. Mohr transcription of Strayer shorthand notes, Dec. 27, 1938, box 10, MSP.

62. Ibid.

63. Roosevelt to Hickok, July 21, 1938, box 5, and Sept. 24, 1937, box 4, LHP.

64. Furman diary, entries for Jan. 31, 1939, Dec. 10, 1938, Mar. 22, 1939, and Oct. 10, 1938, box 1, BFP.

65. Black to Roosevelt, July 28, 1938, Roosevelt to Black, Aug. 4, 1938, and Black to Roosevelt, Oct. 4, 1938, RBP.

66. Roosevelt to Black, Aug. 11, 1938, Black to Victor I. Minahan and John Riedl, July 11, 1938, and Roosevelt to Black, Aug. 11, 1938, all from RBP.

67. Delbert Clark, *Washington Dateline* (New York: Stokes, 1941), pp. 217–18.

68. Beasley interview with Hornaday, May 21, 1979.

69. Furman typescript, Mrs. Roosevelt's press conference, Feb. 13, 1939, and May 4, 1939, box 78, BFP.

70. Interviews with Short and Lide, Nov. 1, 1984.

71. Furman typescript, Mrs. Roosevelt's press conference, Dec. 19, 1938, box 78, BFP.

72. Ibid.

73 Black, *Eleanor Roosevelt*, p. 124; George Gallup, "Mrs. Roosevelt More Popular than President, Survey Finds," *Washington Post*, Jan. 15, 1939, section 3, p. 1.

74. "Oracle," *Time*, Apr. 17, 1939, p. 22.

Chapter 9, "Self-Assertion through the Media"

1. "My Day," Feb. 27, 1939, box 3145, ERP; Furman typescript, notes on Mrs. Roosevelt's press conference, Feb. 27, 1939, BFP; "Mrs. Roosevelt Quits D.A.R. Protesting Anderson Ban," *Washington Post*, Feb. 28, 1939, p. 1.

2. Lash, *Franklin and Eleanor*, p. 686.

3. Furman, typescript, notes on Mrs. Roosevelt's press conference, Feb. 7, 1939, BFP; Hornaday, unpublished typescript on Mrs. Roosevelt's press conferences given to Beasley, May 21, 1979; "My Day," Apr. 6, 1938, box 3172, ERP.

4. Mohr transcription of Strayer shorthand notes, Sept. 27, 1939, box 10, MSP.

5. Ruby A. Black, United Press dispatch from Washington, Sept. 27, 1939, RBP; "Peace Crusade Begun Here by Mrs. Roosevelt," unidentified newspaper clipping, Apr. 7, 1937, RBP; "My Day," Nov. 12, 1940, box 3146, ERP.

6. Beasley interview with Hornaday, May 21, 1979; Winifred Mallon, "Map Party Backing for Doris Stevens," *New York Times*, Feb. 17, 1939, p. 3.

7. Furman typescript, notes on Mrs. Roosevelt's press conferences, Feb. 7, 1939, box 78, BFP; Susan D. Becker, *The Origins of the Equal Rights Amendment: American Feminism Between the Wars* (Westport, Conn.: Greenwood, 1981), pp. 184–85.

8. Albert L. Warner, "Roosevelt Ousts Doris Stevens and Stirs a Women's Tempest," clipping, unidentified newspaper, Feb. 16, 1939, Mallon scrapbooks, box 156, BFP; Furman typescript, notes on Mrs. Roosevelt's press conference, Feb. 27, 1939, box 78, BFP.

9. Furman typescript, notes on Mrs. Roosevelt's press conference, Feb. 27, 1939, BFP.

10. Ibid.

11. Ibid.

12. Furman typescript, notes on Mrs. Roosevelt's press conference, Jan. 17, 1939, box 78, BFP.

13. "First Lady: Press Conferences Help Pet Projects and F.D.R.," p. 24; Strayer typescript, box 2, MSP, pp. 138–39.

14. Roosevelt, *This I Remember*, pp. 6–7.

15. Ibid., pp. 183–84; Furman typescript, notes on Mrs. Roosevelt's press conference, May 22, 1939, box 78, BFP.

16. Kearney, *Anna Eleanor Roosevelt*, pp. 166–67; Mohr transcription of Strayer shorthand notes, May 29, 1939, box 10, MSP; S. J. Woolf, "Energy," *New York Times Magazine*, May 28, 1939, p. 10. For a full discussion of Mrs. Roosevelt's role in Arthurdale, see Tamara K. Hareven, *Eleanor Roosevelt: An American Conscience* (Chicago: Quadrangle, 1968), pp. 102–11.

17. Furman typescript, notes on Mrs. Roosevelt's press conference, May 4, 1939, box 78, BFP.

18. Ibid.

19. Furman, *Washington By-Line*, p. 270.

20. Furman, news story written for Furman Features, June 9, 1939, box 78, BFP.

21. Carlin to Roosevelt, May 23, 1939, box 4873, ERP.

22. Furman typescript, notes of Mrs. Roosevelt's press conference, May 22, 1939, box 78, BFP.

23. "My Day," June 12, 1939, and June 14, 1939, box 3173, ERP.

24. "My Day," May 26, 1939, box 3173, ERP.

25. Marlen E. Pew, Jr., "Mrs. FDR Tells of Writing While Hostess to Royalty," proof sheet from *Editor and Publisher*, June 17, 1939, box 4873, ERP.

26. Arthur Krock, *New York Times*, Aug. 10, 1939, p. 18; "Excerpts Press Conference 570," in *The Public Papers and Addresses of Franklin D. Roosevelt*, vol. 8 (New York: Macmillan, 1949), pp. 432–33; "My Day," Aug. 8, 1939, box 3173, ERP. See also "'My Day' Dominant Influence," *Saturday Evening Post*, Sept. 9, 1939, p. 24.

27. Lash, *Love, Eleanor*, p. 283; John B. Oakes, "Mrs. Roosevelt Hears Witness Sing Dies Song," clipping, *Washington Post*, Dec. 2, 1939; Roosevelt, *This I Remember*, p. 202; "My Day," Dec. 2, 1939, box 3173, ERP.

28. "The *Nation's* Honor Roll for 1939," advance proof for issue of *Nation*, Jan. 6, 1940, RBP; *New York World-Telegram*, Dec. 2, 1939, as quoted in Kearney, *Anna Eleanor Roosevelt*, p. 35.

29. Carlin to Roosevelt, Aug. 8, 1939, box 4873, ERP; "My Day," Aug. 8, 1939, box 3173, ERP.

30. Bromley, "The Future of Eleanor Roosevelt," p. 137; Ruby A. Black, United Press dispatch from Washington, Dec. 19, 1939, RBP.

31. Martha Strayer, "The First Lady Discusses Peace and War and Bustles," *Washington Daily News*, Sept. 29, 1939, p. 8. See also Mohr transcription of Strayer shorthand notes, Mrs. Roosevelt's press conference, Sept. 27, 1939, box 10, MSP.

32. Strayer, "The First Lady Discusses Peace and War and Bustles," p. 8.

33. Dorothy Thompson, "On the Record," *New York Herald-Tribune*, Feb. 16, 1940, as quoted in Kearney, *Anna Eleanor Roosevelt*, pp. 51–52.

34. "My Day," Feb. 12, Feb. 13, and Feb. 15, 1940, box 3174, ERP; Mohr transcription of Strayer shorthand notes, Mrs. Roosevelt's press conference, Feb. 12, 1940, box 10, MSP; Kearney, *Anna Eleanor Roosevelt*, p. 42.

35. Eleanor Roosevelt, "Keepers of Democracy," *Virginia Quarterly Review* 15 (Winter 1939): 2–3.

36. *Time*, Apr. 15, 1940, p. 17; Geneva Kretsinger, "An Analytical Study of Selected Radio Speeches of Eleanor Roosevelt" (M.A. thesis, University of Oklahoma, 1941), pp. 157–79, as cited in Helen Jane Wamboldt, "A Descriptive and Analytical Study of the Speaking Career of Anna Eleanor Roosevelt" (Ph.D. diss., University of Southern California, 1952), p. 178.

37. Black, *Eleanor Roosevelt*, pp. 117–19; *Newsweek*, July 29, 1940, p. 4.

38. Black, *Eleanor Roosevelt*, p. 119.

39. See Eleanor Roosevelt, "Talk to Brides," *Good Housekeeping* 109

(Dec. 1939): 27; "Women in Politics," *Good Housekeeping* (Jan., Mar., and Apr. 1940): 18–19, 45, and 45 respectively; "Good Manners," *Ladies' Home Journal* (June 1939): 21.

40. Eleanor Roosevelt, "Cherry Blossom Time in Washington," *Reader's Digest* 32 (Apr. 1938): 57; Eleanor Roosevelt, "Why I Am Against the People's Vote on War," *Liberty* 16 (Apr. 8, 1939): 7–8.

41. George T. Bye to E. T. Meredith, Sept. 26, 1939, box 313, JOBP.

42. See file of financial statements, United Features Syndicate to Eleanor Roosevelt, box 4873, ERP; Review of *My Days*, *New York Times Book Review*, Aug. 21, 1938, as reprinted by United Features Syndicate, box 4873, ERP; Bromley, "The Future of Eleanor Roosevelt," p. 135.

43. "My Day," Sept. 8, 1939, box 3145; Carlin to Roosevelt, Sept. 8, 1939, box 4873; "My Day," Sept. 13, 1939, box 3145; all from ERP.

44. Furman diary, entry for Feb. 15, 1938, box 1, BFP; Black to Roosevelt, Feb. 16, 1938, RBP.

45. "And Mrs. F. D. R. Said—," *The Guild Reporter*, Jan. 15, 1937, p. 2; Black, *Eleanor Roosevelt*, p. 168; Black to Roosevelt, Dec. 27, 1939, RBP; Westbrook Pegler, "Fair Enough," *New York World-Telegram*, Mar. 17, 1938, as cited in Lash, *Eleanor and Franklin*, p. 564; Pegler, "Fair Enough," *New York World-Telegram*, Aug. 6, 1940, as quoted in *Editor and Publisher*, Aug. 10, 1940, p. 5.

46. Westbrook Pegler, "Fair Enough," clipping, *Washington Post*, Aug. 10, 1940, RBP; "My Day," Aug. 9, 1940, and Sept. 16, 1940, box 3174, ERP; United Press dispatch from Washington, Dec. 30, 1940, RBP.

47. Carlin to Roosevelt, Aug. 17, 1940, as quoted in Lash, *Eleanor and Franklin*, p. 565.

48. Lash, *Eleanor and Franklin*, p. 805.

49. Beasley interview with Hornaday, May 21, 1979.

50. Ibid.

51. Clipping, *Herald and Review* (Decatur, Ill.), Mar. 17, 1940, Malvina Thompson papers (hereafter referred to as MTP), in the possession of her niece, Eleanor Zartman, Bethesda, Md.

52. "My Day," May 17, 1940, box 3146, ERP; Mohr transcription of Strayer shorthand notes, May 13, 1941, box 10, MSP; "My Day," Nov. 2, 1940, and Nov. 12, 1940, box 3146, ERP.

53. Questions submitted to Mrs. Roosevelt attached to Black to Roosevelt, Mar. 15, 1940, and replies, Roosevelt and Thompson to Black [Apr., 1940]; Thompson to Black, July 2, 1940, and Black to Thompson, July 5, 1940; all from RBP.

54. Ruby Black to Rose Feld, Oct. 19, 1940, RBP; Beasley interview

with Hornaday, May 21, 1979; Lash, *Love, Eleanor*, p. 310; "My Day," Oct. 24, 1940, box 3146, ERP.

55. Hickok to Roosevelt, Nov. 11, 1940, box 8, LHP.

56. "Divorce Given to Secretary of First Lady," clipping, *Washington Herald*, Sept. 7, 1938, MTP.

57. Emma Bugbee, "Keeping Up with Mrs. Roosevelt a Joy, Not a Job, Secretary Says," clipping, *New York Herald-Tribune*, Dec. 18, 1939; Vesta Kelling, "She Goes Everywhere with Mrs. Roosevelt," clipping, *St. Louis Post-Dispatch*, May 25, 1941, MTP.

58. Ruby Black to Fred [Essary], Aug. 27, 1940, RBP.

59. Roosevelt to Hickok, Nov. 15, 1940, box 8, LHP; Eleanor Roosevelt, "Men Have to Be Humored," *Woman's Day* 3 (Aug. 1940): 12–13, 58.

60. "Luckiest Wives in U.S.: Married 'Best' Husbands," *Washington Daily News*, Feb. 27, 1940, p. 9.

61. Boorstin, *The Image*, p. 57.

Chapter 10, "The Press as Adversary"

1. Beasley interview with Hornaday, May 21, 1979; Ruby Black, United Press dispatch from Washington, Feb. 17, 1941, RBP; Martha Strayer, "Going to War, Draftees Told, So They'll Work," clipping, *Washington Daily News*, Feb. 25, 1941, MSP; Ruby Black, United Press dispatch from Washington, Apr. 7, 1941, RBP.

2. Mohr transcription of Strayer shorthand notes, Mrs. Roosevelt's press conference, Apr. 1, 1941, box 10, MSP.

3. Eleanor Roosevelt, "Defense and Girls," *Ladies' Home Journal* 58 (May 1941): 25, 54; Interview with Bruce and Beatrice Gould, Oct. 7, 1975, vol. 4, p. 405; "Mrs. Roosevelt's Plan," clipping, *Time*, June 23, 1941, RBP.

4. Mohr transcription of Strayer shorthand notes, Mrs. Roosevelt's press conference, May 29, 1941, box 10, MSP; Susan M. Hartmann, "Women in the Military," in Deutrich and Purdy, eds., *Clio Was a Woman*, pp. 196–98.

5. Lash, *Eleanor and Franklin*, p. 824; Ruby Black, United Press dispatch from Washington, Aug. 25, 1941, RBP; Mohr transcription of Strayer shorthand notes, Aug. 25, 1941, and Sept. 3, 1941, box 10, MSP.

6. Lash, *Eleanor and Franklin*, p. 829.

7. Ruby Black, United Press dispatch from Washington, overnight copy for Sept. 29, 1941, RBP.

8. "My Day," Sept. 7, 1941, box 3175, ERP.

9. Ruby Black, United Press dispatch from Washington, Sept. 29,

1941; clipping, unidentified Washington newspaper, "First Lady is Late for New Job," Sept. 30, 1941; Black, United Press dispatch from Washington, Sept. 15, 1941; all from RBP.

10. Black, United Press dispatch, Sept. 15, 1941, RBP.

11. John O'Donnell and Doris Fleeson, "Capitol Stuff," clipping, *Washington Times-Herald*, May 19, 1941; Ruby Black to Harry Sharpe, memo, May 13, 1941, RBP.

12. List of newspaperwomen eligible to attend Mrs. Roosevelt's press conferences as of June 18, 1941, box 6, Mrs. Roosevelt's Press Conference Association papers (hereafter referred to as PCAP), FDRL.

13. Malvina Thompson to Stephen T. Early, memo, Nov. 1935, as cited in Betty H. Winfield, "Mrs. Roosevelt's Press Conference Association," p. 63; Early to Eleanor Roosevelt, Feb. 10, 1941, box 15, SEP.

14. Early to Thompson, Nov. 17, 1941, box 24, SEP; Frank Freidel, foreword, in Beasley, ed., *The White House Press Conferences of Eleanor Roosevelt*, p. ix.

15. Mohr transcription of Strayer shorthand notes, May 29, 1941, box 10, MSP; Minutes, organizing meeting, Mrs. Roosevelt's Press Conference Association, Dec. 22, 1941, box 6, PCAP.

16. Minutes, organizing meeting, Mrs. Roosevelt's Press Conference Association, Dec. 22, 1941, PCAP.

17. Walter Trohan, *Political Animals: Memoirs of a Sentimental Cynic* (Garden City, N.J.; Doubleday, 1975), p. 101.

18. Minutes of organizing meeting for Mrs. Roosevelt's Press Conference Association, Dec. 22, 1941, PCAP.

19. Hornaday, unpublished typescript on Mrs. Roosevelt's press conferences, 1974, given to Beasley, May 21, 1979.

20. Strayer typescript of shorthand notes for Jan. 5, 1942, box 2, MSP, p. 209.

21. Ibid.

22. Ibid.; Lash, *Eleanor and Franklin*, pp. 832–34.

23. Strayer typescript of shorthand notes for Jan. 5, 1942, box 2, MSP, p. 215; "My Day," Dec. 24, 1941, box 3175, ERP.

24. Walter Lippmann, clipping, *New York Herald-Tribune*, Dec. 16, 1941, and Frank R. Kent, clipping, "The Great Game of Politics," *Washington Star*, Dec. 22, 1941, scrapbook "Amidst Crowded Days," box 3020, ERP.

25. Mohr transcription of Strayer shorthand notes, Jan. 12, 1942, MSP.

26. Ibid.

27. Lash, *Eleanor and Franklin*, p. 839; "My Day," Dec. 16, 1941, box 3175, ERP.

28. Mohr transcription of Strayer shorthand notes, Feb. 9, 1942, box 10, MSP.

29. Lash, *Eleanor and Franklin*, p. 840; "Mrs. Roosevelt Should Resign," clipping, *New York Herald-Tribune*, Feb. 8, 1942, scrapbook "Amidst Crowded Days," box 3020, ERP; *Time*, Feb. 16, 1942, p. 49.

30. Roosevelt, *This I Remember*, p. 232.

31. Mohr transcription of Strayer shorthand notes, Feb. 9, 1942, box 10, MSP.

32. Minutes of temporary standing committee of Mrs. Roosevelt's Press Conference Association, Jan. 31, 1942, box 6, PCAP.

33. Eleanor Roosevelt to Mary Hornaday, Feb. 19, 1942, box 6, PCAP; members of Mrs. Roosevelt's Press Conference Association listed as of 1942, box 2997, ERP.

34. Minutes of temporary standing committee of Mrs. Roosevelt's Press Conference Association, Jan. 31, 1942, PCAP; Mary Hornaday to Malvina Thompson, Feb. 20, 1942, box 33, SEP.

35. Strayer typescript, undated comments on Mrs. Roosevelt's press conferences, box 2, MSP, pp. 7–8.

36. Ibid., p. 221.

37. *Time*, Mar. 2, 1942, p. 51; "Mrs. Roosevelt Resigns," clipping, editorial, *New York Times*, Feb. 21, 1942, scrapbook "Amidst Crowded Days," box 3020, ERP.

38. "My Day," Feb. 23, 1942, box 3176, ERP.

39. Mohr transcription of Strayer shorthand notes, Apr. 25, 1942, box 10, MSP.

40. "Mrs. Roosevelt Expects No Egg-Rolling Fete," clipping, *New York Herald-Tribune*, Mar. 8, 1942, scrapbook "Amidst Crowded Days," box 3021, ERP.

41. Mary Hornaday to Eleanor Roosevelt, May 1, 1942, box 6, PCAP; Beasley interview with Hornaday, May 21, 1979.

42. Mohr transcription of Strayer shorthand notes, May 5, 1942, box 10, MSP; memo to members of Mrs. Roosevelt's Press Conference Association from Mary Hornaday, May 11, 1942, box 6, PCAP; Minutes of Mrs. Roosevelt's Press Conference Association, Feb. 8, 1943, box 6, PCAP; Rules, Mrs. Roosevelt's Press Conference Association, Dec. 1944, box 5, PCAP.

43. Hornaday to Roosevelt, Nov. 28, 1942, and minutes of meeting with Eleanor Roosevelt, Dec. 7, 1942, box 6, PCAP.

44. Virginia Pasley, "Mrs. Roosevelt Lists Herself as 'Housewife,'" clipping, *Washington Times-Herald*, Mar. 17, 1942, scrapbook "Amidst Crowded Days," box 3021, ERP; Mohr transcription of Strayer shorthand

notes, Apr. 25, 1942, box 10, MSP; "Mrs. Roosevelt Decides Slacks Are Not for Her," clipping, *New York Herald-Tribune*, May 15, 1942, scrapbook "Amidst Crowded Days," box 3021, ERP.

45. Mohr transcription of Strayer shorthand notes, June 8, 1942, box 2, MSP; Arthur Krock, "Mrs. Roosevelt's Conversion to Joint Tax Returns," clipping, *New York Times*, June 9, 1942, scrapbook "Amidst Crowded Days," box 3021, ERP.

46. *Time*, Oct. 13, 1941, p. 77.

47. Script of Mrs. Roosevelt's Pan-American Coffee Bureau program, Feb. 22, 1942, RBP.

48. Lash, *Eleanor and Franklin*, p. 564; Robert Bendiner, *Just Around the Corner: A Highly Selective History of the Thirties* (New York: Harper and Row, 1967), p. 232; Westbrook Pegler, "Fair Enough," clipping, *Washington Post*, July 14, 1942, RBP.

49. Script of Mrs. Roosevelt's Pan-American Coffee Bureau program, Jan. 18, 1942, RBP; Raymond Clapper, "Mrs. Roosevelt Sees No Evil," clipping, *Liberty*, Apr. 4, 1942, scrapbook "Amidst Crowded Days," box 3021, ERP.

50. Lash, *Eleanor and Franklin*, p. 847.

Chapter 11, "Promoting the War Effort"

1. Roosevelt, *This I Remember*, pp. 260–61.

2. Lash, *Eleanor and Franklin*, p. 850.

3. Furman typescript, notes on Mrs. Roosevelt's press conference, Nov. 18, 1942, box 78, BFP.

4. Earl J. Johnson to Ruby A. Black, Mar. 20, 1942, RBP; Black to Rosamond Cole, Mar. 22, 1942, personal papers of Cole, Washington, D.C.

5. Black to Cole, Mar. 22, 1942, Cole papers; Furman diary, entry for Oct. 10, 1939, box 2, BFP.

6. Minutes of Mrs. Roosevelt's Press Conference Association meeting, Dec. 19, 1942, box 6, PCAP.

7. Ann Cottrell Free, "Eleanor Roosevelt and the Female White House Press Corps," *Modern Maturity*, Oct.–Nov. 1984, pp. 98–99; Interview with Ann Cottrell Free by Maurine Beasley, May 3, 1979, Bethesda, Md. See also "Ladies of Washington's Working Press: They Get Their Copy— and Their Rights," *Newsweek*, Mar. 1, 1943, p. 64.

8. Beasley interview with Free.

9. Ann Cottrell, "Mrs. Roosevelt Praises Spirit of War-Wounded"

and "Mrs. Roosevelt Assails Stories about Waacs," clippings, *New York Herald-Tribune*, Apr. 12, 1943, and June 8, 1943, respectively, personal papers of Ann Cottrell Free, Bethesda, Md.

10. Free, "Eleanor Roosevelt and the Female White House Press Corps," p. 98.

11. Interview with Esther Van Wagoner Tufty by Maurine Beasley, July 27, 1976, Washington, D.C.

12. Furman to Roosevelt, Nov. 17, 1942, box 33, BFP; Lee B. Wood to George Carlin, Nov. 26, 1943, enclosed in Carlin to Roosevelt, Nov. 27, 1943, box 4873, ERP.

13. "My Day," Sept. 9, 1944, and Feb. 23, 1945, boxes 3177 and 3178 respectively, ERP.

14. Transcript of interview with Jonathan Daniels, Mar. 22, 1972, oral history collection, Columbia University, pp. 133–34; Eleanor Roosevelt, "If I Were a Negro," *Negro Digest*, Oct. 1943, p. 8; "Mrs. F. D. R. Blasts Jim Crow," banner headline, *People's Voice*, Aug. 21, 1943, p. 1.

15. Catherine D. Stallworth to Eleanor Roosevelt, Aug. 18, 1944, and Roosevelt to Stallworth, Aug. 26, 1944, series 100, ERP; "Is It a Grievous Mistake That We Are Americans?" and "Mrs. F. D. R.'s Letter Called Bid for Southern Vote," *Baltimore Afro-American*, Sept. 16, 1944, p. 4.

16. "Eleanor Club Quest Fails," clipping from *Norfolk (Va.) Ledger*, Sept. 22, 1942, FBI file on Eleanor Roosevelt, obtained by Maurine Beasley on June 29, 1983, through Freedom of Information Act, Washington, D.C.; "Colored Guests Rumor of Value to Nazis, Mrs. Roosevelt Says," clipping, *Washington Star*, Dec. 17, 1942, RBP.

17. Transcript of Mrs. Roosevelt's press conference, Feb. 24, 1943, box 2997, ERP.

18. Beasley interview with Tufty, July 27, 1976.

19. "My Day," Aug. 14, 1943, box 3148, ERP.

20. Bert Andrews to Eleanor Roosevelt, telegram, Sept. 25, 1943, box 2997, ERP; James T. Howard, "Males Squirm at First Lady's Parley," clipping, *PM*, Sept. 28, 1943, RBP.

21. Helen Essary, "Dear Washington," clipping, *Washington Times-Herald*, Sept. 28, 1943, RBP.

22. Helen Essary, "Dear Washington," clipping, *Washington Times-Herald*, Apr. 11, 1943, RBP. See also "My Day," Apr. 8, 1943, box 3148, ERP.

23. *Time*, May 22, 1944, p. 43; Eleanor Roosevelt, "How to Take Criticism," *Ladies' Home Journal* 61 (Nov. 1944): 155.

24. As cited in Ted Morgan, *FDR: A Biography* (New York: Simon and Schuster, 1985), pp. 676–77; see also Catherine L. Covert, "Journalism

History and Women's Experience: A Problem in Conceptual Change," *Journalism History* 8 (Spring 1981): 3–4.

25. Eleanor Roosevelt, "American Women in the War," in *Reader's Digest* 44 (Jan. 1944): 44, and "Women at the Peace Conference," *Reader's Digest* (Apr. 1944): 48.

26. Eulalie McDowell, "When Stranger Places Are Discovered, Mrs. Roosevelt Will Show up in Them," clipping, *Washington Daily News* Jan. 19, 1945; "President Looks Much Better, Mrs. Roosevelt Tells Press," clipping, *Washington Times-Herald*, May 2, 1944, RBP; list of those admitted to Mrs. Roosevelt's press conferences in 1945, box 5, PCAP.

27. *New York Times* news copy marked "First Lady," Oct. 11, 1944, box 51, BFP.

28. Ruth Montgomery, *Hail to the Chief* (New York: Coward McCann, 1970), pp. 16–17.

29. *New York Times* news copy marked "First Lady," Oct. 3, 1944, box 51, BFP; "Mrs. Dewey's Press Conference," clipping, *Washington Times-Herald*, July 1, 1944, RBP.

30. Supplemental report on results of meeting of Mrs. Roosevelt's Press Conference Association, Feb. 13, 1945, box 5, PCAP; United Press, "F. D. and His Lady Voice Complaints about Press," clipping, *Washington Daily News*, June 30, 1943, RBP.

31. Furman diary, entry for Jan. 30, 1945, box 2, BFP; copy of *New York Times* news story marked "First Lady," Jan. 30, 1945, box 51, BFP.

32. Supplemental report on results of meeting of Mrs. Roosevelt's Press Conference Association, Feb. 13, 1945, PCAP.

33. Ibid.; "Children's Librarians' Pay Scale Is Too Low, Mrs. Roosevelt's Press Conference Is Told," clipping, *New York Times*, Dec. 4, 1944, scrapbook, box 149, BFP.

34. Supplemental report on results of meeting of Mrs. Roosevelt's Press Conference Association, Feb. 13, 1945, PCAP.

35. Ruth Montgomery to members of Mrs. Roosevelt's Press Conference Association, Feb. 28, 1945, box 5, PCAP.

36. Drew Pearson, "Washington Merry-Go-Round," clipping, *Washington Post*, Apr. 8, 1945, RBP; Roosevelt, *This I Remember*, p. 103; Montgomery to Roosevelt, Apr. 10, 1945, box 6, PCAP.

37. Ruby Black, notes on Mrs. Roosevelt's press conference, Apr. 12, 1945, RBP; Marion Wade Doyle, "Reporters' Right to Ask Any Question Upheld by Mrs. Roosevelt," clipping, *Washington Star*, Apr. 12, 1945.

38. *New York Times* news copy marked "First Lady," Apr. 12, 1945, box 51, BFP.

39. Martha Strayer, "Last Press Conference of Eleanor Roosevelt," clipping [Apr. 20, 1945], *Guild Reporter* [May 1945] scrapbook, box 149, BFP; "My Day," Apr. 18, 1945, box 78, ERP.

Chapter 12, "International Fame"

1. Eleanor Roosevelt to Harold Ickes, May 26, 1945, as quoted in Joseph P. Lash, *Eleanor: The Years Alone* (New York: Signet, 1973), p. 18.

2. *Nation*, Dec. 29, 1945, p. 772; "My Day," Dec. 21, 1945, box 3149, ERP.

3. "My Day," Jan. 3 and Jan. 5, 1946, box 3149, ERP.

4. Ibid., Jan. 12, Jan. 25, Jan. 30, Feb. 8, and Feb. 13, 1946.

5. Eleanor Roosevelt, *On My Own* (New York: Harper, 1945), pp. 42–44; *New York Times*, Feb. 9, 1946, p. 1; Roosevelt to Lash, Feb. 13, 1946, cited in Lash, *Eleanor: The Years Alone*, p. 45.

6. Susanna S. Dado, "Eleanor Roosevelt as a Columnist" (M.A. thesis, California State University, Northridge, 1977), p. 149.

7. Elizabeth Janeway, "First Lady of the U.N.," *New York Times Magazine*, Oct. 22, 1950, p. 12.

8. E. T. Kahn, Jr., "Profiles: The Years Alone — Part I," *New Yorker*, June 12, 1948, p. 33.

9. S. J. Woolf, "The New Chapter in Mrs. Roosevelt's Life," *New York Times Magazine*, Dec. 15, 1946, p. 15; Memorandum for President Truman from Eleanor Roosevelt as quoted in Jason Berger, *A New Deal for the World: Eleanor Roosevelt and American Foreign Policy* (New York: Brooklyn College Press, 1981), p. 55.

10. Lash, *Eleanor: The Years Alone*, p. 17; "My Day," Jan. 25, 1947, and June 22, 1945, box 3149, ERP.

11. See Ted Gup, "Eleanor and Edgar: 'Hoot Owl' vs. the 'Gestapo,' " *Outlook, Washington Post*, June 6, 1982, pp. 1–2. The article is based on the FBI file on Eleanor Roosevelt.

12. Eleanor Roosevelt to J. Edgar Hoover, Jan. 26, 1941, Hoover to Roosevelt, Jan. 24 and Jan. 27, 1941, and Hoover to Harry L. Hopkins, Jan. 24, 1944, FBI file on Eleanor Roosevelt.

13. Notation by J. Edgar Hoover beside clipping "Mrs. R. Lives and Learns," *Washington Times-Herald*, Jan. 16, 1948, FBI file on Eleanor Roosevelt.

14. Notation by Hoover beside clipping of "My Day," *Washington Daily News*, Aug. 19, 1948, and clipping of "My Day," Apr. 4, 1950, FBI file on Eleanor Roosevelt.

15. Notation by Hoover beside clipping of "My Day," *Washington Daily News*, July 14, 1950, FBI file on Eleanor Roosevelt.

16. Eleanor Roosevelt, "If You Ask Me," clipping, *McCall's* magazine, July 1953, FBI file on Eleanor Roosevelt.

17. Transcript of interview with Bruce and Beatrice Gould, May 12, 1976, vol. 5, oral history collection, Columbia University, pp. 591–92; Eleanor Roosevelt to Martha Strayer, June 1949, as quoted in Lash, *Eleanor: The Years Alone*, p. 182.

18. Bruce and Beatrice Gould interview, May 12, 1976, pp. 592–93; Lash, *Eleanor: The Years Aone*, p. 183.

19. Karl Schriftgiesser, "The Literary Summing Up (1949)," *Saturday Review of Literature*, Nov. 5, 1949, p. 1; Arthur Schlesinger, Jr., "A First Lady's Memories," *Saturday Review of Literature*, Nov. 5, 1949, p. 13; Elizabeth Janeway in the *New York Times Book Review*, Nov. 6, 1949, as quoted in Lash, *Eleanor: The Years Alone*, p. 184.

20. Eleanor Roosevelt to Maude and David Gray, undated, as quoted in Lash, *Eleanor: The Years Alone*, p. 183; Eleanor Roosevelt to Anna Dall Boettiger, Sept. 13, 1945, as quoted in Asbell, ed., *Mother and Daughter*, p. 200; Eleanor Roosevelt to John Gunther, June 2, 1950, as quoted in Lash, *Eleanor: The Years Alone*, p. 150.

21. Lash, *Eleanor: The Years Alone*, p. 49; *Time*, Apr. 7, 1952, p. 43.

22. John Reddy to Helen Jane Wamboldt, Nov. 13, 1951, as quoted in Wamboldt, "Speaking Career of Anna Eleanor Roosevelt," pp. 285–86.

23. Review from *Hollywood Reporter* as quoted in Reddy to Wamboldt, Nov. 13, 1951; *Time*, Nov. 22, 1948, p. 46.

24. Philip Hamburger, "Mrs. Roosevelt's Tea Party," *New Yorker*, Feb. 25, 1950, pp. 88–89.

25. *Newsweek*, Feb. 27, 1950, p. 48; Lash, *Eleanor: The Years Alone*, p. 179; Memorandum, L. B. Nichols to Mr. Tolson, Nov. 21, 1950, FBI file on Eleanor Roosevelt.

26. Transcript of interview with Henry Morgenthau III by Emily Williams, Aug. 30, 1978, Eleanor Roosevelt oral history collection, FDRL, p. 3.

27. Ibid., p. 4; Lash, *Eleanor: The Years Alone*, p. 180.

28. News article, *Los Angeles Daily News*, May 7, 1951, as cited in Wamboldt, "Speaking Career of Anna Eleanor Roosevelt," p. 296.

29. Telegram, J. Edgar Hoover to Elizabeth Anne Tucker, Jan. 18, 1951; L. B. Nichols to Mr. Tolson, Apr. 4, 1951; transcript of Eleanor Roosevelt's "Question and Answer" program, WNBC, New York, Apr. 4, 1951, p. 3; all in FBI file on Eleanor Roosevelt.

30. J. Edgar Hoover to Eleanor Roosevelt, Apr. 9, 1951, and Roosevelt

to Hoover, Apr. 12, 1951; Hoover to Roosevelt, Apr. 17, 1951, and Roosevelt to Hoover, May 23, 1951; Hoover notation beside clipping, "Mrs. Roosevelt Says McCarthy Is Menace," *New York Times*, Sept. 21, 1951; all in FBI file on Eleanor Roosevelt.

31. Interview with Elliott Roosevelt by Helen Jane Wamboldt, Oct. 19, 1951, as cited in Wamboldt, "Speaking Career of Anna Eleanor Roosevelt," p. 294; Richard N. Gardner, " 'First Lady' of the Voice of America," *New York Times Magazine*, Feb. 3, 1952, p. 3.

32. *Time*, Dec. 16, 1946, p. 25; "My Day," May 27, 1948, box 3150, ERP.

33. Francis Cardinal Spellman to Eleanor Roosevelt, July 21, 1949, in the *New York Times*, July 23, 1949, p. 24; "My Day," July 23, 1949, box 3151, ERP.

34. Lash, *Eleanor: The Years Alone*, p. 130; Eleanor Roosevelt to Betty Hight, Aug. 15, 1949, as quoted in Lash, *Eleanor: The Years Alone*, p. 151; Spellman to Roosevelt, July 21, 1949.

35. Eleanor Roosevelt to Francis Cardinal Spellman, July 23, 1949, in the *New York Times*, July 28, 1949, pp. 1, 16; Doris Fleeson to Eleanor Roosevelt, Aug. 7, 1949, and May Craig to Eleanor Roosevelt, July 26, 1949, as quoted in Lash, *Eleanor: The Years Alone*, p. 154; *Newsweek*, Aug. 22, 1949, p. 21.

36. Lash, *Eleanor: The Years Alone*, p. 156; "My Day," Aug. 6, 1949, box 3151, ERP.

37. "My Day," Aug. 24, 1949, box 3151, ERP.

38. Eleanor Roosevelt to George Fischer, Sept. 5, 1949, and Roosevelt to George Barsky, Mar. 4, 1950, as quoted in Lash, *Eleanor: The Years Alone*, pp. 160–61.

39. *Time*, Oct. 25, 1948, p. 25; *Saturday Review of Literature*, Jan. 6, 1951, p. 11; *Los Angeles Times*, Jan. 3, 1952, as cited in Wamboldt, "Speaking Career of Anna Eleanor Roosevelt," p. 316.

40. *Newsweek*, Aug. 22, 1949, p. 20.

41. Hornaday interview with Beasley, May 21, 1979.

42. Agnes E. Meyer to Eleanor Roosevelt, July 25, 1952, as quoted in Lash, *Eleanor: The Years Alone*, p. 205.

43. Irene R. Sandifer, *Mrs. Roosevelt As We Know Her* (Silver Spring, Md.: privately printed, 1975), p. 100; Elliott Roosevelt and James Brough, *Mother R*, pp. 207–8.

44. John T. Flynn, *The Roosevelt Myth* (New York: Devin-Adair, 1948), p. 247.

45. Transcript of interview with Minnewa Bell by Emily Williams, Mar. 26, 1979, Eleanor Roosevelt oral history collection, FDRL, pp. 23–24;

Eleanor Roosevelt, "Why Are We Co-operating with Tito?" *Look*, Oct. 5, 1954, pp. 80, 82.

46. Chafe, *The American Woman*, pp. 180–82; Roosevelt, "American Woman's Dilemma," *Life*, June 16, 1947, pp. 101–12.

47. Lash, *Eleanor: The Years Alone*, p. 232; *New York Times* and *New York Herald-Tribune*, Oct. 8, 1954, as quoted in Lash, *Eleanor: The Years Alone*, p. 234.

48. As quoted in Elliott Roosevelt and James Brough, *Mother R*, p. 123.

49. Berger, *A New Deal for the World*, p. 112; transcript of "Meet the Press," Sept. 16, 1956, as quoted in Lash, *Eleanor: The Years Alone*, p. 258.

50. "My Day," Nov. 2, 1956, box 3158, ERP.

51. Lash, *Eleanor: The Years Alone*, p. 262.

52. Alfred Steinberg, *Mrs. R.: The Life of Eleanor Roosevelt* (New York: Putnam, 1958), p. 354.

53. Eleanor Roosevelt, *On My Own* (New York: Harper, 1958), p. 231.

54. Memo from A. H. Belmont to L. V. Boardman, Sept. 16, 1957, FBI file on Eleanor Roosevelt.

55. Notation by J. Edgar Hoover on memo from G. A. Nease to Mr. Tolson, Dec. 11, 1958, attached to clipping of Eleanor Roosevelt's "My Day" column, undated, *Washington Daily News*, FBI file on Eleanor Roosevelt.

56. "My Day," Aug. 17, 1960, box 3162, ERP.

57. Eleanor Roosevelt, *You Learn By Living* (New York: Harper, 1960), pp. 77, 82.

58. Transcript of interview with Henry Morgenthau III, Aug. 30, 1978, pp. 28–29.

59. Ibid.

60. Maurine Christopher, "Videotech Update," *Advertising Age*, Apr. 30, 1984, p. 54; Asbell, ed., *Mother and Daughter*, p. 329; Lash, *Eleanor: The Years Alone*, p. 298.

61. Comment by Esther Peterson to Maurine Beasley during tour titled "Eleanor Roosevelt's Washington" sponsored by Smithsonian Associates, Oct. 28, 1984.

62. Lois Scharf, "ER and Feminism," in Hoff-Wilson and Lightman, eds., *Without Precedent*, pp. 246–49.

63. Comments by Peggy Whedon, American News Women's Club, Washington, D.C., Sept. 27, 1984.

64. Peggy Whedon, *Always On Sunday* (New York: Norton, 1980), pp. 156–57.

65. Eleanor Roosevelt, *Tomorrow Is Now* (New York: Harper, 1963), pp. xvii, 126.

66. Emma Bugbee to Bess Furman, Mar. 9, 1962, box 24, BFP; interview with Dorothy Ducas as quoted in Collins, *She Was There*, pp. 51–52.

Conclusion

1. Remarks by Esther Van Wagoner Tufty, American News Women's Club, Washington, D.C., Sept. 27, 1984; Susan Ware, *Holding Their Own*, p. 24; Ruth Milkman, "Women's Work and the Economic Crisis," in Nancy F. Cott and Elizabeth H. Pleck, eds., *A Heritage of Her Own* (New York: Simon and Schuster, 1979), pp. 511–15.

2. Interview with Beth Campbell Short, Nov. 1, 1984.

3. Remarks by Ann Cottrell Free, Washington Press Club program in honor of Eleanor Roosevelt, National Museum of American History, Washington, D.C., Nov. 20, 1984.

4. Stella K. Hershan, letter to the editor, *New York Times*, July 4, 1986, p. A26.

5. Covert, "Journalism History and Women's Experience," pp. 67, 92.

6. Sally F. Griffith, "Mass Media Come to the Small Town," in Catherine L. Covert and John D. Stevens, eds., *Mass Media Between the Wars: Perceptions of Cultural Tension, 1918–1941* (Syracuse, N.Y.: Syracuse University Press, 1984), pp. 151–53.

7. Maurine H. Beasley and Paul Belgrade, "Eleanor Roosevelt: First Lady as Radio Pioneer," *Journalism History* 11 (Autumn-Winter 1984): 43–45; see also Jacqueline D. St. John, "Sex Role Stereotyping in Early Broadcast History: The Career of Mary Margaret McBride," *Frontiers: A Journal of Women Studies* 3 (Fall 1978): 31–32.

Index

Note on the Author

Maurine H. Beasley is an associate professor in the College of Journalism at the University of Maryland, College Park, where she has taught since she finished work on her Ph.D. (George Washington University) in 1974. Previously she was a staff writer for the *Washington Post*. She is the editor of *The White House Press Conferences of Eleanor Roosevelt* (1983) and author of articles in such journals as *Journalism History*, *Presidential Studies Quarterly*, and *Journalism Quarterly*. She is also the coeditor (with Richard Lowitt) of *One Third of a Nation: Lorena Hickok Reports on the Great Depression* (1981), and (with Sheila Gibbons) of *Women in Media: A Documentary Sourcebook* (1977).